The Forgotten TRINITY

BHP Books by James R. White

Grieving: Our Path Back to Peace
The Forgotten Trinity
Is the Mormon My Brother?
The King James Only Controversy
Letters to a Mormon Elder
Mary—Another Redeemer?
The Roman Catholic Controversy
*What's With the Dudes at the Door?**

*with Kevin Johnson

JAMES R. WHITE

BETHANY HOUSE PUBLISHERS
MINNEAPOLIS, MINNESOTA 55438

Published by Bethany House Publishers
A Ministry of Bethany Fellowship International
11400 Hampshire Avenue South
Minneapolis, Minnesota 55438
www.bethanyhouse.com

Printed in the United States of America by
Bethany Press International, Minneapolis, Minnesota 55438

ISBN 1–55661–725–9

Christian fellowship comprises a little taste of heaven here on earth. Close brothers in the Lord are a treasure not to be taken lightly. One such brother in Christ who has come to mean so much to me and my family is Chris Arnzen. It is with joy that I dedicate this work to a man of God, a brother in the Lord, a true "son of encouragement," a friend who is precious to me. Thank you, Chris, for being a Christian man who loves the Lord and has allowed that love to flow into my life.

Do you have comments?
Please address them to:

Alpha and Omega Ministries
P.O. Box 37106
Phoenix, AZ 85069

For faster response, contact us via E-mail:
orthopodeo@aomin.org

Visit our web page at
http://www.aomin.org
for information about Mormonism,
Jehovah's Witnesses, Roman Catholicism,
and General Apologetics, and
listings of debates, tapes, tracts, etc.

JAMES R. WHITE is director of Alpha and Omega Ministries, a Christian apologetics organization based in Phoenix, Arizona, and is an elder in the Phoenix Reformed Baptist Church. He is also an adjunct professor with the Golden Gate Baptist Theological Seminary. He is a critical consultant for the Lockman Foundation on the New American Standard Bible Update. He is married to Kelli and has two children, Joshua and Summer Marie.

And yet I will exert special effort to the end that they who lend ready and open ears to God's Word may have a firm standing ground. Here, indeed, if anywhere in the secret mysteries of Scripture, we ought to play the philosopher soberly and with great moderation; let us use great caution that neither our thoughts nor our speech go beyond the limits to which the Word of God itself extends. For how can the human mind measure off the measureless essence of God according to its own little measure, a mind as yet unable to establish for certain the nature of the sun's body, though men's eyes daily gaze upon it? Indeed, how can the mind by its own leading come to search out God's essence when it cannot even get to its own? Let us then willingly leave to God the knowledge of himself. For, as Hilary (of Poitiers) says, he is the one fit witness to himself, and is not known except through himself. But we shall be "leaving it to him" if we conceive him to be as he reveals himself to us, without inquiring about him elsewhere than from his Word.

John Calvin, *Institutes of the Christian Religion, I:XIII:21.*

Contents

1. Why the "Forgotten" Trinity? 13
2. What Is the Trinity? 23
3. God: A Brief Introduction 33
4. A Masterpiece: The Prologue of John 47
5. Jesus Christ: God in Human Flesh 65
6. I Am He 95
7. Creator of All Things 105
8. Carmen Christi: The Hymn to Christ as God 119
9. Jehovah of Hosts 131
10. Grieve Not the Holy Spirit 139
11. Three Persons 153
12. A Closer Look 163
13. From the Mists of Time: The Trinity and
    Church History 177
14. Does It Really Matter? Christian Devotion
    and the Trinity 193
    Notes 197
    Index 221

Why the "Forgotten" Trinity?

I love the Trinity. Does that sound strange to you? For most people, it *should* sound strange. Think about it: when was the last time you heard anyone say such a thing? We often hear "I love Jesus" or "I love God," but how often does anyone say, "I love the Trinity"? You even hear "I love the cross" or "I love the Bible," but you don't hear "I love the Trinity." Why not?

Someone might say, "Well, the Trinity is a doctrine, and you don't love doctrines." But in fact we do. "I love justification" or "I love the second coming of Christ" would make perfect sense. What's more, the Trinity isn't just a doctrine any more than saying "I love the deity of Christ" makes Christ just a doctrine.

So why don't we talk about loving the Trinity? Most Christians do not understand what the term means and have only a vague idea of the reality it represents. We don't love things that we consider very complicated, obtuse, or just downright difficult. We are more comfortable saying "I love the old rugged cross" because we *think* we have a firm handle on what that actually means and represents. But we confess how little we understand about the Trinity by how little we talk about it and how little emotion it evokes in our hearts.

Yet we seem rather confused at this point because most Christians take a firm stand on the Trinity and the fundamental issues that lead to it (the deity of Christ, the person of the Holy Spirit). We withhold fellowship from groups like the Mormons and Jehovah's Witnesses because they reject the Trinity and replace it with another concept. We hang a person's very salvation upon the acceptance of the doctrine, yet if we are honest with ourselves, *we really aren't sure exactly why.*

It's the topic we won't talk about: no one dares question the Trinity for fear of being branded a "heretic," yet we have all sorts of questions about it, and we aren't sure who we can ask. Many believers have asked questions of those they thought were more mature in the faith and have often been confused by the *contradictory* answers they received. Deciding it is best to remain confused rather than have one's orthodoxy questioned, many simply leave the topic for that mythical future day "when I have more time." And in the process, we have lost out on a tremendous blessing.

THE BLESSING OF THE TRINITY

A true and accurate knowledge of the Trinity is a blessing in and of itself. Any revelation of God's truth is an act of grace, of course, but the Trinity brings to us a blessing far beyond the worth normally assigned by believers today. Why? Because, upon reflection, we discover that the Trinity is the highest revelation God has made of himself to His people. It is the capstone, the summit, the brightest star in the firmament of divine truths. As I will assert more than once in this work, God revealed this truth about himself most clearly, and most irrefutably, in the Incarnation itself, when Jesus Christ, the eternal Son of God, took on human flesh and walked among us. That one act revealed the Trinity to us in a way that no amount of verbal revelation could ever communicate. God has been pleased to reveal to us that He exists as Father, Son, and Holy Spirit. Since God feels it is important to know, we should likewise. And since God went through a great deal of trouble to make it clear to us, we should see the Trinity as a precious possession, at the very top of the many things God has revealed to us that we otherwise would never have known.

When Paul wrote to the Colossians, he indicated that he was praying for them. He did not pray that they would obtain big houses and fancy chariots. He prayed that they would be blessed by God in the spiritual realm with spiritual wealth. Note his words:

> That their hearts may be encouraged, having been knit together in love, and attaining to all the wealth that comes from the full assurance of understanding, resulting in a true knowledge of God's mystery, that is, Christ Himself, in whom are hidden all the treasures of wisdom and knowledge. (Colossians 2:2–3)

How is one "rich" spiritually? One is rich spiritually who has a "full assurance of understanding." How many people today can honestly claim to have a true understanding of God's nature so as to have "full assurance"? Or do most of us muddle along with something far less than what God would have for us? A person who has such spiritual wealth, seen in a full assurance of understanding, has a "true knowledge" of God's mystery, that is, Christ himself. The goal of the Christian life, including the goal of Christian study and scholarship, is always the same: Jesus Christ, "in whom are hidden all the treasures of wisdom and knowledge." Do we long for a "true knowledge" of Christ? When we sing, "Lord, I want to know you," do we really mean it, and then take advantage of the ways He has given us to attain this "true knowledge" of Him? To know Christ truly is to know the Trinity, for God has not revealed himself in such a way as to allow us to have *true* and *balanced* knowledge of the Father outside of such knowledge of the Son, all of which comes to us through the Spirit. A person who wants to "know Jesus" must, due to the nature of God's revelation, know Him as He is related to the Father and the Spirit. We must know, understand, and love the Trinity to be fully and completely Christian. This is why we say the Trinity is the greatest of God's revealed truths.

WHY "FORGOTTEN"?

Why has the Trinity become a theological appendage that is more often misunderstood than rightly known? I believe there are many reasons. There is the utterly false idea that God does not want us to use our minds in loving and worshiping Him (anti-intellectualism), as well as the idea that "theology is for cold, unfeeling people. We want a living faith." This last reason is the most irrational because a living faith is one that is focused upon the truths of God's revelation. The deepest feelings and emotions evoked by the Spirit of God are not directed toward unclear, nebulous, fuzzy concepts, but toward the clear revealed truths of God concerning His love, the work of Christ, and the ministry of the Holy Spirit. It makes no sense whatsoever in human relations to say "I love my wife" while doing our best to remain ignorant of her personality, likes, dreams, etc. And even worse, if my wife has put forth the effort to make sure that I *can* know these things about her, and I go about *ignoring* her efforts, what does that say about how much I really *love* her? The idea that there is some kind of contradiction between the in-depth study of God's Word, so as to know what God has revealed about himself, and a living, vital faith is inherently self-contradictory.

Whatever the reasons for the general ignorance of the specifics of the Trinity, the result is plain. Most Christian people, while remembering the term "Trinity," have forgotten the central place the doctrine is to hold in the Christian life. It is rarely the topic of sermons and Bible studies, rarely the object of adoration and worship—at least worship *in truth*, which is what the Lord Jesus said the Father desires (John 4:23). Instead, the doctrine is *misunderstood* as well as *ignored*. It is so misunderstood that a majority of Christians, when asked, give *incorrect* and at times downright *heretical* definitions of the Trinity. For others, it is ignored in such a way that even among those who correctly understand the doctrine, it does not hold the place it should in the proclamation of the Gospel message, nor in the life of the individual believer in prayer, worship, and service.

THE SOLUTION

Thankfully, the solution to this problem is near at hand. The Holy Spirit of God always desires to lead God's people to a deeper knowledge of God's truth. This is the wonderful "constant" that every minister and teacher can rely upon: every true believer is indwelt by the Holy Spirit of God, and the Spirit is always going to fulfill the promise to lead us into all truth. Any believer who honestly seeks God's truth, and is willing to lay aside any preconceptions and traditions that might stand contrary to that truth, will find strength and encouragement for the *work* (yes, "work") that is required to come to that true knowledge and full assurance of which Paul spoke. We do not just sit back and expect God to zap us with some emotional surge. Instead, the Spirit drives us into His Word, enlightening our minds and filling our hearts with love for the truths we discover.

Many theological works flow from an intellectual, scholarly stance. There is nothing wrong with such works, for there is a need for them. However, this work, while incorporating necessary elements of scholarship, is written from a position of "passion." Passion, not in the sense of unordered, chaotic feelings, but passion in the sense of a burning love for something—in this case, the truth about God we call "Trinity." This book is not meant to be a handbook of all the "arguments" you can use to "prove" a point. There are plenty of such works in existence. Instead, this work is written *by* a believer *for* other believers. While I must explain and teach, illustrate and document, I do so to achieve a higher goal.

I wish to invite you, my fellow believer, to a deeper, higher, more intense love of God's truth. It is my longing that when you complete this work, you will not simply put it down and say, "I got some good ammunition to use the next time I debate the Trinity." Instead, I hope that God, in His grace, will use this to implant in your heart a deep longing to know Him even more. I pray that longing will last the rest of your life, and that it will result in your loving Him more completely, worshiping Him more fully, honoring Him with the totality of your life. I desire that you will join with me in being able to say, "I love the Trinity." A person who *loves* this truth of God will likewise be able to explain and defend it, but the *motivation* for doing so will be so much richer, and the end result will be the edification of the believer and the church at large rather than a mere "victory" in a particular debate or argument. And one thing is for sure: a person who speaks God's truth from *conviction* and *love* does so far more convincingly than the person who lacks such motivations.

True worship must worship God *as He exists,* not as we wish Him to be. The essence of idolatry is the making of images of God. An image is a shadow, a false representation. We may not bow before a statue or figure, but if we make an image of God in our mind *that is not in accord with God's revelation of himself,* then we are not worshiping in truth. Since sin and rebellion are always pushing us toward false gods and away from the true God, we must seek *every day* to conform our thinking and our worship to God's straight-edge standard of truth, revealed so wonderfully in Scripture. We must to be willing to love God *as He is,* and that includes *every* aspect of His being that might, due to our fallen state, be offensive to us, or beyond our limited capacities to fully comprehend. God is not to be edited to fit our ideas and preconceptions. Instead, we must always be asking Him to graciously open our clouded mind and reveal himself to us so that we may love Him truly and worship Him aright.

THE EXAMPLE OF EDWARDS

I have always been challenged by the example of Jonathan Edwards[1] when it came to this matter of loving God *as He has revealed himself* rather than loving an image I have created of Him in my mind:

> Sometimes, only mentioning a single word caused my heart to burn within me; or only seeing the name of Christ, or the name of some attribute of God. And God has appeared glorious to me on account of the Trinity. It has made me have exalting thoughts of God, that he subsists in three persons; the Father, Son and Holy Ghost. The sweetest joys and delights I have experienced, have not been those that have arisen from a hope of my own good estate, but in a direct view of the glorious things of the gospel.
>
> Once, as I rode out into the woods for my health, in 1737,

having alighted from my horse in a retired place, as my manner commonly has been, to walk for divine contemplation and prayer, I had a view that for me was extraordinary, of the glory of the Son of God, as Mediator between God and man, and his wonderful, great, full, pure and sweet grace and love, and meek and gentle condescension. This grace that appeared so calm and sweet, appeared also great above the heavens. The person of Christ appeared ineffably excellent with an excellency great enough to swallow up all thought and conception—which continued, as near as I can judge, about an hour; which kept me the greater part of the time in a flood of tears and weeping aloud. I felt an ardency of soul to be, what I know not otherwise how to express, emptied and annihilated; to lie in the dust, and to be full of Christ alone; to love Him with a holy and pure love; to trust in Him; to live upon Him; to serve and follow Him; and to be perfectly sanctified and made pure, with a divine and heavenly purity. I have, several other times, had views very much of the same nature, and which have had the same effects.[2]

When people today talk about "spiritual experiences," I am often forced to reflect upon the fact that rarely are these experiences focused upon *God*, but rather upon what that person believes God has done for him or her, or what that person has *accomplished* "for God." How much deeper, how much more meaningful, is the experience of Edwards. The object of his reflection is unchanging, for it is nothing other than the eternal truth of God. The world, and his circumstances, cannot take away from him what is most precious: his God.

I confess that the times when my soul is so enraptured by such divine joys is far too infrequent in comparison with how often it is taken up with worldly things and distracted by much less worthy objects of consideration. It seems as though the whole world does its best to keep me from enjoying myself in my God, in contemplating His nature, His attributes, and His works. But I read of great men of God in the past and realize there are two common elements in their lives: suffering and a love of the contemplation of God's attributes and works. When I compare myself with Edwards, or any other of the great godly men and women of the past, I quickly see how influenced I am by worldly standards and worldly priorities.

But most importantly, Edwards was drawn heavenward by the very attributes of God that turn the worldly person cold and, in fact, are often the most offensive to the natural or unsaved man. Do we love God—*all of God, including the "tough" parts of His nature*—or do we refuse to bow before those elements that cause us "problems"? If we love Him and worship Him as He deserves, we will not *dare* to "edit" Him to fit *our* desires. Instead, we will seek to worship Him in truth.

GOD IS GREAT

The Trinity is a truth that tests our dedication to the principle that God is smarter than we are. As strange as that may sound, I truly believe that in most instances where a religious group denies the Trinity, the reason can be traced back to the founder's unwillingness to admit the simple reality that God is bigger than we can ever imagine. That is really what Christians have always meant when they use the term "mystery" of the Trinity. The term has never meant that the Trinity is an inherently irrational thing. Instead, it simply means that we realize that God is completely unique in the way He exists, and there are elements of His being that are simply beyond our meager mental capacity to comprehend. The fact that God is eternal is another facet of His being that is beyond us. We cannot really grasp eternity, nor how God exists eternally rather than in time. Yet this truth is revealed to us in Scripture, and we believe it on the logical basis that God is trustworthy. It is a "mystery" that we accept on the basis of faith in God's revelation.

When men approach God's truth with a haughty attitude, they often decide that particular elements of that truth are not "suitable" to them, so they "modify" the message of the faith to fit their own notions. Since the Trinity is the highest of God's revelations concerning himself, it is hardly surprising to discover that many groups deny it. If one denies any of the preceding truths upon which the Trinity is based, one will end up rejecting the entire doctrine *en toto*. An unwillingness to worship God *as God is and has revealed himself* lies behind every denial of the Trinity that appears down through history. We want a God we can fit in a box, and the eternal, Triune God does not fit that mold.

William G. T. Shedd saw the truth when he wrote,

> The doctrine of the Trinity is the most *immense* of all the doctrines of religion. It is the foundation of theology. Christianity, in the last analysis, is Trinitarianism. Take out of the New Testament the person of the Father, the Son, and the Holy Spirit, and there is no God left. Take out of the Christian consciousness the thoughts and affections that relate to the Father, the Son, and the Holy Spirit, and there is no Christian consciousness left. The Trinity is the constitutive idea of the evangelical theology, and the formative idea of the evangelical experience. The immensity of the doctrine makes it of necessity a mystery; but a mystery which like night enfolds in its unfathomed depths the bright stars—points of light, compared with which there is no light so keen and so glittering. Mysterious as it is, the Trinity of Divine Revelation is the doctrine that holds in it all the hope of man; for it holds within it the infinite pity of the Incarnation and the infinite mercy of the Redemption.
>
> And it shares its mysteriousness with the doctrine of the Divine Eternity. It is difficult to say which is most baffling to human comprehension, the all-comprehending, simultaneous, successionless consciousness of the Infinite One, or his trinal personality. Yet no theist rejects the doctrine of the Divine Eternity because of its mystery. The two doctrines are antithetic and correlative. On one of the Northern rivers that flows through a narrow chasm whose depth no plummet has sounded, there stand two cliffs fronting each other, shooting their pinnacles into the blue ether, and sending their roots down to the foundations of the earth. They have named them Trinity and Eternity. So stand, antithetic and confronting, in the Christian scheme, the trinity and eternity of God.[3]

One attitude of the heart struggles against an eternal God, desiring to make Him "more like us." But a godly attitude, the attitude that is imparted by the Spirit of God, bows in humble reverence, and instead of *struggling,* it *embraces* in love the God who is beyond all comprehension. Such an attitude cannot be forced on anyone. It takes a miracle for the naturally hostile[4] soul to be made willing to love God and seek His face. That miracle is the work of regeneration, of causing one to be "born from above,"[5] made "a new creature."[6] Hence, such truths as the eternality of God, and His Triune nature, are doctrines *for Christians,* in the sense that to truly love, accept, and hunger for these things, the miracle of salvation must take place.

The more exhaustive our knowledge of God's revelation, the deeper our love for Him will be. So we must delve into God's revelation, "put our waders on," so to speak, and explore the Scriptures so that we can properly understand the pinnacle of God's revelation about himself the Trinity.

A BRIEF WORD ABOUT THE FORMAT

I wish to bring my love for the Trinity into the hearts of many of my fellow believers. As a result, I have done my best to avoid the temptation that comes from having defended this great truth against those who deny it: to attempt to be *exhaustive* at every point. Anyone who has spent a great deal of time "debating" with someone who denies the Trinity knows how one must, at times, get very, *very* particular in responding to certain arguments and points. But since I am not writing specifically for those who *don't* believe, but for those who *do,* I have tried to be brief, concise, and direct. There are many passages of Scripture I *could* have presented, objections I *could* have addressed, but I did not. My reason was simply to make sure that the final result was readily available to the widest possible audience.

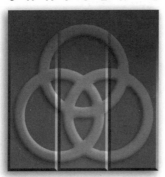

What Is the Trinity?

The single greatest reason people struggle with the doctrine of the Trinity is miscommunication. It is *very* rare that anyone actually argues or debates about the *real* doctrine of the Trinity. Most arguments that take place at the door, or over coffee, or at the workplace involve two or more people fighting vigorously over two or more *misrepresentations* of the doctrine itself. It is no wonder so many encounters create far more heat than they do light.

It is basic to human communication to define terms. Yet so many people have so much emotional energy invested in the Trinity that they often skip right past the "definitions" stage and charge into the "tooth and claw" stage. And this is not only true today. Historically speaking, many of the early battles over the doctrine centuries ago had to do with one side using a certain set of terms in one way, and the other the same set of terms in another way. This was made even more a difficulty by the fact that you had Greek-speaking people trying to understand what

1. Creer en la Trinidad

Latin-speaking people were saying, and *vice versa*. Today we can look back and realize that early on both sides were saying the same thing, only they were saying it with different words. If someone had just sat down and defined terms clearly and forcefully, a lot of arguments could have been avoided.

When it comes to the central affirmation of the triune nature of God, most of the time we leap right past the "formalities" and directly into a tug-of-war with passages of Scripture. The result is almost always the same: both sides go away thinking the other is utterly blind. Such frustrating experiences could be minimized if we remember that we cannot *assume* that the other person shares our knowledge or understanding of the specifics of the doctrine under discussion. As tedious as it may seem at first, we must resist the temptation to bypass the necessary "groundwork" and insist that everyone define what they believe the Trinity to be, and how they are going to be using many of the key terms that come into play. Without this first step, little else will be accomplished.

BUT CAN YOU DEFINE THE UNDEFINABLE?

Before we present a definition of the Trinity, it is important to point out that we face a real difficulty right at the start: language itself. Christians have struggled for centuries to express, within the limitations of human language, the unique revelation God makes of His mode of existence. We struggle because language is a finite means of communication. Finite minds are trying to express in words infinite truths. At times we simply cannot "say" what we need to say to adequately express the grandeur that is our God.

Humans communicate by means of examples. When little children start asking the endless series of questions that suggest themselves to little minds, we often find ourselves using analogies and examples in our replies. When asked what a new food tastes like, we compare it to known foods in the child's life. We might say, "It tastes a little bit like crackers with honey on them," knowing the child has had crackers with honey. That may not be *exactly* what it tastes like, but they get the idea. As their "database" of knowledge grows, so we can expand our analogies. We never escape this element of our language. When we encounter new thoughts, new ideas, it is natural for us to fit them into preexisting categories by comparing them with past experiences or facts.

This process works just fine for most things. But for unique things, it doesn't. If something is *truly* unique, it cannot be compared to anything else, at least not without introducing some element of error. One might be able to draw a parallel to a certain *aspect* of the truly unique thing, but if it's really unique, the analogy will be limited, and, if pressed too far, downright erroneous. But since we don't encounter too many *completely* unique things in our lives, we manage to get along.

The problem is, of course, God is *completely unique.* He is God, and there is no other. He is totally unlike anything else, and as He frequently reminds us, "To whom then will you liken Me?" (Isaiah 40:25). There is no answer to that question, because to compare God to anything in the created order is, in the final analysis, to deny His uniqueness. When we say, "God is like . . ." we are treading on dangerous ground. Yes, we might be able to illustrate a certain *aspect* of God's being in this way, but in every instance the analogy, if pushed far enough, is going to break down.

Our language fails us in two other ways as well. First, our language is based upon time. We speak of the past, the present, and the future. As we will see in the next chapter, God is not limited to time as we are. Thus, when we speak of Him with our language, we are forced to place misleading limitations upon His being. This often causes real problems for us in discussing His triune nature, for we slip into the all-too-human mode of thinking as time-based, time-limited creatures.

The second way in which our language fails us has to do with what I call "excess baggage." Words often carry with them "baggage" that has become attached to the meaning of a word. The way we use the word may cause us to conjure up particular mental images every time we hear it. The most glaring example of this is the word "person," a word that is often used when discussing the Trinity. When we use the word "person," we attach to it all sorts of "baggage" that comes from our own personal experiences. We think of a physical body, an individual, separate from everyone else. We think of a spatial location, physical attributes like height, weight, age—all things associated with our common use of the word "person." When we use this word to describe a divine person (Father, Son, or Holy Spirit), we tend to drag along with it the "baggage" that comes from our common use of the term in everyday life. Many people, upon hearing the word "person" used of the Father, for example, conjure up an image of a kind old grandfatherly figure who is the "person" of the Father. He's separate, different, limited—everything we think of when we think of the term "person." It will be our task (and it is a difficult one!) to labor to separate such "baggage" from our thinking and use such terms in very specific, limited ways so as to avoid unneeded confusion.

A BASIC DEFINITION

It is time to lay down a basic, fundamental definition of the Trinity. At the end of our study we will look a little closer at this definition, expand upon it some, and examine a few of the issues it raises.

But we need a short, succinct, accurate definition to start with. Here it is:

> **Within the one Being that is God, there exists eternally three coequal and coeternal persons, namely, the Father, the Son, and the Holy Spirit.**

You would think that a belief that can be expressed in one sentence would be fairly simple as a result, but such would be a mistake. I have chosen my words very carefully. Each is very important, each has a specific function. More importantly, I have *avoided* certain words, too. Let's look briefly at some of the major issues presented by this definition.

First, the doctrine rests completely upon the truth of the first clause: there is only one God. "The one Being that is God" carries within it a tremendous amount of information. It not only asserts that there is only one God—the historic belief, shared by Christians and Jews known as *monotheism*—but it also insists that God's "Being" (capitalized so as to contrast it with the term "persons" found in the next clause) is one, unique, undivided, indivisible. As you can see already, there is a lot packed into each phrase. We will "unpack" all of this in time. But for now, the emphasis of the first clause is *monotheism* and the assertion that there is only one true God.

Second, the definition insists that there are three divine persons. Note immediately that we are not saying there are three Beings that are one Being, or three persons that are one person. Such would be self-contradictory. I emphasize this because, *most often,* this is the misrepresentation of the doctrine that is commonly found in the literature of various religions that deny the Trinity. The second clause speaks of three divine persons, not three divine Beings. As I warned before, we must not succumb to the temptation to read the term "person" as if we are talking about finite, self-contained human beings. What "person" means when we speak of the Trinity is quite different than when we speak of creatures such as ourselves. These divine persons are identified in the last clause as the Father, the Son, and the Holy Spirit.

Hank Hanegraaff, president of the *Christian Research Institute* (*CRI*), has often expressed this point in a wonderfully simple and clear way: when speaking of the Trinity, we need to realize that we are talking about one *what* and three *who's*. The one *what* is the Being or essence of God; the three *who's* are the Father, Son, and Spirit. We dare not mix up the *what's* and *who's* regarding the Trinity.

Thirdly, we are told that the relationship among these divine persons is eternal. They have *eternally existed* in this unique relationship. Each of the persons is said to be eternal, each is said to be coequal with the others as to their divine nature. Each fully shares the one *Being* that is God. The Father is not ⅓ of God, the Son ⅓ of God, the Spirit ⅓ of God. Each is fully God, coequal with the others, and that eternally. There never was a time when the Father was not the Father; never a time when the Son was not the Son; never a time when the Spirit was not the Spirit. Their relationship is eternal, not in the sense of having been for a *long* time, but existing, in fact, outside the realm of time itself.

The three foundations of the Trinity, then, are already clearly visible. Here they are:

Foundation One:	Monotheism: There Is Only One God
Foundation Two:	There Are Three Divine Persons
Foundation Three:	The Persons Are Coequal and Coeternal

These three foundations not only provide the grounds upon which the Trinity is based, they explain to us *why Christians who accept all of the Bible believe this doctrine.* This is very important. Often the discussions Christians have with others about the Trinity flounder and go in circles because we do not identify these three truths as *biblical teachings.* When someone says, "How can you claim to only believe the Bible, when you use terms like 'Trinity' that don't appear in the Bible?" we must be quick to point out that we are *forced* to do so by the teaching of the Bible itself on these three points. *Every error and heresy on this doctrine will find its origin in a denial of one or more of these truths.*

THE THREE FOUNDATIONS AND THE BIBLE

This book is based upon establishing, as divine truths, plainly revealed in Scripture, the three foundations listed above. I do not approach the Trinity as a philosophical issue or a theological speculation that may interest a person for a while. I approach the Trinity as *a revealed truth.* I do not believe in the Trinity because it is "traditional" to do so. I believe in it for the same reason Athanasius[1] did so long ago: the Scriptures compel me to this conclusion. I cannot hold the Bible in my hand while denying the Trinity. There is a fundamental contradiction there. The Trinity is a doctrine *for Bible-believing people.*

It is quite common for those who deny the Trinity to make Christians feel as if they are somehow inconsistent in believing in a doctrine that is not "biblical." "Where do you find the word 'Trinity' in the Bible?" they ask. Yet just the opposite is the case. The only folks who are truly *biblical* are those who believe *all* the Bible has to say on a given topic. If I believe *everything* the Bible says about topic X and use a term not found in the Bible to describe the full teaching of Scripture on that point, am I not being more truthful to the Word than someone who limits themselves to only biblical terms, but rejects some aspect of God's revelation? Christians believe in the Trinity not because the term itself is given in some creedlike form in the text of Scripture. Instead, they believe in the Trinity because the Bible, taken in its completeness, accepted as a self-consistent revelation of God, *teaches* that there is one Being of God (Foundation One) that is shared fully (Foundation Three) by three divine persons (Foundation Two), the Father, the Son, and the Holy Spirit. There is, therefore, no contradiction between being a "Bible believer" and holding to the Trinity. The one leads naturally, and inevitably, to the other.

The majority of this work will demonstrate from the text of Scripture each of the three foundational truths that lead us inexorably to the historic doctrine of the Trinity. After we have established these truths, we will briefly expand upon our definition. While it is sufficient to explain the doctrine in broad terms, Christian theologians over the centuries have found it necessary to carefully explain various elements of the doctrine in greater depth. Most of this more technical discussion has been to safeguard each of the three foundations from subtle, yet destructive, erosion and redefinition. These technical definitions are generally negative; that is, they tell us more about what the Trinity *isn't* than what it *is*. This shouldn't be surprising, however. We must always remember that we are trying to define and describe something that is absolutely, universally *unique*. It is far easier to say, "I don't mean this," than it is to say, "Well, it's like this," since there is nothing in the created universe that really, fully is *like* an absolutely unique thing. That's what makes it unique in the first place! Consequently, theologians have had much more success at saying, "The Trinity *is not this*," than positively saying, "The Trinity *is this*."

WHAT WE ARE NOT SAYING—

The errors that result from denying, or misunderstanding, any one of the foundational truths presented above can be graphically illustrated through the use of the following triangle diagram:

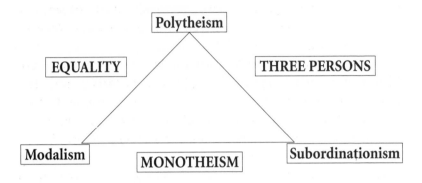

Each of the three sides represents a foundational truth. When any one of these truths is denied, the other two sides form an arrow that point to the resultant error. For example, if one denies *monotheism*, the other two sides of the triangle point to "polytheism." If one denies the *equality* of the persons, the result is "subordinationism." And if one denies the existence of *three persons*, the result is "modalism." This diagram also points out how *balanced* we must be in our study of this important subject. Failing to believe one fundamental element of God's revelation will lead us into grave danger and error.

The large majority of people with whom I have spoken who insisted they did not believe in the Trinity actually did not believe in a *misrepresentation* or *misunderstanding* of the doctrine itself. Most often people confuse *modalism*, the belief that God exists in three "modes" (Father, Son, and Spirit), but is only one *person*, with the real doctrine of the Trinity. "But Jesus prayed to the Father! How could He *be* the Father?" is what I often hear. It is important to emphasize that we are *not* saying that the Father is the Son, nor that the Son is the Spirit. That is not the doctrine of the Trinity, despite how many people in honest ignorance think otherwise. No true Trinitarian believes the Father was a "ventriloquist" at the baptism of Jesus, nor that Jesus was praying to himself in the Garden of Gethsemane.

A WORD TO APOLOGISTS

I write as a Christian theologian and *apologist*. A Christian apologist is a person who gives a defense, a reason for the Christian faith. As a Christian apologist, I have often undertaken to define, and defend, the biblical doctrine of the Trinity.

I do not intend this book to be an exhaustive defense of the Trinity. There are all sorts of objections I simply will not address, not for lack of desire to do so, but for another more important reason. It is my desire that this work function to introduce, explain, and make understandable a doctrine that, while at the center of our faith, is often ignored and misunderstood. I am attempting to explain and, as a result, cause Christians to love and understand the doctrine of the Trinity. I do provide some responses to the common objections raised against the truth of the Trinity, mainly through the use of endnotes, but if I allowed too much of the "debate" to enter into the work itself, I would lose the very audience I so desire to see fall in love with the Trinity. Beyond this, the very space that would be required to respond to every possible objection would remove this book from the hands of the Christian who is simply seeking to understand accurately the great God whom we worship as Father, Son, and Holy Spirit.

CHAPTER 3

God: A Brief Introduction

He dragged a big, thick, foreboding-looking book from under the podium and held it up high. "I am sick and tired of theology!" he yelled, slamming the book down. "Don't give me theology, just give me Jesus!" The crowd, with the notable exception of my wife and me, seated in the back row, roared its approval. *Yeah, but as soon as you make one statement about Jesus,* I thought to myself, *you are speaking theology.*

I love theology. Not the cold, stuffy, lifeless stuff you find in some corners of the church, but the living, exciting, Bible-based, life-changing, "wow, isn't God incredible" theology that you encounter in every verse of the New Testament. I love reading great writers of the faith like Augustine, Athanasius, Wycliffe, Luther, Calvin, the Puritans, Charles Haddon Spurgeon (oh, that we had a dozen like him today!), Hodge, Machen, Warfield, and modern writers like R. C. Sproul, John Armstrong, and John MacArthur. I remember sitting up till early in the morning reading Sproul's *The Holiness of God.* I wasn't able to put it down. Some writers can transport you into the very presence of God by accurately and forcefully explaining God's truth.

If you are a Christian, you are a theologian. You have no choice. Theology is simply *knowing about God.* In fact, since Christians are called to grow in their knowledge of God, part of the very *goal* of the Christian life is theology. Theology is a normal part of the Christian life—a part that gives rise to everything else.

The primary focus of this chapter is to establish the very foundation of the doctrine of the Trinity: absolute, uncompromised monotheism. Monotheism—the belief in one true and eternal God, maker of all things—is the first truth that separates Christianity from the pagan religions of the world. Any discussion of the Trinity that does not begin with the clear, unequivocal proclamation that there is one, indivisible Being of God is a discussion doomed to failure. Anyone who thinks that the doctrine of the Trinity *compromises* absolute monotheism simply does not understand what the doctrine is teaching.

A PROPER ATTITUDE

We dare not embark on our examination of the Scriptures' testimony to the nature of our Creator without recognizing that it is He who sets the limits to our study. If we wish to know God *truly,* we must be willing to allow Him to reveal to us *what* He wants us to know, and He must be free as to *how* He wants to reveal it. He has given us a treasure trove of truth about Him, but He has not deemed it proper to reveal *everything* there is to know (if such is even possible). We dare not go beyond the boundaries He himself has set in His Word. The Scriptures put it this way:

> The secret things belong to the LORD our God, but the things revealed belong to us and to our sons forever, that we may observe all the words of this law. (Deuteronomy 29:29)

God's revelation is a gift to His people, and we are free to delve as deeply as we desire into its eternal truths. But we can never allow pride and arrogance to cause us to think that we can "put God in a box" and remove from Him the supremacy that is His. As He reminds us:

> "For My thoughts are not your thoughts, neither are your ways
> My ways," declares the LORD. "For as the heavens are higher than
> the earth, so are My ways higher than your ways and My thoughts
> than your thoughts" (Isaiah 55:8–9).

THE MORNING PRAYER

Each morning the faithful Jew repeated the words that defined his faith and provided the foundation of his religion. This prayer is known as the *Shema,* taken from the Hebrew word "to hear":

> Hear, O Israel! The LORD[1] is our God, the LORD is one! You
> shall love the LORD your God with all your heart and with all your
> soul and with all your might. These words, which I am com-
> manding you today, shall be on your heart. (Deuteronomy 6:4–6)

Monotheism. One God, Yahweh. No other gods beside Me. These are basic and fundamental truths confessed by Jews and Christians alike. God chose to begin His revelation of His truth not by arguing for His existence, but by asserting that He alone is God, the Creator of all things (Genesis 1:1). As the one God of Israel, He is to be loved with all the heart, soul, mind, and strength. The Lord Jesus said this is the greatest commandment—there is no higher calling than to love this one God. God's people have always accepted God's claims about him-self:

> Behold, to the LORD your God belong heaven and the highest
> heavens, the earth and all that is in it. (Deuteronomy 10:14)

It was truly novel, in the days when polytheism reigned supreme as the religious "consensus" of the world, for anyone to claim that *their* God was the Creator of all things. But God would not allow His wor-ship to be polluted by the false idea that He was but one God among many true deities. He is distinguished from all the false gods of the peoples around Israel by the fact that He *alone* is God, and He *alone* created all things.

God often had to remind His people Israel of the most basic of His truths. They were always wandering off into idolatry, attempting to join His worship with the worship of other deities. The Old Testament is a tribute to His longsuffering patience with them, and His constantly bringing them back into the fold. A constant cycle of punishment, repentance, and restoration unfolds for us in the Scriptures, and it is always associated with the confession on the part of the penitent Israelites that they had indeed sinned in going after "other gods."

In Isaiah's prophecy we find the most explicit testimony to God's utter uniqueness and to the resultant truth of absolute monotheism. Here, in chapters 40 through 48, we find what I like to call the "Trial of the False Gods." God sets up His cosmic courtroom and invites those gods vying for the attention of His people to take the stand and experience a little celestial cross-examination. God is unrelenting in pressing His claims against these false gods, and in the process, He reveals a tremendous number of fundamental truths about himself. By comparing the *real thing* with all the pretenders, God exposes them all for the frauds they truly are.

> "You are My witnesses," declares the LORD, "and My servant whom I have chosen, in order that you may know and believe Me and understand that I am He. Before Me there was no God formed, and there will be none after Me" (Isaiah 43:10).

Here Yahweh (the LORD) calls as a witness in His suit against the false gods His own people, Israel. He chose Israel for a purpose: that they might know and believe Him. As a result, they are witnesses to the truth of the statement "Before Me there was no God formed, and there will be none after Me."[2] God is saying, "Israel, I alone am God. There are no true gods beside me. There were none before Me, for I am eternal. And there will be none after Me, for I do not age, and will not pass away. There is no room for other gods, for I alone am God, the Creator."

> "Thus says the LORD, the King of Israel and his Redeemer, the LORD of hosts: 'I am the first and I am the last, and there is no

God besides Me. Who is like Me? Let him proclaim and declare it; yes, let him recount it to Me in order, from the time that I established the ancient nation. And let them declare to them the things that are coming and the events that are going to take place. Do not tremble and do not be afraid; have I not long since announced *it* to you and declared *it*? And you are My witnesses. Is there any God besides Me, or is there any *other* Rock? I know of none' " (Isaiah 44:6–8).

Again, Yahweh speaks and reminds us that He is the first and the last. Such a phrase is exhaustive. "There is no God besides Me." Idolatry is inherently foolish simply because there is no worthy object of worship other than the one true God.

God then asks, "Who is like Me?" There is no answer given, for this is celestial rhetoric—anyone who attempts to answer is guilty of idolatry.

God then challenges anyone who would claim to be like Him to do what only He can do: reveal the future with exacting and minute detail and accuracy. God knows the future, not because He has some kind of crystal ball, but because, as these passages assert over and over again, He is the Creator of all things, *including* time, past, present, and future.

God comforts His people by saying that they need not be fearful of the gods of the peoples, for those gods have no existence in reality. He then asks a question that should end all discussion: "Is there any God besides Me?" The believer can only answer, "No."

> "Declare and set forth *your case;* indeed, let them consult together. Who has announced this from of old? Who has long since declared it? Is it not I, the LORD? And there is no other God besides Me, a righteous God and a Savior; there is none except Me. Turn to Me and be saved, all the ends of the earth; for I am God, and there is no other" (Isaiah 45:21–22).

The scene is still the courtroom, and here God demands that the idols present their case as to why Israel should give them worship. You will note the idols never respond. Aside from the fact that they are dumb (mute and blind as well), even if they could speak, what would they say? They have no defense. So basic is the realization that there is only one true God that centuries later Paul can refer to idols as those that "by nature are no gods" (Galatians 4:8). A god other than Yahweh is, *by nature*, a "no-god."

ONE OF A KIND

Uniqueness. Otherness. It is part of the meaning of the word "holy" itself, and God makes it plainly known that He is holy. No images, no likenesses of Him are to be allowed, for such would create a connection that does not exist. He is Creator, everything else is created. He is infinite, everything else is finite. God asks the questions of anyone who would compare Him to anything in the created order:

> Who has directed the Spirit of the LORD, or as His counselor has informed Him? With whom did He consult and who gave Him understanding? And who taught Him in the path of justice and taught Him knowledge and informed Him of the way of understanding? Behold, the nations are like a drop from a bucket, and are regarded as a speck of dust on the scales; behold, He lifts up the islands like fine dust. Even Lebanon is not enough to burn, nor its beasts enough for a burnt offering. All the nations are as nothing before Him, they are regarded by Him as less than nothing and meaningless. To whom then will you liken God? Or what likeness will you compare with Him? (Isaiah 40:13–18)

These questions are rhetorical—there are no answers. If you can come up with answers to those questions for the God you worship, you have the wrong God. This tremendous passage continues:

> Do you not know? Have you not heard? Has it not been declared to you from the beginning? Have you not understood from the foundations of the earth? It is He who sits above the circle of the earth, and its inhabitants are like grasshoppers, who stretches out the heavens like a curtain and spreads them out like a tent to dwell in. He it is who reduces rulers to nothing, who makes the judges of the earth meaningless. Scarcely have they been planted, scarcely have they been sown, scarcely has their stock taken root

in the earth, but He merely blows on them, and they wither, and the storm carries them away like stubble. "To whom then will you liken Me that I would be his equal?" says the Holy One. Lift up your eyes on high and see who has created these stars, the One who leads forth their host by number, He calls them all by name; because of the greatness of His might and the strength of His power, not one of them is missing. Why do you say, O Jacob, and assert, O Israel, "My way is hidden from the LORD, and the justice due me escapes the notice of my God"? Do you not know? Have you not heard? The Everlasting God, the LORD, the Creator of the ends of the earth does not become weary or tired. His understanding is inscrutable. (Isaiah 40:21–28)

This is the only God worthy of worship and adoration. And God expects us to know this truth—He upbraids those who have forgotten by asking, "Do you not know? Have you not heard?" That this has *always* been known is plainly proclaimed. There is no excuse for idolatry, no defense for polytheism. This is the true Creator, the Maker of heaven and earth, and the men who dwell on the earth.

The fact that God rules and reigns over His creation is often placed in the context of demonstrating God's true nature. Listen to these words from Scripture:

> "Remember the former things long past, for I am God, and there is no other; I am God, and there is no one like Me, declaring the end from the beginning, and from ancient times things which have not been done, saying, 'My purpose will be established, and I will accomplish all My good pleasure' " (Isaiah 46:9–10).

None but the true God can say, "My purpose will be established." James wisely warned us against boasting of tomorrow, for we don't know what tomorrow will hold. Instead, he taught that we, as finite creatures, should say, "If the Lord wills I will do such and so" (James 4:13–16). But God is completely different than man: He can say that His purpose will be established, and beyond all question, *it will be*.

Jeremiah ministered to a people who were surrounded by the pressures of idolatry. They were constantly being enticed to go after other gods. Hear his antidote to idolatry:

> But the LORD is the true God; He is the living God and the everlasting King. At His wrath the earth quakes, and the nations cannot endure His indignation. Thus you shall say to them, "The gods that did not make the heavens and the earth shall perish from the earth and from under the heavens" (Jeremiah 10:10–11).[3]

God provides His people with the very words to say to those who would lead them after other gods: unless those gods created the heavens and the earth, they will perish from the earth. The irony of a god "perishing" is meant to point out the foolishness of making a god out of anyone but the Creator himself.

GOD IS SPIRIT

God does not exist in the same *mode* or *way* we do. He is utterly unlike us in many aspects. One truth about God's existence that is very difficult for us to grasp (but very important for us to struggle with) is that He is not limited to time and space. Theologians refer to this as His spirituality, not in the sense of simply being one spirit among many spirits, but that He exists as *spirit* and is therefore "omnipresent." It is best to think of omnipresence more in the realm of "lack of spatial limitations" than anything else. As with most things, God is far beyond our creaturely categories. When we speak of His omnipresence, we are saying something that is primarily negative (He does not have limitations of space, just as His eternal existence is basically a statement of His not having limitations based in time).

When speaking with the woman at the well in Samaria, the Lord Jesus ended the controversy regarding the *place* of worship by pointing out a basic truth:

> "God is spirit,[4] and those who worship Him must worship in spirit and truth" (John 4:24).

The worship of God is not a matter of *where* but of *how*. Whether Mount Gerazim (where the Samaritans thought one must worship) or in Jerusalem is not the issue. Spatial location is irrelevant, as space does not limit God, for He is spirit. The important thing is the *how* of worship (in spirit and in truth), not the *where.*

It is not Jesus' intention in this passage to lay out an entire discourse on the nature of God. He is instead addressing the matter of worship. But in doing so, He bases His teaching upon a belief that was a given, a truth that had been revealed in the Scriptures long before: God is not limited to time and space. He, unlike man, is *spirit,* and His worship cannot be limited to a particular place. Some of the Old Testament passages that informed the people of this truth include these words from Jeremiah:

> "Can a man hide himself in hiding places so I do not see him?" declares the LORD. "Do I not fill the heavens and the earth?" declares the LORD. (Jeremiah 23:24)

Likewise, Solomon knew the truth that no man-made temple could contain God's presence:

> "But will God indeed dwell with mankind on the earth? Behold, heaven and the highest heaven cannot contain You; how much less this house which I have built" (2 Chronicles 6:18).

God's omnipresence flows from the fact that He created all things: how could His creation be greater than He? How could there be anyplace in His creation beyond His presence?

God's *being* is not limited. And since God is omnipresent, another important truth can be seen: *God's being cannot be divided.* What is half of omnipresence? How can the infinite be divided into parts? We will see why this is important when we consider how *all* the fullness of the being of God is shared *completely* by each of the Divine Persons of the Trinity.

BEYOND THE REALM OF TIME

We have already seen a number of passages witness to the eternal nature of God. One of the clearest comes from Moses:

Before the mountains were born or You gave birth to the earth and the world, even from everlasting to everlasting,[5] You are God. (Psalm 90:2)

From everlasting *to* everlasting. Without limitation. God has existed *as God* eternally. There has never been a time *when God was not God.*

For thus says the high and exalted One Who lives forever, whose name is Holy, "I dwell *on* a high and holy place, and *also* with the contrite and lowly of spirit in order to revive the spirit of the lowly and to revive the heart of the contrite" (Isaiah 57:15).

"Of old You founded the earth, and the heavens are the work of Your hands. Even they will perish, but You endure; and all of them will wear out like a garment; like clothing You will change them and they will be changed. But You are the same, and Your years will not come to an end" (Psalm 102:25–27).

The psalmist here makes the same contrast that Moses made in Psalm 90:2: creation is temporal, passing, and limited. God, the true God, is none of those things.

We struggle with God's eternity. We cannot grasp it. Our lives are conditioned by the passing of time. Our language itself is based upon tenses: past, present, future. We are creatures, and as such, we have been created to exist *temporally,* that is, within the realm of time. God is not a creature and does not exist *temporally,* but *eternally.* Rather than thinking of eternity as a long, long time, think of it here as a *way* of existence that does not involve a progression of events and moments. That is how God lives. He defies our categories and our feeble efforts to comprehend Him. If He didn't, He wouldn't be God. And if we struggle mightily to even begin to envision the eternity of God, which is part of the most *basic* truth He has revealed about himself, how can we expect to probe all the recesses of His *highest* revelation, His Triune nature?

Since God exists eternally He is unchanging. He is not growing, progressing, evolving, or in any way moving from a state of imperfection to a state of perfection. This is the teaching of the Scriptures. Indeed, the very fact that God is *unchangingly faithful* to His promises to Israel is based upon the understanding that Yahweh himself does not change with time:

> "For I, the LORD, do not change; therefore you, O sons of Jacob, are not consumed" (Malachi 3:6).

God says He does not change. Change involves movement over time, yet God is eternal and does not change as men do. Our very salvation is dependent upon God's unchanging nature, for His faithfulness is based upon His being the same yesterday, today, and tomorrow.

> "God is not a man, that He should lie, nor a son of man, that He should repent; has He said, and will He not do it? Or has He spoken, and will He not make it good?" (Numbers 23:19)

What is the solid foundation of God's trustworthiness? He is God, not man. Man lies. Man changes his mind. Man says many things but cannot fulfill his promises. But God is not man. There is a fundamental distinction between God and man on the level of *being*. The same theme is struck many centuries later in Hosea:

> I will not execute My fierce anger; I will not destroy Ephraim again. For I am God and not man, the Holy One in your midst, and I will not come in wrath. (Hosea 11:9)

CREATOR OF ALL

The Scriptures claim that since God is *Creator,* He must, of necessity, be the *only* true God. It's an obvious conclusion: if God made everything, and is himself not dependent upon anything else, then any other "god" that might exist would have to be dependent upon Him and, therefore, would not be true deity.

> By the word of the LORD the heavens were made, and by the breath of His mouth all their host. . . . For He spoke, and it was done; He commanded, and it stood fast. (Psalm 33:6, 9)

All that exists—heaven and earth being exhaustive, in Hebrew thought, of creation itself—does so because God made it.

> "Who has performed and accomplished *it*, calling forth the generations from the beginning? I, the LORD, am the first, and with the last. I am He" (Isaiah 41:4).

God created *all* things, including "the generations." The Eternal One, Yahweh, the first and the last, is the Lord of time itself. Later in the same chapter God mocks the idols who do not exist beyond the realm of time as He does. He challenges them to do two things that only the true God can do to perfection. One is easy to see: tell us the future. This is a common challenge, one God can fulfill because He *created* time and is not limited to it. Secondly, God asks the idols to tell us what has taken place in the past, and, even more importantly, *the purpose of what happened.* It is one thing to recount past events as a historian, but to know *why* they happened—only the Sovereign Lord of eternity itself can do that. He challenges all would-be gods:

> Let them bring forth and declare to us what is going to take place; as for the former *events*, declare what they *were*, that we may consider them and know their outcome. Or announce to us what is coming; declare the things that are going to come afterward, that we may know that you are gods; indeed, do good or evil, that we may anxiously look about us and fear together. Behold, you are of no account, and your work amounts to nothing; he who chooses you is an abomination. (Isaiah 41:22–24)

We worship the very Lord of time and space itself, the Creator of both. He *alone* made the heavens and the earth:

> Thus says the LORD, your Redeemer, and the one who formed you from the womb, "I, the LORD, am the maker of all things, stretching out the heavens by Myself and spreading out the earth all alone" (Isaiah 44:24).

> For thus says the LORD, who created the heavens (He is the God who formed the earth and made it, He established it *and* did not create it a waste place, *but* formed it to be inhabited), "I am the

LORD, and there is none else" (Isaiah 45:18).

There is none else. No other God, no other deity, no other Savior. One God, absolute, eternal, Creator of all things.

The doctrine of the Trinity is based upon this firm foundation. We are no proclaimers of a plurality of gods. We have no allegiance but to the same God who appeared to Moses in the burning bush. The Trinity in no way, shape, or form compromises this fundamental truth—*it does, however, fulfill it, bring it to full realization, and reveal to us how this one true and eternal God exists as three coequal and coeternal persons.*

A Masterpiece: The Prologue of John

I wonder how long it took. Surely it wasn't something that was written carelessly, without planning, without thought. He must have spent a good deal of time and energy on it. I refer to the prologue of John, the first eighteen verses of the Gospel that bears his name. Some people are a little uncomfortable with the idea of one of the writers of Scripture working hard on a particular passage, a special section. There are others that think the writers of the Bible must have gone into some kind of "trance" while being led by the Holy Spirit to speak God's truth. But such is not a truly biblical idea. These holy men indeed spoke from God, but that does not exclude at all the use of their highest efforts to present God's truth (2 Peter 1:20–21; 2 Timothy 3:16–17).

The prologue of John is a literary masterpiece. Its balance is almost unparalleled. It is a carefully crafted work of art, a revelation that has inspired believers for almost two thousand years. The brightest minds have been fascinated by it and have always marveled at its beauty. It is an inexhaustible treasure.

Few passages of Scripture are more important to our study of the Trinity, and in particular, of the person of the Son, than the prologue of John. You see, John clearly intended this passage to function as a lens, a window of sorts, through which we are to read the rest of his Gospel. If we stumble here, we are in danger of missing so much of the richness that is to be found in the rest of the book. But if we work hard to grasp John's meaning here, many other passages will open up for us of their own accord, yielding tremendous insights into the heart of God's revelation of himself in Jesus Christ.

I live in Arizona, and we have a number of old abandoned mines out in the desert, including the famous, though not yet located, "Lost Dutchman Mine." Most of these mines required a *tremendous* amount of work to open and run. But the hoped-for reward, the precious commodity of gold, was worth the effort on the part of the miners. In the same way, the prologue of John calls us to do some work, to stretch ourselves beyond what might be our "comfort zone," but the reward is more than worth it.

As you scan through the next few pages you will see some Greek terms. Don't let them stop you. I will explain what each one means, and for the person who is intent upon reaching the goal and truly entering into the treasure John has placed in these verses for us, they are necessary. No one studies Shakespeare solely in German or French—the subtleties of Shakespeare's language, his turning of a phrase, his use of synonyms or double meanings, can be lost in translation. So it is with John. John didn't write the prologue in English, and the person who wishes to delve deeply into his meaning will seek to hear him speaking *as he once spoke* in the beautiful Greek language.

> ¹In the beginning was the Word, and the Word was with God, and the Word was God. ²He was in the beginning with God. ³All things came into being through Him, and apart from Him nothing came into being that has come into being. (John 1:1–3)

Here is the translation with the important Greek terms provided.

The Greek term *follows* the English term that translates it.

> (John 1:1–3) In the beginning [ἐν ἀρχῇ] was [ἦν] the Word [ὁ λόγος], and the Word was with God [πρὸς τὸν θεόν], and the Word was God [θεὸς ἦν ὁ λόγος]. [2]He was in the beginning with God. [3]All things came into being through Him [πάντα δὶ αὐτοῦ ἐγένετο], and apart from Him nothing came into being that has come into being.

Each of the terms provided above is very important, and as we work through the prologue, you will see how each word reinforces the truth of the Christian belief in the inspiration of the Scriptures as well as in the deity of Jesus Christ.

IN THE BEGINNING

"In the beginning" should sound somewhat familiar. Many see this as a purposeful reference to Genesis 1:1, "In the beginning God created the heavens and the earth." Just as Genesis introduces God's work of creation, so John 1:1 introduces God's work of redeeming that people, and that work has been going on just as long as creation itself. Yet we do not need to focus solely upon the same point of origin in creation that is found in Genesis 1:1, for John is yet to give us some very important information about the time frame he has in mind.

THE WORD

We must keep foremost in our thinking the purpose of John's prologue. It can be summed up rather simply: Who is the Word? From verse 1 through verse 18, John is telling us about the Word. We dare not take our "eye off the ball," so to speak, and miss the fact that throughout this passage, the identity of the Word is at issue. Right at the start we must ask why John would use such a term as "the Word." What is he attempting to communicate?

The Greek term translated "Word" in this passage is *logos*. It is certainly not an unusual term. It appears three hundred and thirty times as a noun in the Greek New Testament alone. It has a wide range of meanings, from the basic "word" to merely a "matter" or a "thing."

So why would John choose such a word for such an important task?

The Greeks had used the term *logos* in their philosophical explanations regarding the functioning of the world. The *logos* was for them an impersonal ordering force, that which gave harmony to the universe. The *logos* was not personal in their philosophy, but it was very important.

In the Old Testament there are dim reflections upon a similar concept. The "Word of the Lord" came to have deep significance to the Jewish people. Such passages as Psalm 33:6, "By the word of the LORD the heavens were made, and by the breath of His mouth all their host," lent themselves to the idea that there was more to the "word" than one might see at first glance. During the few centuries prior to the coming of Christ, Jewish theologians and thinkers would see in such phrases as "word of the Lord" and in the "wisdom of God" references to a personal rather than an abstract concept.

But John went beyond everything that came before in his use of the term *logos*. In fact, as we proceed, we will see that it would be better to write *Logos* than *logos,* for John is using the word as a name, not merely a description. He fills the impersonal *logos* that came before him with personality and life, and presents to us the living and personal *Logos,* the Word who was in the beginning.

THE LITTLE WORD "WAS"

The English word "was" is about as bland a term as you can find. Yet in Greek, it is most expressive. The Greeks were quite concerned about being able to express subtleties in regard not only to *when* something happened, but *how* it happened as well. Our little word "was" is poorly suited to handle the depth of the Greek at this point. John's choice of words is deliberate and, quite honestly, beautiful.

Throughout the prologue of the Gospel of John, the author balances between two verbs. When speaking of the *Logos* as He existed in eternity past, John uses the Greek word ἦν, *en.* The tense[1] of the word expresses *continuous action in the past.* Compare this with the verb he chooses to use when speaking of everything else—found, for example, in verse 3: "All things *came into being* through Him," ἐγένετο, *egeneto.*

This verb[2] contains the very element missing from the other: a point of origin. The term, when used in contexts of creation and origin, speaks of a time when something came into existence. The first verb, *en*, does not. John is *very* careful to use only the first verb of the *Logos* throughout the first thirteen verses, and the second verb, *egeneto*, he uses for everything else (including John the Baptist in verse 6). Finally, in verse 14, he breaks this pattern, for a very specific reason, as we shall see.

Why emphasize the tense of a little verb? Because it tells us a great deal. When we speak of the Word, the *Logos,* we must ask ourselves: how long has the *Logos* existed? Did the *Logos* come into being at a point in time? Is the *Logos* a creature? John is very concerned that we get the right answer to such questions, and he provides the answers by the careful selection of the words he uses.

Above we noted that John gave us some very important information about the time frame he has in mind when he says "in the beginning." That information is found in the tense of the verb *en.* You see, as far back as you wish to push "the beginning," the Word is already in existence. The Word does not come *into* existence at the "beginning," but is already *in* existence when the "beginning" takes place. If we take the beginning of John 1:1, the Word is already there. If we push it back further (if one can even do so!), say, a year, the Word is already there. A thousand years, the Word is there. A billion years, the Word is there.[3] What is John's point? The Word is eternal. The Word has always existed. The Word is not a creation. The *New English Bible* puts it quite nicely: "When all things began, the Word already was."

Right from the start, then, John tells us something vital about the Word. Whatever else we will learn about the Word, the Word is *eternal.*[4] With this John begins to lay the foundation for what will come.

WITH GOD

The next phrase of John 1:1 tells us something new about the Word. The Word is eternal, but the Word was not alone in eternity past. "The Word was with God (πρὸς τὸν θεόν)." Yes, it is the same word "was," again pointing us to an eternal truth. The Word has eternally been "with God." What does this mean?

Just as Greek verbs are often more expressive than their English counterparts, so too are Greek prepositions. Here John uses the preposition πρός (*pros*). The term has a wide range of meanings, depending on the context in which it is found. In this particular instance, the term speaks to a personal *relationship*, in fact, to *intimacy*. It is the same term the apostle Paul uses when he speaks of how we presently have a knowledge comparable to seeing in a dim mirror, but someday, in eternity, we will have a clearer knowledge, an intimate knowledge, for we shall see "face to (*pros*) face" (1 Corinthians 13:12). When you are face-to-face with someone, you have nowhere to hide. You have a relationship with that person, whether you like it or not.[5]

In John 1:1b, John says the Word was eternally face-to-face with God, that is, that the Word has eternally had a relationship with God. Immediately, questions about how this can be pop into our minds, but for the moment we must stick with the text and follow John's thought through to its conclusion. He will answer our question about the identity of "God" in due time. For now, we note it is the normal word for God, θεόν (*theon*).[6] It is the word any monotheistic[7] Jew would use to describe the Almighty God, Yahweh, the Creator of all things. Someone such as John would never think that there were *two* eternal beings. John will explain himself soon enough.

WAS GOD

The third clause of John 1:1 balances out the initial presentation John is making about the Word. We read, "and the Word was God (θεὸς ἦν ὁ λόγος)." Again, the eternal *en*. John avoids contradiction by telling us that the Word was *with* God, and the Word *was* God. If John were making this an equation, like this:

$$\text{All of the "Word"} = \text{All of "God"}$$

he would be contradicting himself. If the Word is "all" of God, and God is "all" of the Word, and the two terms are interchangeable, then how could the Word be "with" himself? Such would make no sense.

But John beautifully walks the fine line, balancing God's truth as he is "carried along" by the Holy Spirit (2 Peter 1:21, NIV). John avoids equating the Word with all of God through his use of the little Greek article, the equivalent of our word "the" (ὁ).

It may seem "nit-picking" to talk about such a small thing as the Greek article, but as my friend Daniel Wallace points out, "One of the greatest gifts bequeathed by the Greeks to Western civilization was the article. European intellectual life was profoundly impacted by this gift of clarity."[8] He also notes, "In the least, we cannot treat it lightly, for its presence or absence is the crucial element to unlocking the meaning of scores of passages in the NT."[9] The writers of Scripture used the article to convey meaning, and we need to be very careful not to overlook the information they provide to us through the use, or nonuse, of the article.

The third clause of John 1:1 provides us with an example of what is known in grammar as a *predicate nominative* construction.[10] That is, we have a noun, the subject of the clause, which is "the Word." We have an "equative" or "copulative" verb, "was," and we have another noun, in the same case or form as the subject, which is called the *nominative* case, that being "God." We need to realize that in Greek the order in which words appear is not nearly as important as it is in English. The Greeks had no problem putting the subject of a sentence, or its main verb, *way* down the line, so to speak. Just because one word comes *before* another in Greek does not *necessarily* have any significance. What does this have to do with John 1:1? Well, in English, the final phrase would be literally rendered, "God was the Word." But in English, we put the *subject* first, and the predicate nominative later. The Greeks used the article to communicate to us which word is the subject, and which is the predicate. If one of the two nouns has the article, it is the subject. In this case, "Word" has the article, even though it comes *after* "God," and hence is our subject. That is why the last phrase is translated "the Word was God" rather than "God was the Word."

Stay with me now, for there is another important point to be seen in the text. If both of the nouns in a predicate nominative construction like this one have the article, or if both *lack* the article, this is significant as well. In that case, *the two nouns become interchangeable.* That is, if "Word" had the article, and "God" did, too, this would mean that John is saying that "God was the Word" and the "Word was God." Both would be the same thing. Or, if neither of them had the article, we would have the same idea: an equating of *all* of God with *all* of the Word. "God" and "Word" would be interchangeable and equal terms.

You see, much has been made, especially by Jehovah's Witnesses, of the fact that the word "God" in the last clause of John 1:1 is *anarthrous,* that is, without the article. You will notice that there is no form of the Greek article preceding the term θεός (*theos*). Because of this, they argue that we should translate it "a god." This completely misses the point of why the word *theos* does not have the article. If John had put the article before *theos,* he would have been teaching *modalism,* a belief we mentioned earlier that denies the existence of three divine persons, saying there is only one person who sometimes acts like the Father, sometimes like the Son, sometimes like the Spirit. We will discuss modalism (which is also often called "Sabellianism") later. For now, we see that if John had placed the article before *theos,* he would have been making "God" and the "Word" equal and interchangeable terms. As we will see, John is very careful to differentiate between these terms here, for He is careful to differentiate between the Father and the Son throughout the entire Gospel of John.[11]

One commentator has rightly noted regarding the prologue, "John is not trying to show who is God, but who is the Word."[12] The final phrase tells us about the *Word*, emphasizing the *nature* of the Word. F. F. Bruce's comments on this passage are valuable:

> The structure of the third clause in verse 1, *theos en ho logos,* demands the translation "The Word was God." Since *logos* has the article preceding it, it is marked out as the subject. The fact that *theos* is the first word after the conjunction *kai* (and) shows that the main emphasis of the clause lies on it. Had *theos* as well as *logos* been preceded by the article the meaning would have been that the Word was completely identical with God, which is impossible if the Word was also "with God." What is meant is that the Word

shared the nature and being of God, or (to use a piece of modern jargon) was an extension of the personality of God. The NEB paraphrase "what God was, the Word was," brings out the meaning of the clause as successfully as a paraphrase can.[13]

In the same way, the *New Living Translation* renders John 1:1, "In the beginning the Word already existed. He was with God, and he was God."

INDEFINITE, DEFINITE, QUALITATIVE, OR WHAT?

Before leaving John 1:1, we need to wrestle with the controversy that surrounds how to translate the final phrase. We've touched a bit on it above, but it would be good to lay out the possibilities. Without going into all the issues,[14] the possible *renderings* fall into three categories:

Indefinite: hence, "a god."
Definite: hence, "God."
Qualitative: hence, "in nature God."

Arguments abound about how to translate an "anarthrous preverbal predicate nominative," and most people get lost fairly quickly when you start throwing terms like *those* around. Basically, the question we have to ask is this: how does John intend us to take the word θεός in the last clause? Does he wish us to understand it as *indefinite*, so that no particular "god" is in mind, but instead, that Jesus is *a god*, one of at least two, or even more?[15] Or is θεός definite, so that *the God* is in view? Or does the position of the word (before the verb, adding emphasis), coupled with the lack of the article, indicate that John is directing us to a *quality* when he says the Word is θεός? That is, is John describing the *nature* of the Word, saying the Word is deity?

In reference to the first possibility, we can dismiss it almost immediately. The reasons are as follows:

Monotheism in the Bible—certainly it cannot be argued that John would use the very word he always uses of the one true God, θεός, of one who is simply a "godlike" one or a lesser "god." The Scriptures do not teach that there exists a whole host of intermediate beings that can truly be called "gods." That is gnosticism.

The anarthrous θεός —If one is to dogmatically assert that any anarthrous noun must be indefinite and translated with an indefinite article, one must be able to do the same with the 282 other times θεός appears anarthrously. For an example of the chaos that would create, try translating the anarthrous θεός at 2 Corinthians 5:19 (i.e., "a god was in Christ . . ."). What is more, θεός appears many times in the prologue of John anarthrously, yet no one argues that in these instances it should be translated "a god." Note verses 6, 12, 13, and 18. There is simply no warrant in the language to do this.[16]

No room for alternate understanding—It ignores a basic tenet of translation: if you are going to insist on a translation, you must be prepared to defend it in such a way so as to provide a way for the author to have expressed the alternate translation. In other words, if θεὸς ἦν ὁ λόγος is "the Word was a god," how could John have said "the Word was God?" We have already seen that if John had employed the article before θεός, he would have made the terms θεός and λόγος interchangeable, amounting to modalism.

Ignores the context—The translation tears the phrase from the immediately preceding context, leaving it alone and useless. Can He who is eternal (first clause) and who has always been with God (second clause), and who created all things (verse 3), be "a god"?

F. F. Bruce sums up the truth pretty well:

> It is nowhere more sadly true than in the acquisition of Greek that "a little learning is a dangerous thing." The uses of the Greek article, the functions of Greek prepositions, and the fine distinctions between Greek tenses are confidently expounded in public at times by men who find considerable difficulty in using these parts of speech accurately in their native tongue.[17]

A footnote appears after the comment on the article, and it says:

> Those people who emphasize that the true rendering of the last

clause of John 1.1 is "the word was a god," prove nothing thereby save their ignorance of Greek grammar.

So our decision, then, must be between the *definite* understanding of the word and the *qualitative*. If we take θεός as *definite*, we are hard-pressed to avoid the same conclusion that we would reach if the word had the article; that is, if we wish to say *the God* in the same way as if the word had the article, we are making θεός and λόγος interchangeable. Yet the vast majority of translations render the phrase "the Word was God." Is this not the definite translation? Not necessarily.

The last clause of John 1:1 tells us *about the nature* of the Word. The translation should be *qualitative*. We have already seen in the words of F. F. Bruce that John is telling us that the Word "shared the nature and being of God."[18] The *New English Bible* renders the phrase "what God was, the Word was." Kenneth Wuest puts it, "And the Word was as to His essence absolute deity."[19] Yet Daniel Wallace is quite right when he notes:

> Although I believe that θεός in 1:1c is qualitative, I think the simplest and most straightforward translation is, "and the Word was God." It may be better to clearly affirm the NT teaching of the deity of Christ and then explain that he is *not* the Father, than to *sound* ambiguous on his deity and explain that he is God but is not the Father.[20]

Here we encounter another instance where the English translation is not quite up to the Greek original. We must go beyond a basic translation and ask what John himself meant.

In summary, then, what do we find in John 1:1? In a matter of only seventeen short Greek words, John communicates the following truths:

The Word is eternal—He has always existed and did not come into existence at a point in time.
The Word is personal—He is not a force, but a person, and that eternally. He has always been in communion with the Father.
The Word is deity—The Word is God as to His nature.

We would all do well to communicate so much in so few words! But he did not stop at verse 1. This is but the first verse of an entire composition. We move on to examine the rest.

MORE ON THE ETERNAL WORD, THE CREATOR

In verses 2 and 3, John continues his work of introducing us to the *Logos*, the Word. He reemphasizes the startling statement of verse 1 by insisting that "He was in the beginning with God." Again the English is not quite as expressive as the Greek, for John puts the Greek word translated "He" at the beginning of the phrase so that we could very well understand him to be saying, *"This One"* was in the beginning, or *"This is the One"* who has eternally existed in personal relationship with God (the Father, as we shall see in verse 18, and as John himself says in 1 John 1:2).

Verse 3 then introduces another evidence of the deity of the *Logos*: His role in creation. "All things came into being through Him, and apart from Him nothing came into being that has come into being." Here is a phrase that can *only be used of the one true God.* Creation is always *God's work.* If the *Logos* created all things, then the *Logos* is divine—fully.[21] John is very careful. He doesn't say "most things," or "some things," but *all things* came into being, were made, by the *Logos.* Creation took place *through* Him, by His power. Apart or separately from Him, *nothing was made which has been made.*[22] This is clearly an *exhaustive* assertion. Just as Paul in Colossians 1:16–17 uses the entirety of the Greek language to express the unlimited extent of Christ's creative activity, so, too, John makes sure that we do not leave room for *anything* that is not made by the *Logos.* If it exists, it does so because it was created by the *Logos.*

John continues his work of introducing us to the Word by stating that in Him was life, and that life was the light of men. He goes on to speak of the preparation for the coming of the *Logos* into the world through the ministry of John (vv. 6–8). He then turns to the matter of the rejection, by some, of the *Logos*, and the acceptance by others, resulting in regeneration and salvation (vv. 10–13). In these verses John speaks to us about what the *Logos* does by coming into the world. But starting in verse 14 John returns to the subject of *who* the *Logos* is. And what he says is as amazing as what we saw in the first few verses.

ETERNITY INVADES TIME

Throughout the first thirteen verses of the gospel of John, our author has carefully distinguished the eternal *Logos* from that which is made by Him through the use of the verbs *en* and *egeneto*. But in verse 14 he communicates a deep truth to us by changing his pattern, and that for a clear reason. He writes:

> And the Word became flesh, and dwelt among us, and we saw His glory, glory as of the only begotten from the Father, full of grace and truth.

"And the Word *became* flesh." Here John uses *egeneto*, a verb that refers to an action in time. And the reason is clear: the Word entered into human existence, "became flesh," at a particular point in time. The *Logos* was not eternally flesh. He existed in a nonfleshly manner in eternity past. But at a blessed point in time, at the Incarnation, the *Logos* became flesh. The Eternal experienced time.

We need to stop and consider this truth for just a moment. Sometimes Christians who have known God's truth for a long time become somewhat hardened to the impact such a declaration was meant to carry. The Word, the Creator of all things, the Eternal One, *became flesh*. Maybe we think so highly of ourselves that we are not properly struck by such a statement. We need to be amazed by the assertion, "The Word became flesh." How can the unlimited enter into limitation? John does not tell us. The mechanics of *how* are not revealed to us, for God is under no obligation to answer every prying question. We are simply told that the eternal Word became flesh. Faith rests in God's revelation.

The Word *became* flesh. He did not simply *appear* to be flesh. He was not "faking it," to use modern terminology. Jesus was not simply some phantom or spirit masquerading as a real human being. He became *flesh*. John uses a term that was easily understandable in his day. It's not an unusual word. At times it refers solely to *flesh*, as in the material stuff of our bodies. At other times it refers to the whole human nature. In any case, its meaning could not be missed. The *Logos* entered into the physical realm. He became a human being, a real, living, breathing human being.

John is so concerned that his readers understand that he points out that He "dwelt among us, and we saw His glory." John is not reporting a second- or third-hand story. He is giving an eyewitness account. Jesus dwelt among us. He lived His life in the middle of the mass of humanity. He rubbed shoulders with sinners and saints. He walked dusty roads, thirsted for water on hot days, and reclined at the table with friends, and even with enemies. He really existed, He really lived.

Why is John so concerned about this? We note that he repeats this emphasis in 1 John 1:1–5, and then goes so far as to say that anyone who denies that Jesus Christ came in the flesh is the antichrist (1 John 4:2–3)! The reason is found in the fact that even while the apostles lived on earth, false teachers were entering into the church. Specifically, there were men teaching a system that would eventually become known as "Gnosticism." This belief system teaches that everything that is spirit is good, and everything that is material (including flesh) is evil. This is known as the belief in "dualism." Spirit is good, matter is evil.

What, then, does a person do who believes in dualism but wants to make some room for the message of Jesus? He has to get around the plain fact that Jesus Christ came *in the flesh*. So these teachers, known to the early church by the term *Docetics*,[23] denied that Jesus truly had a physical body so that they could keep the idea that He was good and pure and holy. They even spread stories about disciples walking with Jesus along the beach, and when one of the disciples turned around, he saw only one set of footprints, because, of course, Jesus doesn't leave footprints! John is *tremendously* concerned that his beloved readers do not fall for this kind of teaching, so he strongly emphasizes the reality of Christ's physical nature. He leaves no stone unturned in his quest to make sure we understand: the eternal *Logos*, fully deity by nature, eternal Creator, the very source of life itself, *became a human being*. This is the only way to understand his words.

John insists that he and his companions observed the glory of the "only begotten from the Father." It would be good to stop for a moment and make sure we have a firm understanding of what "only begotten" means. Huge misunderstandings have arisen about the use of this term. For those interested in the in-depth story, an extended note is attached to this chapter. To summarize that information for our purposes here, the Greek term used is μονογενής (*monogenes*). The term does not refer to *begetting*, but to *uniqueness*. While the traditional translation is "only-begotten," a better translation would be "unique" or "one of a kind."

In verse 14, John uses the term as a title, "the glory of the One and Only" (NIV). Immediately we see that the term *monogenes* has special meaning for John, for he speaks of the One and Only having "glory." The One and Only comes "from the Father." This is the first time John has specifically identified the Father by name in this Gospel. He differentiates the Father from the *Logos*, the "One and Only," clearly directing us to two *persons,* the one coming *from* the other. Yet the *Logos* is seen to have glory, to have a divine origin with the Father, and is said to be "full of grace and truth."

John moves on to again make note of John's testimony to Jesus in verse 15, and finally makes it plain that he is speaking of Jesus Christ by using that phrase for the first time in verse 17. But before he closes his prologue, John uses what is often called the "bookends" technique. He provides a closing statement that sums up and repeats, in a different form, what he said in his introduction. And this is found in the final verse of the prologue, verse 18.

THE ONLY SON, WHO IS GOD

When you are speaking to someone, it is usually the last thing you say that will be remembered. That's what we are taught in classes on "How to Make a Great Presentation." John seemed to understand that concept, because in John 1:18 he provides us with a summary statement, the second bookend, so to speak, for his prologue. Here's what he wrote:

No one has seen God at any time; the only begotten God who

is in the bosom of the Father, He has explained Him. (NASB)

Let's note a couple of other translations:

> No one has ever seen God, but God the One and Only, who is at the Father's side, has made him known. (NIV)

> No one has ever seen God. It is God the only Son, who is close to the Father's heart, who has made him known. (NRSV)

Yet if you have a KJV or NKJV, your translation reads differently at a very key point. Note the NKJV translation:

> No one has seen God at any time. The only begotten Son, who is in the bosom of the Father, He has declared *Him.*

The KJV and NKJV follow a later, less primitive text in reading "the only begotten Son" rather than "the only begotten God" (NASB). We have here a textual variant, pitting the earliest, oldest manuscripts of the gospel of John against the later bulk of manuscripts. Without going into a lot of detail,[24] there is every reason to accept the reading of the earliest manuscripts, and to see the later emendation as a natural mistake made by scribes who were accustomed to the phraseology "only begotten son."

But even once we have established the proper reading of the text, how do we translate it? The phrase in question is μονογενὴς θεός (*monogenes theos*). The renderings given above provide a wide range of translation, from the very literal "the only begotten God" (NASB) through the NIV's "God the One and Only" to the NRSV's "God the only Son." There are excellent summaries of the issue available,[25] so we won't go into the technicalities here. Suffice it to say that I find the NRSV's translation to be the best, "God the only Son." If we wanted something a little more literal, I would suggest, "the only Son, *who is* God." This preserves the word order that John uses, placing *monogenes* as a title immediately preceding *theos* (God).

What is John telling us by using such an unusual phrase? One thing is for certain: he is *not* telling us that Jesus Christ was "created" at some time in the past. He is *not* denying everything he said in the previous seventeen verses and turning Jesus into a creation! Such ideas flow from wrong thinking about what *monogenes* means. Remember that the term means "unique" or "one of a kind." In light of this, John's meaning is clear. In fact, I would submit that outside of a Trinitarian understanding of this passage, John is making no sense at all! What do I mean?

John tells us that no one has seen God at any time. Is this true? Are there not many instances of men seeing God in the Old Testament? Did not Isaiah say that he saw the Lord sitting upon His throne in the temple (Isaiah 6:1–3)? So what is John saying? How can we understand his words?

The key is found in the final phrases of verse 18, specifically, "who is at the Father's side." When John says "no one has seen God at any time," he is referring to the *Father*. No man has seen the *Father* at any time. So how do we have knowledge of the Father? The μονογενής has "made Him known" or "explained Him."[26] The *unique One* has made the Father known. Or, in light of the use of the term Father, *the Only Son* has revealed the Father. But this is not merely a dim reflection, a partial revelation, provided by the Only Son. This is the *monogenes theos*, the Only Son *who is God*. The divine nature of the μονογενής is again plainly asserted, just as it was in verse 1. This is what forms the "bookend," the assertion in verse 1 that the *Logos* is divine, repeated and reaffirmed here in verse 18 with the statement that the Only Son is *God*.[27]

Another important fact to note from this verse is that if indeed no one has seen *the Father*, then what does this tell us of the Son? Who did Isaiah see in Isaiah 6? Who walked with Abraham by the oaks of Mamre (Genesis 18:1)? None other than the preincarnate Jesus Christ, the eternal *Logos*. John will develop this thought later in his Gospel, as we shall see when we examine those passages that identify Jesus as Yahweh.

With the great truths proclaimed in the prologue in mind, I would strongly encourage you to take the time to *read the entire gospel of John.* It's barely an evening's reading, and with the prologue acting as a "lens," giving you the proper perspective of who Jesus Christ truly is, you will find passages leaping from the page, all of which confirm and substantiate the proclamation of John 1:1–18: Jesus Christ is God in human flesh, the eternal Creator of all things, "the Only Son, *who is* God!"

CHAPTER 5

Jesus Christ: God in Human Flesh

There is a particular group of passages in the Holy Scriptures that uses the word "God" of the Lord Jesus. While we could wish this would be enough to banish all doubt, obviously it is not. The deity of Christ is the constant object of attack and denial, and the verses that bear testimony to this divine truth have been mistranslated, twisted, and in various other ways undermined by nearly every false prophet and false teacher over the past seventeen hundred years.

Just as the writers of the New Testament and the early Christians did not hesitate to confess Jesus as their God, so we, too, must be bold in our profession of this divine truth. We will, in this chapter, see how the early Christians called Jesus "God." Each passage has been attacked in almost every imaginable way; thus, we will have to explain why we believe these passages proclaim the deity of Christ, and why others should accept this truth.

There are many extensive and exhaustive works on each of these verses of Scripture, and we will not seek to recreate those works here. Instead, I desire my fellow servants of Christ to be encouraged in their faith in our Lord and to be strengthened in their faith and their testimony to the Lord of glory, the one Thomas called "my Lord and my God."

RIGHT AT THE START

It seems an appropriate time to settle one of the most important issues regarding the Trinity and the text of Scripture. If all Christians would simply understand the following statement, their task of explaining and defending the Trinity would be much easier. Here is a basic, simple truth that is lost in the vast majority of discussions (or arguments) on this topic:

Difference in function does not indicate inferiority of nature.

Not exactly an earth-shattering concept? It isn't, but *the vast majority of material produced by those who oppose the deity of Christ ignores this basic truth.* What do I mean? It's really quite simple. Let's take a common argument against the deity of Christ: "The Father is the Creator of all things. He creates *through* Jesus Christ. Therefore, Jesus Christ is not fully God." Or here's another argument against the deity of the Spirit: "The Spirit is sent to testify of Jesus Christ and convict the world of sin. Since the Spirit is sent by the Father, the Spirit cannot truly be God." Both arguments share the same error: they ignore the above cited truth, *difference in function does not indicate inferiority of nature.* That is, just because the Father, Son, and Spirit *do* different things does not mean that any one of them is *inferior* to the others *in nature.*[1]

Think of it this way: in eternity past[2] the Father, Son, and Spirit *voluntarily and freely chose the roles they would take in bringing about the redemption of God's people.* This is what is called the "Eternal Covenant of Redemption." The Father chose to be the fount and source of the entirety of the work; the Son chose to be the Redeemer and to enter into human flesh as one subject to the Father; and the Spirit chose to be the Sanctifier of the church, the indwelling Testifier of Jesus Christ.

Each took different roles of necessity—they could not all take the same role and do the same things.

The large portion of arguments against the deity of Christ and the Trinity make one major unspoken (and false) assumption: that for either the Son or the Spirit to be truly and fully God, *they have to do the exact same things as the Father in the exact same way.* That is, they assume there cannot possibly be any differentiation in the persons of the Trinity without introducing an automatic inferiority on the part of those who do something "different" than the Father. Any difference in function, they assume, results in an inferiority of nature. To put it simply, they *assume* a unitarian view of God (as opposed to the Trinitarian view), and *assume* that God could never do what He has revealed He has done in the work of redemption.

The truth of the matter is, however, that just because the Son takes a different role in the eternal covenant of Redemption, it does not follow that He is inferior in nature to the Father or the Spirit. The different role He takes *distinguishes* Him from the Father and the Spirit, but it does not make Him *less* than the Father or the Spirit. It is quite true that Jesus is normally described as the *agent* of creation and the Father as the *source* of creation, but it does not logically follow that the Son is therefore *inferior.* It only follows that He is *different.* In the same way, the Spirit is indeed *sent* by the Father and the Son, but this only makes Him *different* than the Father and the Son, not *less than* the Father and the Son.

When you dig past the rhetoric and really examine the *best* writings against the Christian confession of the Trinity and the deity of Christ, you find that these arguments are circular at their core. They assume that Yahweh is *uni-personal,* or *unitarian,* and then use that assumption to attack and deny all evidence to the contrary. Keeping this one truth in mind will help you evaluate the passages that describe the Lord Jesus Christ as God, even while distinguishing Him from the Father.

There is one other thought to keep in mind *whenever* we engage in dialogue on the issue of the deity of Christ. Christians often get so caught up in the "battle" that they lose sight of some basic considerations. When we encounter someone who denies the deity of Christ, we often "let them off the hook" by not asking them to defend *their* view on the basis of each passage we are considering. We don't apply the same arguments to *their* position that they are applying to *ours*.

The most obvious example is provided by Jehovah's Witnesses. They have a positive belief that Jesus is actually an angelic creature, Michael, the Archangel.[3] When dialoguing with Witnesses about the deity of Christ, we must not only give a positive defense of our own faith, but we must constantly be asking if the descriptions of Christ found in Scripture could possibly be applied to Michael the Archangel. Could we describe Michael as the Way, the Truth, and the Life? (John 14:6). Could an angel say, "Come to Me, all who are weary and heavy-laden, and I will give you rest"? (Matthew 11:28). Is an angel King of kings and Lord of lords? (Revelation 19:16). Does divine grace come from God the Father and Michael the Archangel? (1 Corinthians 1:3). Can Michael say, "He who has seen Me has seen the Father"? (John 14:9). What could it possibly mean to say, "For to me, to live is Michael the Archangel and to die is gain"? (Philippians 1:21). We can go on and on in this way, for many of the strongest proofs of the deity of Christ are found in recognizing that no mere creature could ever say the words Jesus said, do the things Jesus did, or be described in the way Jesus is described.

Keeping these two concepts in mind will assist the follower of Christ in accurately handling the testimony of Scripture to the majesty of the Lord Jesus.

THOMAS'S CONFESSION

It is one of the most touching scenes in all of Scripture. Its meaning is clear, unambiguous, and plain. Its translation is not questionable on any serious grounds. And the only way around it is to engage in the greatest sorts of mental gymnastics. For the Christian, it is but an echo of the heart that loves Christ. For the person who denies the truth about Jesus Christ, it is an insurmountable barrier.

In God's providence, Thomas had been absent the first time the risen Lord Jesus Christ appeared to His disciples. John records the incident for us:

But Thomas, one of the twelve, called Didymus, was not with them when Jesus came. So the other disciples were saying to him, "We have seen the Lord!" But he said to them, "Unless I see in His hands the imprint of the nails, and put my finger into the place of the nails, and put my hand into His side, I will not believe" (John 20:24–25).

The Lord was well aware of the word of His skeptical disciple, even though He was not physically present at the time. The encounter between the risen Lord and Thomas follows quickly:

After eight days His disciples were again inside, and Thomas with them. Jesus came, the doors having been shut, and stood in their midst and said, "Peace *be* with you." Then He said to Thomas, "Reach here with your finger, and see My hands; and reach here your hand and put it into My side; and do not be unbelieving, but believing" (John 20:26–27).

Thomas surely was struck to his heart when the Lord immediately turned His attention to him and demonstrated that the words he had spoken were known to the risen Lord. How will Thomas respond? He has been invited to believe. We are not told if he actually put forth his hand to dispel his skepticism. All we are told is what he said, and how the Lord responded:

Thomas answered and said to Him, "My Lord and my God!" Jesus said to him, "Because you have seen Me, have you believed? Blessed *are* they who did not see, and *yet* believed" (John 20:28–29).

Thomas's answer is simple and clear. It is directed to the Lord Jesus, not to anyone else, for John says, "he said *to Him*." The content of his confession is plain and unambiguous. "My Lord and my God!" Jesus is Thomas's Lord. Of this there is no question.[4] And there is simply no reason—grammatical, contextual, or otherwise—to deny that in the very same breath Thomas calls Jesus Christ his "God."[5]

Jesus' response to Thomas's confession shows not the slightest discomfort at the appellation "God." Jesus says Thomas has shown *faith*, for he has "believed." He then pronounces a blessing upon all who will believe like Thomas without the added element of physical sight. There is no reproach of Thomas's description of Jesus as his Lord and God. No created being could *ever* allow such words to be addressed to him personally. No angel, no prophet, no sane human being, could ever allow himself to be addressed as "Lord and God." Yet Jesus not only accepts the words of Thomas but pronounces the blessing of faith upon them as well.

What could be clearer? Should not such a passage banish all doubt? Should we not be able to simply cite this verse and see every person who denies the deity of Christ repenting of their error in its glaring light? Of course, such is wishful thinking. Man finds ways around everything, and the most common means of avoiding the weight of this passage is to move the conversation back a few verses:

> Jesus said to her, "Stop clinging to Me, for I have not yet ascended to the Father; but go to My brethren and say to them, 'I ascend to My Father and your Father, and My God and your God'" (John 20:17).

Why cite this passage? Because the truth I noted at the beginning of this chapter really *is* frequently ignored! The idea is simple: if Jesus can speak of His "God," then He can't really be *God*, but must be something less (i.e., a creature) who is called "God" but only in a "sort of" fashion. Remember the maxim: *Difference in function does not indicate inferiority of nature.* Here the Father is described as Jesus' "God." Since this is so, Jesus must be some inferior being, and therefore, John 20:28 can't mean what it so obviously says.[6] Note how one writer has expressed it:

> Such a confession, as in the case of Thomas, is *qualified* not only by the context (John 20:17), but also by the whole of Scripture. The use of later Chalcedonian christology does not come into play in verses such as John 20:17, either. Here Jesus, in the same state Thomas addressed him, says that the Father is his God, again

differentiating between the two in terms of *theos,* as well as acknowledging the Father's superiority over him, as his God.[7]

And just here we see the circularity of the arguments of those who deny the deity of Christ: why can't Thomas mean what he said? Because, of course, the Father is *different* than the Son. It was the *Son* who became Incarnate, and since the Son, as the perfect man, acknowledged the Father as His God, He, himself, can't be fully deity. The argument assumes that God *could not enter into human form.* Why? Well, what would the God-man be like? If one of the divine persons entered into human flesh, how would such a divine person act? Would He be an atheist? Would He refuse to acknowledge those divine persons who had *not* entered into human existence? Of course not. Yet when we see the Lord Jesus doing exactly what we would expect the Incarnate Son to do, we find this being used as an argument against His deity! So those who put forward such arguments have already made up their minds. They are not deriving their beliefs *from* the Scriptures but are forcing those beliefs *onto* the Scriptures. Thomas's confession is in perfect harmony with the fact that the Incarnate Son spoke of the Father as His God. As long as one recognizes that the word "God" can refer to the Father, to the Son, to the Spirit, or to all three persons at once, the asserted contradiction is seen to be nothing more than a circular argument designed to avoid having to make the same confession that Thomas made long ago.

GOD OVER ALL

Romans 9:5 presents us with another reference to the deity of Christ. However, this passage also carries some challenges along with it:

> . . . whose are the fathers, and from whom is the Christ according to the flesh, who is over all, God blessed forever. Amen.

As the translation will be the key, let's look at some other renderings. Some translations directly identify Jesus as God in this passage:

> Theirs are the patriarchs, and from them is traced the human

ancestry of Christ, who is God over all, forever praised! Amen. (NIV)

. . . of whom *are* the fathers and from whom, according to the flesh, Christ *came,* who is over all, *the* eternally blessed God. Amen. (NKJV)

Their ancestors were great people of God, and Christ himself was a Jew as far as his human nature is concerned. And he is God, who rules over everything and is worthy of eternal praise! Amen. (NLT)

They are descended from the patriarchs and from their flesh and blood came Christ who is above all, God for ever blessed! Amen. (JB)

Others leave the issue somewhat undecided:

Whose are the fathers, and of whom as concerning the flesh Christ came, who is over all, God blessed for ever. Amen. (KJV)

To them belong the patriarchs, and from them, according to the flesh, comes the Messiah, who is over all, God blessed forever. Amen. (NRSV)

And others insert a complete break into the text, leaving no room for the deity of Christ in the passage:

Theirs are the patriarchs, and from them, in natural descent, sprang the Messiah. May God, supreme above all, be blessed for ever! Amen. (NEB)

They are descended from the patriarchs, and Christ, as a human being, belongs to their race. May God, who rules over all, be praised forever! Amen. (TEV)

So what do we do with the text? We are able to clearly discern Paul's intentions here in reference to the deity of Christ. It just takes a little work and a little background.

We should remember that punctuation did not exist in the most primitive manuscripts of the New Testament. Hence, punctuation is an interpretational issue. We have to decide where to place periods and commas on the basis of Paul's style and his statements elsewhere.

The most often repeated argument *against* viewing this passage as speaking of the Christ as "God" is that Paul nowhere else refers to the Lord in that way. But such is a circular argument, for not only can one refer to Titus 2:13 (see below) where Paul does this very thing, but would it be a valid argument against Titus 2:13 to likewise say that Paul doesn't call Jesus "God" elsewhere? Seemingly the person offering this argument is not so much seeking to interpret the passage as to substantiate a particular theology.

The arguments in favor of seeing this passage as a reference to the deity of Christ are many. I will summarize them here:[8]

(1) It is the natural reading of the text to see the entire verse as referring to Christ. Breaking the sentence up into two parts leads to difficulties in translation and interpretation. Some words become superfluous,[9] and the balance of the sentence is thrown off.[10]

(2) The phrase "who is" is used by Paul elsewhere to modify a word in the preceding context (as in 2 Corinthians 11:31, a very close parallel), and would naturally do so here as well.

(3) The form of the doxology simply will not allow for it to be separated from the preceding context. Paul's consistent usage connects the doxology to the discussion of Christ. In his other doxologies[11] he follows this pattern.

(4) In the Greek New Testament, and in the Greek translation of the Old Testament (the Septuagint), the word "blessed" always[12] comes *before* the word "God," but here in Romans 9:5 it follows, which would indicate that the "blessing" is tied to what came before (i.e., the discussion of Christ). So strong is this last point that Metzger said it is "altogether incredible that Paul, whose ear must have been perfectly familiar with this constantly recurring formula of praise, should in this solitary instance have departed from established usage."[13]

Add to these weighty considerations the testimony of many of the early

Fathers as well,[14] and the conclusion is inescapable: Paul breaks into praise at the majesty of the person of the Messiah who has come into the world through the Jewish race. The very God who is over all has entered into flesh, and for this, Paul gives glory and honor.

THE ANGELS WORSHIP HIM

> And when He again brings the firstborn into the world, He says, "AND LET ALL THE ANGELS OF GOD WORSHIP HIM." And of the angels He says, "WHO MAKES HIS ANGELS WINDS, AND HIS MINISTERS A FLAME OF FIRE." But of the Son *He says,* "YOUR THRONE, O GOD, IS FOREVER AND EVER, AND THE RIGHTEOUS SCEPTER IS THE SCEPTER OF HIS KINGDOM" (Hebrews 1:6–8).

We will have occasion to enter into the first chapter of Hebrews searching for golden nuggets on the deity of Christ a total of three times.[15] But first we look at the use of the term "God" of the Lord Jesus in this passage, specifically in verse 8.

There is debate over the translation of the passage, for on a strictly grammatical basis, one could render it "God is Your throne" rather than "Your throne, O God," and, of course, this is exactly the argument presented by all who deny the deity of Christ. But again the context indicates otherwise. Without going into a lot of detail,[16] the writer to the Hebrews is demonstrating the superiority of Jesus Christ to the angels. He says that all the angels of God worship the Firstborn.[17] This is true religious worship, as the context demands.[18] Such worship is only given to God. He contrasts this worship by the angels of the Son[19] with the description God uses of angels as mere "winds" and "flames of fire." But, in opposition to this, the description God uses of the Son is striking. Quoting from Psalm 45:6–7, God (the Father) makes reference to God (the Son), saying, "Your throne, O God, is forever and ever."

It should be noted that the passage the writer quotes, Psalm 45, was a "wedding" psalm written in reference to the king of Israel.[20] As with so many other passages in the Old Testament, it takes on a much greater meaning when applied to the King of kings, Jesus Christ. While the Israelite king's reign was temporary, the reign of Christ will truly be forever and ever. In summarizing the teaching of this passage, Murray Harris said:

> The appellation ὁ θεός that was figurative and hyperbolic when applied to a mortal king was applied to the immortal Son in a literal and true sense. Jesus is not merely superior to the angels. Equally with the Father he shares in the divine nature (ὁ θεός, v. 8) while remaining distinct from him (ὁ θεός σου, v. 9). The author places Jesus far above any angel with respect to nature and function, and on a par with God with regard to nature but subordinate to God with regard to function. There is an "essential" unity but a functional subordination.[21]

That Dr. Harris is correct is seen by noting how the context supports his conclusions. Not only is Jesus the object of divine worship in verse 6, but we will see that in verses 10 through 12 He is identified as Yahweh.[22] Since Christ is shown receiving worship immediately before this passage, and identified with Yahweh immediately thereafter, there can be nothing strange about the Father referring to the Son as "God" in verse 8.

Finally, in another place where Christ is identified as God, Isaiah 9:6 (which will be examined below), the same truth that Christ's kingdom is an everlasting kingdom is found. The only One whose throne will *truly* be forever and ever is God himself.

OUR GREAT GOD AND SAVIOR

Paul describes Christians as faithful people who are looking for a blessed event: the coming of Jesus Christ. Here are his words:

> . . . looking for the blessed hope and the appearing of the glory of our great God and Savior, Christ Jesus, who gave Himself for us to redeem us from every lawless deed, and to purify for Himself a people for His own possession, zealous for good deeds. (Titus 2:13–14)

The appearing of Christ is described as our "blessed hope," and indeed it is. The key phrase is obviously the description of Jesus as "our great God and Savior." Do both terms refer to Jesus? That is the issue. But before we demonstrate that indeed both words are being used of Christ, we dare not rush past the context itself. Could it be that Christians have a blessed hope that is anchored in looking for the appearance of a mere creature, say, Michael the Archangel?

Paul says that the Lord Jesus "gave Himself for us to redeem us from every lawless deed." This is in reference to the atoning sacrifice of Jesus Christ upon the cross of Calvary. Since it is plainly the coming of the Lord Jesus that we are expectantly awaiting, and since it is the Lord Jesus who gave himself for us on the Cross, what reason is there, contextually, for introducing another person into the passage? Simply put, there is none. The only reason some attempt to do so is to avoid the clear identification of Jesus Christ as "God and Savior."

Another contextual clue confirms the assertion of the deity of Christ by Paul. Verse 14 says that Christ intends to "purify for Himself a people for His own possession, zealous for good deeds." To the person whose ear is attuned to the words of the Old Testament, this is a phrase that would bring to mind none other than Yahweh himself:

> O Israel, hope in the LORD;
> For with the LORD there is lovingkindness,
> And with Him is abundant redemption.
> And He will redeem Israel from all his iniquities. (Psalm 130:7–8)

What is not immediately apparent by simply looking at the English text is that this passage from the psalms uses the same terms[23] found in Titus 2:14. Specifically, "to redeem" in the psalm is the same term used by Paul of the redeeming work of Christ, and the term "iniquities" in the psalm is the term translated "lawless deed" in Titus. While it is Yahweh who redeems His people in the Old Testament, here it is Christ. But there is more:

> "They will no longer defile themselves with their idols, or with their detestable things, or with any of their transgressions; but I will deliver them from all their dwelling places in which they have

sinned, and will cleanse them. And they will be My people, and I will be their God" (Ezekiel 37:23).

Here Yahweh again speaks of His redemption of His people, and again Paul uses the same terms to describe the work of Christ. Specifically, the word "cleanse" is the same in both passages, as is the word "people." Just coincidence? Not at all, for there is more:

"Now then, if you will indeed obey My voice and keep My covenant, then you shall be My own possession among all the peoples, for all the earth is Mine" (Exodus 19:5).

The phrase "My own possession" is the same in Exodus, where Yahweh speaks of His special people, and in Titus, where Christ has a people for His own possession. Deuteronomy 7:6 and 14:2 make the same statement. Anyone familiar with a "redeemed people" in the Old Testament would recognize that Paul is applying the same terms used of Yahweh there to the Lord Jesus here. The context, then, is one that would find no problem at all in calling Jesus "God and Savior," since it has freely applied to Him words that had been used by God's people for centuries to describe Yahweh, their Savior.

The focus of attention in Titus 2:13 has always been on whether we should understand Paul to be applying *both* terms "God" and "Savior" to Christ. We have seen that before addressing the grammatical concerns, the context gives us no reason whatsoever to think that two persons are in view here. Only Christ is under discussion. One must wonder, then, why anyone would *wish* to find a second person, since the context does not push us in that direction.

As with every other such passage, large numbers of papers and articles have been written regarding the proper translation of Titus 2:13. In fact, an entire grammatical rule finds its primary application in this passage. The rule has been dubbed Granville Sharp's Rule,[24] after Granville Sharp who first formulated it. In reality, Sharp's Rule is more of a set of rules, all relating to the use of nouns and the Greek connective καί, "and." Without going into great detail, Sharp's study of the text of the New Testament led him to recognize that when the writer used a particular construction of "article (the word "the")—substantive (noun)—καί —substantive," and when the personal nouns involved were singular and not proper names, they *always* referred to the same person.[25] The significance to Titus 2:13 is found in the fact that the phrase "our great God and Savior" fits this pattern exactly:

τοῦ μεγάλου θεοῦ καὶ σωτῆρος ἡμῶν Ἰησοῦ Χριστοῦ

The word "God" has the definite article ("the") before it. It is connected by the word καί with the word "Savior." There is only one person in the context to which both terms, then, can be applied: Jesus Christ. He is our God and Savior.

Various attempts have been made to short-circuit this rule of Greek grammar, all prompted by an unwillingness to believe what the text itself says. Dr. Daniel Wallace's work on the subject in recent years has only further strengthened the validity of Sharp's Rule, and its application at Titus 2:13.[26]

But we only see half the evidence when we look only at Titus 2:13. There is another very important passage that adds further evidence to the validity of this understanding of the text of the New Testament:

> Simon Peter, a bond-servant and apostle of Jesus Christ, to those who have received a faith of the same kind as ours, by the righteousness of our God and Savior, Jesus Christ. (2 Peter 1:1)

We can immediately see the Granville Sharp construction: "our God and Savior, Jesus Christ." But this passage does not contain the surrounding context of Titus 2:13, so is it less certain? Not at all, for here we find that the use of other Granville Sharp constructions in 2 Peter provides us with the same kind of external support that Paul provided with his allusions to the Old Testament. There are a total of four[27] such constructions in this small epistle (1:1, 1:11, 2:20, 3:18), the second being found in 2 Peter 1:11:

> . . . for in this way the entrance into the eternal kingdom of our Lord and Savior Jesus Christ will be abundantly supplied to you. (2 Peter 1:11)

Here the construction is "our Lord and Savior Jesus Christ." By comparing the actual texts the similarity in these passages is clearly seen:

1:1: τοῦ θεοῦ ἡμῶν καὶ σωτῆρος Ἰησοῦ Χριστοῦ
1:11: τοῦ κυρίου ἡμῶν καὶ σωτῆρος Ἰησοῦ Χριστοῦ

1:1: *tou theou hemon kai soteros Iesou Christou*
1:11: *tou kuriou hemon kai soteros Iesou Christou*

1:1: our God and Savior Jesus Christ
1:11: our Lord and Savior Jesus Christ

The phrases are identical outside of the fact that in 1:1 the term is "God," and in 1:11 it is "Lord." No one hesitates to translate 2 Peter 1:11 as "Lord and Savior," so why do so at 2 Peter 1:1? The repetition of this construction in 2:20 and 3:18 only strengthens the argument. As Wallace concludes, "This being the case, there is no good reason for rejecting 2 Peter 1:1 as an explicit affirmation of the deity of Christ."[28] And I add that there is simply no reason, outside of *theological* reasons (which should not drive our translation in the first place), to avoid the proper rendering of either Titus 2:13 or 2 Peter 1:1. Both testify to the deity of Jesus Christ.

Someone might point out that some older translations, such as the *King James Version* of the Bible, do not translate these passages well. The main reason[29] the KJV does not clearly render the passages has to do with the fact that Sharp did his work long *after* the KJV was translated. The Latin usage had a great influence on the KJV translators, and being unaware of the proper relationship discovered by Sharp's inquiry, they could not be expected to provide the best rendering. But why do some other older versions incorrectly translate these passages? The great American Greek scholar A. T. Robertson maintained that it is mainly due to the influence of George B. Winer and his grammatical work. For three generations Winer's work was supreme, and many scholars did not feel inclined to disagree with him and insist on the correct translation of these passages. However, Winer himself, an antitrinitarian, admitted that it was not grammatical grounds that led him to reject the correct rendering of Titus 2:13, but theological ones. In the Winer-Moulton Grammar (as cited by Robertson), page 162, Winer said, "Considerations derived from Paul's system of doctrine lead me to believe that σωτῆρος is not a second predicate, coordinate with θεοῦ, Christ being first called μέγας θεός, and then σωτήρ." However, Robertson put it well when he said, "Sharp stands vindicated after all the dust has settled. We must let these passages mean what they want to mean regardless of our theories about the theology of the writers."[30]

THE MIGHTY GOD

Long before the blessed night of the Incarnation, Isaiah was led by the Spirit of God to utter these words:

> For a child will be born to us, a son will be given to us;
> And the government will rest on His shoulders;
> And His name will be called Wonderful Counselor,
> Mighty God, Eternal Father, Prince of Peace. (Isaiah 9:6)

As this prophecy was originally given, it had a particular and immediate application in Isaiah's day. But we know that its true fulfillment went far beyond the days of Isaiah. Christians have always seen this passage applying to the Lord Jesus Christ. There are a number of reasons why this is true. Isaiah says a "child" will be "born" to us. Both terms are the normal words for the natural birth of children. But when Isaiah says a "son will be given to us," he uses the literal word for "given." One cannot help but think of the fact that the one born in Bethlehem was truly a child, *born* as children are born (that is to say, truly man, truly flesh), but was also the Son, given to us so as to redeem us.

The passage is definitely Messianic, referring to the coming Messiah and His rule and reign (v. 7). But before speaking of what the Messiah will *do*, the passage tells us who the Messiah will *be*. Here we have a string of descriptive names, all of which are filled with high meaning. We must focus, however, upon that name that indicates the deity of the coming One, that being the name *El gibbor*, "Mighty God."[31]

Very few deny that this phrase is being used of the Messiah, the Son of God. Instead, two routes are taken to avoid the impact of the description. Some say that the phrase simply means "Mighty Hero" or something along these lines, drawing from the use of the Hebrew term *gibbor* in other contexts. Others are willing to allow the normal translation to stand, "Mighty God," but will quickly say, "Yes, He is a mighty God, but He is not the *Almighty God*." This is the normal response given by Jehovah's Witnesses when faced with this passage.

Apart from the problem introduced by having two "true" Gods, all of these attempted ways around the force of the verse run smack dab into a brick wall provided by Isaiah himself. F. Delitzsch put it this way:

> But all these renderings, and others of a similar kind, founder, without needing any further refutation, on ch. x. 21, where He, to whom the remnant of Israel will turn with penitence, is called *El gibbor* (the mighty God). There is no reason why we should take *El* in this name of the Messiah in any other sense than in *Immanu-El*; not to mention the fact that *El* in Isaiah is always a name of God, and that the prophet was ever strongly conscious of the antithesis between *El* and *âdâm* [i.e., between God and man], as ch. xxxi. 3 (cf. Hos. xi. 9) clearly shows. And finally, *El gibbor* was a traditional name of God, which occurs as early as Deut. x. 17, cf. Jer. xxxii. 18, Neh. ix. 32, Ps. xxiv. 8, etc. The name *gibbor* is used here as an adjective, like *shaddai* in *El shaddai*. The Messiah, then, is here designated "mighty God." Undoubtedly this appears to go beyond the limits of the Old Testament horizon; but what if it should go beyond them? It stands written once for all, just as in Jer. xxiii. 6 *Jehovah Zidkenu* (Jehovah our Righteousness) is also used as a name of the Messiah. . . . Still we must not go too far. If we look at the spirit of the prophecy, the mystery of the incarnation of God is unquestionably indicated in such statements as these. But if we look at the consciousness of the prophet himself, nothing further was involved than this, that the Messiah would be

the image of God as not other man ever had been.[32]

The use, then, of *El gibbor* of Yahweh in Isaiah 10:21, a scant chapter later, makes the attempted excuse that the phrase indicates an inferiority and does not indicate true deity untenable. The Incarnate One will be the Mighty God, truly, Immanuel, God with us.

THE CHURCH OF GOD

> "Be on guard for yourselves and for all the flock, among which the Holy Spirit has made you overseers, to shepherd the church of God which He purchased with His own blood" (Acts 20:28).

As Paul traveled to Jerusalem, sure of the chains and imprisonment awaiting him there, he called the elders of the church at Ephesus to meet him along the seashore. There he exhorted them to remain faithful to the cause of Christ. He strongly impressed upon them the need to watch over the flock, recognizing that it was the Holy Spirit himself who had placed them in that position of leadership. Then Paul described the church they were to shepherd as that which He "purchased with His own blood." The phrase has prompted a large amount of discussion,[33] and, of course, controversy. Here are the two major issues in looking at this passage:

(1) The passage contains an important "textual variation" in the Greek manuscripts.[34] Many manuscripts read "the church of the Lord" rather than "the church of God."[35]

(2) There is great debate over whether the last phrase should be translated "His own blood" or, as it is rendered in other translations, "blood of His own Son" (*so* NRSV, NJB).

As a result, we cannot, with certainty, insist that this passage is a reference to the deity of Christ. It can be understood in the following ways:

(1) The passage is, in fact, a reference to the deity of Christ, and the phrase "with His own blood" would refer directly to the term "God," making Jesus God.

(2) The passage is actually a Trinitarian passage, with all three divine Persons being mentioned: the Holy Spirit (who sets apart the overseers for their duties in the church), God the Father ("the church of God"), and Jesus Christ ("the blood of His own," or "His own Son").

(3) If we read the passage as "church of the Lord," the phrase "with His own blood" would naturally refer to the blood of Christ.

I believe the evidence favors the second choice, though certainly the first choice remains a valid possibility. But in light of the possibilities, one cannot be dogmatic on the passage.

THE TRUE GOD AND ETERNAL LIFE

The same must be said regarding an inability to be dogmatic concerning the last passage we will examine, where the specific word "God" may be used of Christ, that being 1 John 5:20:

> And we know that the Son of God has come, and has given us understanding so that we may know Him who is true; and we are in Him who is true, in His Son Jesus Christ. This is the true God and eternal life.

Two possible understandings are easily seen: the phrase "the true God and eternal life" can refer, logically and grammatically, to *either* the Father ("Him who is true") *or* to Jesus Christ. The demonstrative pronoun "this one" normally refers to the closest antecedent, in this case, "Jesus Christ." But one can even argue that "His Son Jesus Christ" would make the "His" (i.e., the Father) the antecedent. In either case, we cannot say with absolute certainty what the antecedent is, nor, really, do we have to be overly concerned to know. Why? The relationship between the Father and the Son in John's writings is so close, so intimate, and so perfect, that in reality, the description "the true God and eternal life" can be used of *either one* or *both*. Think about it: Jesus said that it is eternal life to know the Father *and* to know the One sent by the Father, Jesus Christ (John 17:3). It is not eternal life, in John's theology, to know the Father *without the Son*. He had just written these words:

> The one who believes in the Son of God has the testimony in himself; the one who does not believe God has made Him a liar, because he has not believed in the testimony that God has given concerning His Son. And the testimony is this, that God has given us eternal life, and this life is in His Son. He who has the Son has the life; he who does not have the Son of God does not have the life. (1 John 5:10–12)

So to have eternal life, one must have *both* the Father and the Son (cf. 1 John 2:23!). Thus, we might well be completely missing the point in trying to find out whether it is the Father *or* the Son who is being referred to in 1 John 5:20. There is a third possibility that has the added advantage of explaining why John would allow the phrase to be ambiguous. He may well have done so on purpose, for the phrase may need to be understood as describing *both* the Father and the Son, for to know *them* is to have eternal life. Given the established fact that John has already referred to Jesus as God (John 1:1, 20:28), we should not be surprised to find such a usage in 1 John.

OTHER TESTIMONIES TO HIS DEITY

There are literally hundreds—no, thousands—of passages that testify to the deity of Christ once we understand that no creature could possibly do or say the things that the Lord Jesus did and said. And we certainly cannot catalog them in this brief work. Instead, I would like to focus upon just a few more passages that, while not using the term "God" of Jesus, communicate the very same idea but in different terms.

When Paul wrote to the Colossians, he emphasized over and over again the supremacy of Jesus Christ. I again remind my fellow believers that the descriptions of our Lord found throughout the New Testament defy any attempted application to a mere[36] creature. Only true deity can be described as our Lord is. This is especially true in Paul's description of Christ to the Colossians as the one in whom are hidden all the treasures of wisdom and knowledge (Colossians 2:3). Paul then makes Jesus Christ the standard of all human knowledge and thought:

See to it that no one takes you captive through philosophy and empty deception, according to the tradition of men, according to the elementary principles of the world, rather than according to Christ. For in Him all the fullness of Deity dwells in bodily form. (Colossians 2:8–9)

Why is Christ the standard? Why is He worthy to be the benchmark by which everything else is to be measured? Because all the "fullness of Deity" dwells in Him. Each word is full of meaning. When we read of the "fullness of Deity," we find here a claim to the deity of Christ that is, in some respects, stronger than if Paul had used the very word "God" of the Lord in this passage. Why? Because the word itself is very strong. The *King James Version* renders it "godhead," which is not only ambiguous, but since the KJV elsewhere renders other *less strong* terms by the same word (e.g., Romans 1:20), it can be quite confusing. The Bauer, Arndt, Gingrich, and Danker lexicon renders the word "deity, divinity, used as an abstract noun for θεός."[37] Thayer's lexicon says, "deity, i.e. the state of being God, Godhead: Col. ii. 9."[38] Dr. Thayer is here giving us the words of Dr. Grimm. However, he then goes on to provide some important information on his own:

[SYN. θεότης, θειότης: θεότ. *deity* differs from θειότ. *divinity*, as essence differs from quality or attribute]

What does this mean? Basically, this lexical source is indicating that the word we have at Colossians 2:9 is different from the weaker term used at Romans 1:20. The term Paul uses here of Christ refers to the very *essence* of deity rather than a mere quality or attribute.[39] Thayer notes as one of his sources the work of Richard Trench on synonyms in the New Testament. Trench said of these two terms:

. . . yet they must not be regarded as identical in meaning, nor even as two different forms of the same word, which in process of time have separated off from one another, and acquired different shades of significance. On the contrary, there is a real distinction between them, and one which grounds itself on their different derivations; θεότης being from Θεός, and θειότης not from τὸ θειόν, which is nearly though not quite equivalent to Θεός, but from the adjective θεῖος . . . But in the second passage (Col. ii. 9) St. Paul is declaring that in the Son there dwells all the fulness of absolute Godhead; they were no mere rays of divine glory which gilded Him, lighting up his person for a season and with a splendour not his own; but He was, and is, absolute and perfect God; and the Apostle uses θεότης to express this essential and personal Godhead of the Son.[40]

This is why B. B. Warfield hit it on the head when he said of this passage, "that is to say, the very Deity of God, that which makes God God, in all its completeness, has its permanent home in Our Lord, and that in a 'bodily fashion,' that is, it is in Him clothed with a body."[41]

ALPHA AND OMEGA

In the book of Revelation we read the following passages:

> BEHOLD, HE IS COMING WITH THE CLOUDS, and every eye will see Him, even those who pierced Him; and all the tribes of the earth will mourn over Him. So it is to be. Amen. "I am the Alpha and the Omega," says the Lord God, "who is and who was and who is to come, the Almighty" (Revelation 1:7–8).

> When I saw Him, I fell at His feet like a dead man. And He placed His right hand on me, saying, "Do not be afraid; I am the first and the last, and the living One; and I was dead, and behold, I am alive forevermore, and I have the keys of death and of Hades" (Revelation 1:17–18).

> "Behold, I am coming quickly, and My reward *is* with Me, to render to every man according to what he has done. I am the Alpha and the Omega, the first and the last, the beginning and the end" (Revelation 22:12–13).

Christians have used the title "Alpha and Omega" of the Lord Jesus from the very beginning. Alpha (A) was the first letter of the Greek alphabet, and Omega (Ω) was the last. It would be the same as saying "the A and the Z" in the English language. It carries the same meaning as "first and last"[42] and "beginning and end."[43]

Is Jesus identified as the Alpha and Omega, the first and the last, the beginning and the end? Certainly He is. Revelation 22:12 speaks of the coming of Christ and continues directly into verse 13. There is no reason, grammatical or otherwise, to insert a break here and separate verse 13 from verse 12.[44] This chapter ends with the words "Come, Lord Jesus." There is no reference to the "coming" of the Father, and the attempts to find such a reference are feeble at best.[45] Logically, if Jesus is the Alpha and Omega in 22:13, He is likewise everywhere else, for there can be only one first and last, only one beginning and end. Does this exclude the Father? Of course not. Since Jehovah is the first and the last (Isaiah 41:4), and each of the divine Persons is likewise identified as Yahweh (see chapter 9), the phrase "Alpha and Omega" would apply equally to the Father, to the Son, or to the Spirit.

EQUAL WITH GOD

When Jesus healed a man on the Sabbath, a controversy ensued that sheds light on the deity of Christ:

> For this reason the Jews were persecuting Jesus, because He was doing these things on the Sabbath. But He answered them, "My Father is working until now, and I Myself am working." For this reason therefore the Jews were seeking all the more to kill Him, because He not only was breaking the Sabbath, but also was calling God His own Father, making Himself equal with God. Therefore Jesus answered and was saying to them, "Truly, truly, I say to you, the Son can do nothing of Himself, unless *it is* something He sees the Father doing; for whatever the Father does, these things the Son also does in like manner" (John 5:16–19).

Jesus healed on the Sabbath. The Jews objected to this, alleging He was breaking God's law. Jesus' response is often missed in the rush to get to the phrase, "making Himself equal with God." The Jews took great offense when He said that His Father was working till then, and He himself was working. The reason they were so upset is that they had a belief that Yahweh "broke" the Sabbath. That is, Yahweh kept the world spinning in its orbit, kept the sun shining or the rain falling, even on the Sabbath day. Thus, in one sense, God was above the Sabbath law because He continued to "work" in maintaining the universe. You can see, then, why Jesus' words offended them. He claimed the same right for himself! They are enraged that by calling God "Father" in a way that was unique and special to himself, He was making himself equal with God. They knew that to be *the* Son of God was to be deity. The son is always like the father, and if Jesus is the Son of the Father in a special and unique way, He must be deity.

Now, many are confused by the discourse that follows, for in it Jesus says that "the Son can do nothing of Himself." All through the discourse the dependence of the Son upon the Father is stressed. Many use this to argue against the deity of Christ. Yet, in reality, just the opposite is true. The Son of God is not here repudiating the allegation of His equality with the Father. Instead, He is *expanding* upon it, and in the process correcting it. That is, He is making sure that no one misunderstands what it means for Him to be equal with the Father. How does He do this?

First, the Jews, while rightly sensing the exalted nature of the Lord's claim, misunderstand the claim and phrase in the context of *competition* between the Father and the Son. That is, the Jews use a term of the Son that is technically incorrect—it speaks of an equality of *persons*, which would confuse the distinction that exists between the Father and the Son.[46] Rather than using the term in the way Paul does when speaking of the equality the Son had with the Father in Philippians 2:6, they use the term in a different form. Jesus corrects their misapprehension in the following verses by carefully distinguishing Himself from the Father, while maintaining the truth of the claim He has made in verse 17.

Secondly, Jesus makes it clear in the following discourse that there is no competition between the Father and the Son. There are no differences of opinion, no disagreements to be ironed out. The Son is not a "loose cannon" off on His own, doing His own thing. No, monotheism and the singular glory of God is not in any danger by the coming of the Son in human flesh. Instead, the Son's actions are in *perfect accord* with the Father, in *everything*. And again, no mere creature could possibly utter such words. Jesus did indeed claim equality with God by healing on the Sabbath—and in the rest of the chapter He makes sure that we recognize that equality with God does not mean He and the Father are at odds. Instead, He and the Father are "one" (John 10:30) in all things.

TWO FINAL TESTIMONIES TO THE DEITY OF CHRIST

As I indicated at the outset, it is not my purpose to provide an exhaustive apologetic for the doctrine of the Trinity. Instead, I have attempted to provide helpful information along the way that is designed to assist those who so love this truth about God's nature that they have to tell others about it! One such hopefully helpful bit of information is found in looking at two passages that are often cited *against* the deity of Christ, but which, in fact, when properly understood, testify *to* the deity of Christ. These passages have the added advantage of removing from the hands of the detractors of the Trinity some of their "favorite" texts, and causing them to reconsider what they have been taught.

As the Lord Jesus walked with His disciples on the night of His betrayal, He taught them many deep truths about himself, the Father, and the soon coming Spirit. He told them that He was going to be leaving them and returning to the presence of the Father. In the midst of this discourse, Jesus says,

> "You heard that I said to you, 'I go away, and I will come to you.' If you loved Me, you would have rejoiced because I go to the Father, for the Father is greater than I" (John 14:28).

Probably no passage comes to the lips of the person who denies the deity of Christ faster than John 14:28. Yet if we will but consider the passage, and avoid embracing surface-level uses of it, we will find that it does not lead us to deny the deity of Christ, but rather to embrace it.

Most of the time we see this passage only partially quoted. The last few words are recited as if they by themselves settled all question of the deity of Christ. "The Father is greater than I." Doesn't that say it all? No one is greater than God; therefore, Jesus can't possibly be God if, in fact, there is anyone greater than Him. How could it get any simpler than that? But such an argument ignores what Jesus himself is saying. Why does He refer to the Father as being greater than He is? He does so because He is reproaching the disciples for their selfishness. He had told them that He was going back to the presence of the Father. If they truly loved Him (and were not simply thinking about themselves), this announcement would have caused them to rejoice. Why? Because the Father is greater than the Son.

Now immediately we can see what the term "greater" means. If it meant "better" as in "a higher type of being," these words would have no meaning. Why would the disciples rejoice because Jesus was going to see a being who is greater than He? Why would that cause rejoicing? But the term does not refer to "better" but "greater" as in *positionally* greater. The Son was returning back to the place He had with the Father before the world was (John 17:5, see below). He would no longer be walking the dusty roads of Galilee, surrounded by sin and sickness and misery. He would no longer be the subject of attack and ridicule by legions of scribes and Pharisees. Instead, He would be at the right hand of the Father in heaven itself. So we see that the term "greater" speaks to the position of the Father in heaven over against the position of the Son on earth. The Son had voluntarily (Philippians 2:6) laid aside His divine prerogatives and *humbled* himself by entering into human flesh. He would soon be leaving this *humbled* position and returning to His position of *glory.* If the disciples had been thinking of the ramifications of Jesus' words, they would have rejoiced that He was going to such a place. Instead, they were focused upon themselves and their own needs, not upon the glorification of their Lord.

So we can see that rather than denying the deity of Christ, John 14:28 implies it, for the position into which the Son was returning is a position fit only for deity, not for mere creatures. This is brought out plainly in the words of Jesus in John 17 and His prayer to the Father:

> "This is eternal life, that they may know You, the only true

God, and Jesus Christ whom You have sent. I glorified You on the earth, having accomplished the work which You have given Me to do. Now, Father, glorify Me together with Yourself, with the glory which I had with You before the world was" (John 17:3–5).

Amazingly, even this passage is sometimes cited against the truth of the Trinity. How can a passage that connects eternal life itself with knowledge of *both* the Father and the Son, and that speaks of the Son sharing the very glory of the Father in eternity past (cf. Isaiah 48:11), be used *against* the deity of Christ? Again, it requires one to make a couple of false assumptions right at the start. First, one must assume unitarianism and refuse to see that "God" can refer either to the person of the Father, or can be used more generically of the godhead *en toto*. Secondly, one must assume that if there is any difference between the Father and the Son, then the Son is not truly deity, the old "*difference in function does not indicate inferiority of nature*" issue. So the argument is, "Jesus said the Father was the only true God. Hence, Jesus is not God and is an inferior creature." Yet what Jesus said was that to have eternal life one must know *both* the one true God *and* Jesus Christ, who was sent by the Father. This is exactly what we read in 1 John, where having eternal life involves knowing *both* the Father and the Son.

But what of the phrase "the only true God"? Doesn't this mean that Jesus isn't God? Of course not. How else would Jesus make mention of the truth of monotheism? Since He is not a separate *God* from the Father (He is a separate person, sharing the one Being that is God), how could His confession of the deity of the Father be taken as a denial of His own deity? As the perfect God-man, we again encounter the question of how the Incarnate One would behave and relate to the Persons who did not enter into human existence (i.e., the Father and the Spirit), just as we discussed above in reference to John 20:17. Would Jesus deny the deity of the Father? Would He say that the Father is *not* the only true God? What is often missed by those who present John 17:3 as an argument against the deity of Christ is that they have only two options as to what the passage is saying, if, in fact, it is not supporting the deity of Christ. Either (1) Jesus is a *false* god, separate from the Father, or (2) Jesus would have to make some statement supporting polytheism, like "You are one of a couple of true Gods" or some other such absurd statement. Instead, Jesus speaks the truth: There is only one true God. And as the God-Man, He prayed to the one true God, just as we would expect.

Having seen the misuse of the passage, we can then see how it is directly relevant to John 14:28, in that it describes the exalted position the Son had before the Incarnation, sharing the very glory of the Father. It is no surprise to recall that John himself had insisted that when Isaiah saw the glory of Jehovah, Isaiah was, in fact, seeing the glory of Christ and was speaking about Him (John 12:39–41, see chapter 9). Therefore, we can easily understand that the Father was, during the entire time of the Incarnation, positionally *greater* than the Son, who voluntarily subjected himself to the Father, taking a subordinate position, doing the Father's will, all to fulfill the eternal covenant of redemption.

We close by looking at our final passage, which has again been presented as if it denies the deity of Christ, when in reality it is beyond understanding outside of that truth:

> Therefore concerning the eating of things sacrificed to idols, we know that there is no such thing as an idol in the world, and that there is no God but one. For even if there are so-called gods whether in heaven or on earth, as indeed there are many gods and many lords, yet for us there is *but* one God, the Father, from whom are all things and we *exist* for Him; and one Lord, Jesus Christ, by whom are all things, and we *exist* through Him. (1 Corinthians 8:4–6)

Here some wish us to believe that, just like in John 17:3, Paul's use of the phrase "one God, the Father" excludes Jesus from the realm of deity. Of course, we immediately recognize that there is a real problem here: that's not all Paul says. If "one God, the Father" is meant to be taken exclusively, then does it not follow that "one Lord, Jesus Christ" also excludes the Father from the realm of Lordship? When we see the distinctive use of the terms "God" and "Lord," we should realize that the Scriptures are not here introducing a competition or contest between the two. God is just as much Lord as the Lord is God. The two terms are merely being used to describe different Persons in their relationship to one another. They are not being used to say that God is more "Lord" than the Lord is "God." But beyond this, B. B. Warfield very accurately sums up the beautiful testimony of this passage of sacred Scripture:

> In the very act of asserting his monotheism Paul takes our Lord up into this unique Godhead. "There is no God but one," he roundly asserts, and then illustrates and proves this assertion by remarking that the heathen may have "gods many, and lords many," but "to us there is one God, the Father, of whom are all things, and we unto him; and one Lord, Jesus Christ, through whom are all things, and we through him" (I Cor. vii. 6). Obviously, this "one God, the Father," and "one Lord, Jesus Christ," are embraced together in the one God who alone is. Paul's conception of the one God, whom alone he worships, includes, in other words, a recognition that within the unity of His being, there exists such a distinction of Persons as is given us in the "one God, the Father" and the "one Lord, Jesus Christ."[47]

I Am He

John's literary artistry was not limited to the prologue of his Gospel, nor was it confined to the direct assertion of the deity of Christ through calling Him "God" (1:1; 20:28). He found subtle ways of teaching this truth as well. One method that John presented, that the other Gospel writers did not use, is found in Jesus' use of the phrase *I am.*

Look at these passages from the gospel of John:

"Therefore I said to you that you will die in your sins; for unless you believe that I am *He,* you will die in your sins" (John 8:24).

Jesus said to them, "Truly, truly, I say to you, before Abraham was born, I am" (John 8:58).

"From now on I am telling you before *it* comes to pass, so that when it does occur, you may believe that I am *He*" (John 13:19).

They answered Him, "Jesus the Nazarene." He said to them, "I am *He*." And Judas also, who was betraying Him, was standing with them. So when He said to them, "I am *He*," they drew back and fell to the ground. (John 18:5–6)

In each of these verses a particular Greek phrase appears: ἐγὼ εἰμί (*ego eimi*). The *New American Standard Bible* renders this Greek phrase as "I am *He*." The fact that the word "He" is italicized is very important, for this means the word itself is not found in the Greek[1] and is being supplied by the translators in an effort to smooth out an awkward English phrase. John makes sure, through the use of context, that we do not miss the point he is making by recording these words of Jesus. One might wonder, "Why don't the other gospel writers pick up on this?" Mark does record an example of the phrase (Mark 14:62), but he does not emphasize it the way John does. There might well be a simple answer to the question. When Mark wrote his gospel, it was not his purpose to emphasize the same truths about Christ's nature as John would decades later. It seems quite probable that John, with more time to reflect upon the events of the Lord's ministry, found in these words an insight that later events and developments in the church proved useful and necessary.

The first question that we have to tackle is straightforward: how do you translate the phrase properly? This is not a controversy in most of the instances above. The vast majority of scholarly translations render it the same way: "I am *He*," with the "He" in italics. But when we come to the clearest and most obvious of the passages, John 8:58, a few translations give a different rendering, emphasizing the idea that Jesus is merely claiming *preexistence*. How then should the phrase be translated at John 8:58? Once we consider this, we need to establish some Old Testament background, and *then* we can take all the appearances of the phrase in John as a group and determine what John is communicating to us.

HOW SHOULD WE TRANSLATE IT?

There are a very small number of translations that avoid a direct translation of the phrase at John 8:58 (in particular). Moffat renders it, "I have existed before Abraham was born!" *The Twentieth Century New Testament* has "before Abraham existed I was." The Jehovah's Witnesses' *New World Translation* renders *ego eimi* as "I have been."

Allegedly many of these translations are viewing the phrase as what Dr. A. T. Robertson called a "progressive present."[2] There are many instances in historical narrative or conversation where the Greek will use a present tense verb that is best rendered in English by the perfect tense. John 15:27 would be a good example: "because you have been with me from the beginning." The verb is in the present tense, but the context makes it clear that it is in reference to both the past and the present. Robertson notes that this is a common idiom in the New Testament, though he also adds the fact that, in his opinion, John 8:58 is "absolute" and should be rendered as such (which he always does in his works[3]). It should also be noted that it is the deficiency of the English that is to blame for the rendering—to place weight on the meaning of the English perfect tense when rendering the Greek present tense in this way would be in error.[4]

So why should John 8:58 *not* be rendered in this way? Why do so few translations follow this path? Because to translate it that way is to miss the entire context and content of what is being said! The vast majority of translators see, as do many commentators, that there is a clear differentiation being made here between the derivative existence of Abraham and the eternal existence of the Lord Christ. Many scholars rightly point out the same contrasting of verbs as seen in the prologue of John[5] as well as the same kind of differentiation found in the Septuagint Greek rendering of Psalm 90:2. They also recognize that the response of the Jews would be rather strong if this was simply a claim of preexistence. The oft-repeated charge of blasphemy as found in John makes this clear. Rather, the usage of a term used of God himself (as will be shown later) would be sufficient to bring the response of verse 59, where the Jews pick up stones so as to kill Him.

The phrase was so understood by the early church as well. Irenaeus showed familiarity with it as "I am,"[6] as did Origen[7] and Novatian.[8] Chrysostom wrote, "As the Father used this expression, 'I Am,' so also doth Christ; for it signifieth continuous Being, irrespective of time. On which account the expression seemed to them to be blasphemous."[9] The context of this passage is far too strong to allow this to be rendered as a simple historical narrative, resulting in the conversion of the present indicative into a perfect tense.[10]

OLD TESTAMENT BACKGROUND OF EGO EIMI

It happens all the time: we are in a hurry to make a point, so we jump from one point to another quickly, skipping a few necessary points in between. There's always that one person in the bunch who stops you and makes you go back and trace your argument, step by step, rather than allowing you to condense things a bit and make better speed.

When dealing with theological issues, we often condense things and make connections that, in reality, take a little more proof than we have offered. This is nowhere better illustrated than in the connection that is alleged to exist between Jesus' words in John 8:58 and the words of Yahweh in Exodus 3:14, "I am that I am." You will find references to Exodus 3:14 in most commentaries on John 8:58, yet those who deny the deity of Christ cry "foul!" and argue that such an immediate connection can't be made. The strongest argument they can present is that the *ego eimi* portion of Exodus 3:14 isn't really the assertion of divinity: the *ho ohn* portion is (*ho ohn* being translated as "the Being" or "the One Existing").

As far as the argument goes, this is true. However, the claim that Jesus' words in John 8:58 (and the other passages) should be connected to Exodus 3:14 does not exist in a vacuum. There is a line of argumentation, a very solid one, that leads us from John 8 back through Isaiah to Exodus 3. We need to trace that path before we can make the statement that Jesus is, in fact, using a name of deity of himself in John's gospel.

The closest and most logical connection between John's usage of *ego eimi* and the Old Testament is to be found in the Septuagint rendering of a particular Hebrew phrase, *ani hu*, in the writings (primarily) of Isaiah.[11] The Septuagint translates the Hebrew phrase *ani hu* as *ego eimi* in Isaiah 41:4; 43:10; and 46:4. In each of these instances the phrase *ani hu* appears at the end of the clause, and is so rendered (or punctuated) in the LXX (just as in these seven examples in John). The phrase *ego eimi* appears as the translation of a few other phrases in Isaiah as well that are significant to this discussion. It translates the Hebrew *anoki anoki hu* as *ego eimi* in 43:25 and 51:12. Once (52:6) *ani hu* is translated as *ego eimi autos* (basically an even more emphasized form). And once (45:18) we find *ego eimi kurios* for *ani Yahweh!* This last passage is provocative in that it is in the context of creation, an act ascribed to Jesus by John (John 1:3) and other New Testament writers (Colossians 1:16–17; Hebrews 1:2–3).

The use of *ani hu* by Isaiah is a euphemism for the very name of God himself. Some see a connection between *ani hu* and Yahweh as both referring to being.[12] That it carried great weight with the Jews is seen in 8:59 and their reaction to the Lord's usage of the phrase. If one wishes to say that Jesus was not speaking Greek, but Aramaic, the difficulty is not removed, for the identification would have been just that much clearer!

There seems to be a direct connection between the *Septuagint* and Jesus' usage of *ego eimi*. In Isaiah 43:10 we read, "In order that you may know and believe Me and understand that I am He."[13] In John 13:19, Jesus says to the disciples, "From now on I am telling you before it comes to pass, so that when it does occur, you may believe that I am He."[14] When one removes the extraneous words (such as the phrase that connects the last clause to the first) and compares these two passages, this is the result:

> Isaiah 43:10: *hina pisteusete . . . hoti ego eimi*
> John 13:19: *hina pisteusete . . . hoti ego eimi*

Even if one were to theorize that Jesus himself did not attempt to make such an obvious connection between himself and Yahweh (which would be difficult enough to do!), one must answer the question of why John, being obviously familiar with the LXX, would so intentionally insert this kind of parallelism.

Another parallel between the usage of *ego eimi* in John 13:19 and its usage in Isaiah has to do with the fact that in 13:19 Jesus is telling them the future—one of the very challenges to the false gods thrown down by Yahweh in the passages from Isaiah under consideration (the so-called "trial of the false gods.") This connection is direct in Isaiah 41:4, "Who has performed and accomplished *it*, calling forth the generations from the beginning? 'I, the LORD, am the first, and with the last. I am He.' " Here the "calling forth" of the generations—time itself—is part of the usage of *ani hu*. The same is true in John 13:19. In the same chapter of the book of Isaiah referenced above, in verse 22 we read, "Let them bring forth and declare to us what is going to take place; as for the former *events*, declare what they *were*, that we may consider them and know their outcome. Or announce to us what is coming." That this reference to knowledge of the future would appear in the same section that uses *ani hu* as the name for God, and that this would be introduced by the Lord himself in the same context in John 13:19 is significant indeed.

Hence, though some would easily dismiss the *ani hu/ego eimi* connection,[15] or ignore it altogether,[16] the evidence is overwhelming that this connection is intended by John himself.

UNDERSTANDING JOHN'S MESSAGE

It is not hard to understand why there have been many who have not wished to make the connection that John makes between Jesus and Yahweh. One cannot make this identification outside of a Trinitarian understanding of the Gospel itself, as one can certainly not identify Jesus as the Father in John's Gospel. If Jesus is identified as *ego eimi* in the sense of the Old Testament *ani hu*, then one is left with two persons sharing the one nature that is God, and this, when it encounters John's discussion of the Holy Spirit, becomes the basis of the doctrine of the Trinity![17] An interpreter who is unwilling to dismiss the words of Scripture as simply "tradition" (and hence nonauthoritative) or to interpret Scripture in contradiction with itself (as in a violation of strict monotheism in the positing of a being who is quasi-god, mighty, but not "almighty") will be hard-pressed to avoid the obvious conclusions of John's presentation. Lest one should find it hard to believe that John would identify the carpenter from Galilee as Yahweh himself, it might be pointed out that he did just that in John 12:39–41 by quoting from Isaiah's temple vision of Yahweh in Isaiah 6 and then concluding by saying, "These things Isaiah said because he saw His glory and he spoke about Him." The only "Him" in the context is Jesus; hence, for John, Isaiah, when he saw Yahweh on His throne, was in reality seeing the Lord Jesus. John 1:18 says as much as well.[18]

It is self-evident that such a far-reaching and in reality astounding claim as is made by the Lord Jesus in John 8:24, 58 is hard to accept outside of the highest estimation of His person. Indeed, Augustine wrote,

> Weigh the words, and get a knowledge of the mystery. "Before Abraham was made." Understand, that "was made" refers to human formation; but "am" to the Divine essence. "He was made," because Abraham was a creature. He did not say, Before Abraham was, I was; but, "Before Abraham was made," who was not made save by me, "I am." Nor did He say this, Before Abraham was made I was made; for "In the beginning God created the heaven and the earth;" and "in the beginning was the Word." "Before Abraham was made, I am." Recognize the Creator—distinguish the creature. He who spake was made the seed of Abraham; and that Abraham might be made, He Himself was before Abraham.[19]

But can the usage of *ego eimi* withstand that much weight? A large number of believing Christian scholars certainly think so. Leon Morris has written,

> "I am" must have the fullest significance it can bear. It is, as we have already had occasion to notice . . . in the style of deity.[20]

B. B. Warfield has written concerning this,

> . . . and again, as the most impressive language possible, He declares. . . : "Verily, verily, I say unto you, Before Abraham was, I am," where He claims for Himself the timeless present of eternity as His mode of existence.[21]

The great expositor J. C. Ryle noted,

Let us carefully note what a strong proof we have here of the pre-existence and divinity of our Lord Jesus Christ. He applies to Himself the very name by which God made Himself known when He undertook to redeem Israel. It was "I AM" who brought them out of the land of Egypt. It was "I AM" who died for us upon the cross. The amazing strength of the foundation of a sinner's hope appears here. Believing on Jesus we rest on divinity, on One who is God as well as man. There is a difference in the Greek verbs here employed which we should carefully notice. The Greek for "was" is quite different from the Greek for "am." It is as if our Lord said, "Before Abraham has born, I have an existence individual and eternal."[22]

Luther, like Augustine before him, wrote in no uncertain terms,

The Lord Christ is angry below the surface and says: "Do you want to know who I am? I am God, and that in the fullest sense. Do as you please. If you do not believe that I am He, then you are nothing, and you must die in your sin." No prophet, apostle, or evangelist may proclaim and say: "Believe in God, and also believe that I am God; otherwise you are damned.[23]

A. T. Robertson certainly did not see any linguistic problems here:

I am (*ego eimi*). Undoubtedly here Jesus claims eternal existence with the absolute phrase used of God. The contrast between *genesthai* (entrance into existence of Abraham) and *eimi* (timeless being) is complete. See the same contrast between en in 1:1 and egeneto in 1:14. See the contrast also in Psa. 90:2 between God (*ei*, art) and the mountains (*genethenai*).[24]

And finally, William Hendrickson put it rather bluntly:

The "I am" here (8:58) reminds one of the "I am" in 8:24. Basically, the same thought is expressed in both passages; namely, that Jesus is God!"[25]

There simply is no way that John could have been any more obvious in his intention to invest in *ego eimi* a significance far beyond the simple function of identification that it can, and does at times, perform. In 8:58 the Jews pick up stones to stone Jesus. The other two times this occurs are right on the heels of claims to deity as well—first in John 5 where Jesus has just claimed equality with the Father both by calling God His own Father in very special terms as well as claiming the same right to work on the Sabbath as the Jews understood to be God's in upholding the universe; secondly in John 10 after Jesus claims that He and the Father are one in their role of bringing salvation to God's elect—His "sheep." In both instances John spells it out clearly that these claims were understood to be claims to equality with God—can 8:58 then be different?

In John 13:19, the introduction of the phrase in the context of the revelation of future events, just as is found in Isaiah, even to the point of nearly *quoting* the LXX rendering, is far too specific to be overlooked. And in 18:5–6, John even *repeats himself* just to make sure no one can possibly miss the reason why the soldier fell back upon the ground:

> They answered Him, "Jesus the Nazarene." He said to them, "I am *He.*" And Judas also, who was betraying Him, was standing with them. So when He said to them, "I am *He,*" they drew back and fell to the ground.

Twice John repeats the phrase *ego eimi,* emphasizing that it is the uttering of these words that causes the soldiers to draw back and fall down. Some have tried to say that the soldiers were simply amazed that Jesus would so boldly identify himself and that they stumbled in the darkness.[26] But such is far beyond the realm of meaningful interpretation, for it not only reads a good bit *out of* the immediate text, but it also isolates this passage from the rest of John's gospel. When 8:24, 8:58, and 13:19 are allowed to speak their peace, as well, the reason for the soldiers' discomfort and humiliation is all too obvious. John's meaning cannot be mistaken.

If each of these instances were examined solely in a vacuum, separated from the others, without any thought of the entire book of John, one might see how their collective significance could be missed. But this is not the way of scholarly interpretation. These statements are not made in a vacuum—they are placed in a book that is rich with meaning and purpose. We have asserted that John intends the entire Gospel to be read through the "interpretive window" of the prologue of 1:1–18. Given the teachings of that passage, can one seriously doubt the meaning of *ego eimi* in the above examined passages? It would seem not.

We might do well, then, with this understanding in mind, to look at Jesus' words at John 8:24: "Unless you believe that I am *He*, you will die in your sins." Jesus here gives us the content and object of saving faith—real faith is that which focuses on the real Jesus. A faith that demands a change in *Jesus* before a commitment is made is not real faith at all. The Jews standing around Him during this conversation most assuredly would not have denied that He was a man—but that was not sufficient for faith. Some had only recently proclaimed Him as Messiah—but that was not sufficient for faith. Some might hail Him as a prophet or a miracle worker, blessed by God—but that was not sufficient for faith. Some today say He was a great moral teacher and philosopher—but that is not sufficient for faith. Some call Him "a god" or a great angel—but that is not sufficient for faith. No, Jesus himself laid down the line. Unless one believes Him for who He says He is—the *ego eimi*—one will die in one's sins. There is no salvation in a false Christ. If we are to be united with Christ to have eternal life, then we must be united with the true Christ, not a false representation. It is out of love that Christ uttered John 8:24. We would do well to heed His words.

Creator of All Things

It is instinctive, something simply built into us. When we pray, we recognize, intuitively, that God is the Creator, and we are the created. Our hearts are filled with awe when we consider the One who has given us our being.

There is no greater proof of deity than to be the Creator. As we saw earlier, God constantly upbraided the idols of the people of Israel for the very reason that they could not claim to have created the world (Jeremiah 10:10–11). A god who is not the Creator is not worthy of our worship and adoration. Such is a plain biblical teaching.

In light of this, we can hardly underestimate how important it is that the New Testament often speaks of Jesus Christ as the Creator. No discussion of the deity of Christ would be complete without dealing with the fact that the Man from Galilee was described by His immediate followers as the Maker of the heavens and the earth!

Of course, if Jesus is described as the *Creator*, another truth is therefore established. He who *creates* cannot himself be *created*. Hence, the eternality of Christ is directly related to His being the Maker of all things. Obviously, then, those who wish to deny the deity of Christ, whether they do so because they belong to a non-Christian cultic group, or simply reject the bare possibility that Jesus was more than a mere man (as in liberal Protestantism or liberal Catholicism), focus quite strongly on the passages that assert both His creatorship and His eternality. The first group attempts to get around the passages, either by misinterpretation or even mistranslation. The second group dismisses the passages as later "reflections" that have little if anything to do with the "historical Jesus." But the fact of the matter is that we have the plain assertions of the earliest Christian writings that they believed Jesus Christ *created the entire universe.* And as we shall see in the next chapter, this belief fits perfectly with the earliest forms of worship in the Christian church, where we find the highest thoughts and confessions about Christ's eternity, power, and might.

The first passage we will examine is one of the most important in all the New Testament, Colossians 1:15–17. But before we can properly understand this passage, we need to establish some of the background of the passage.[1] While many have argued about what these words mean, rarely is that debate played out in full light of the reasons that prompted Paul's letter to the church at Colossae. If we wish to deal with Paul's words, we must understand one of the major religious movements of that day, Gnosticism.

GNOSTICISM

One of the greatest struggles of the early Christian faith was against a mortal foe, an enemy that believers recognized as one of the most dangerous threats to the infant church. Today most Christians have never heard of this movement, yet, in some senses, we are still threatened by it. Gnosticism was a religious movement that prompted many of the early literary efforts of the early church. Many of the leaders of the church in the second and third centuries wrote blistering denunciations of Gnosticism. At times, and in certain places, Gnosticism threatened the very existence of orthodox Christian faith.

By its very character Gnosticism was dangerous, for it was an eclectic movement. That is, it was willing to "make room" in its theology for religious leaders and beliefs it encountered as it spread west into the Roman Empire and south into the academic strongholds of Egypt. Like some religious faiths today, it could adapt and change its own views to "make room" for new religious concepts, heros, theories, or dogmas. It was, to use a modern term, a very "inclusive" movement. That is not to say that there were not fundamental concepts that marked the general movement we today call Gnosticism. There were. But the Gnostics were willing to add your favorite deity to their system, as long as it resulted in your "going along" with their program.

Two main ideas will help us to get a handle on Gnostic belief. First, the very term "gnosticism" comes from the Greek term *gnosis*,[2] meaning "knowledge." Devotees of Gnostic thinking believed that salvation was primarily a matter of obtaining certain knowledge (normally available only through their particular group, often disseminated by secret rituals). This knowledge, in turn, allowed a person to "escape" from the corruption of the world and their physical bodies.

Second, Gnostic belief was marked by dualism. Dualism is the idea that what is material (matter, flesh, the world) is inherently evil, while that which is spiritual (the soul, angels, God) is inherently good. Much of Greek thought was dualistic in nature. Salvation was found through "escaping" the body, for it was believed that man is basically a good spirit trapped inside an evil body. This is one of the reasons that when Paul made mention of the resurrection in his sermon on Mars Hill (Acts 17:32) they began to mock, for anyone who sees salvation as being freed *from* the body will hardly find the message of the resurrection *of* the body to be good news.

The acceptance of dualism led to two extremes of behavior. Some became ascetics, depriving the body through fasts and monastic living, often demanding that followers abstain from sexual conduct, even to the point of forbidding marriage. For some strange reason, these groups often died out in a couple of generations. On the other extreme, you had the hedonists who reasoned that since the goal of salvation was to be rid of your physical body, and since your spirit really wasn't impacted by what your body did, why not just have fun, eat, drink, and be merry? These folks would engage in extremes of immorality, figuring that what the physical body did was irrelevant to the pure, immortal "soul."

Most important for our study and for the background of Colossians is the question of how the Gnostics explained the creation of the world. If you think about it, you see they had a problem. If all matter is evil, how could the pure, good God of Gnosticism be responsible for the creation of evil matter? Over time they developed an elaborate scheme to explain how evil matter made its appearance in the universe. As it is a bit complex, I provide a graphical explanation below.

We begin with the good, pure, spiritual God at the top of the diagram. From this one true God flows a long series of "emanations" known to the Gnostics as "aeons." These aeons are godlike creatures, often identified as angels when Gnosticism encountered Jewish or Christian beliefs (possibly alluded to in Colossians 2:18). All of the aeons, taken as a group, comprised the "pleroma," the Greek word for "fullness."[3] Each of these aeons along the line of emanation from God is a little less "pure," a little further away from the one true God. Eventually, the line extends far enough that you encounter the "Demiurge," a divine being who has

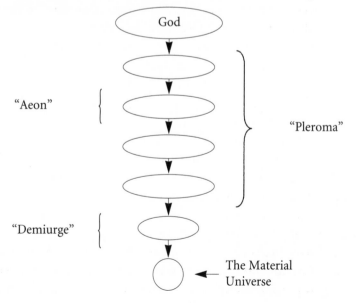

the capacity to create and is sufficiently "less pure" than the true God so as to create, and come in contact with, matter. In the second century of the church's history, some Gnostic teachers identified this evil Demiurge with the God of the Old Testament, Yahweh.

One other element of Gnostic teaching and influence should be noted. The concept of dualism led to one of the most forcefully denounced heresies of the apostolic era: *Docetism.* The Docetics were individuals who denied that Jesus had a real physical body. They were called Docetics because the Greek term *dokein*[4] means "to seem." Hence, Jesus only *seemed* to have a physical body, when in fact He didn't. As we noted earlier, Docetics would tell stories about Jesus and a disciple walking by the seashore, talking about the mysteries of the kingdom. At some point the disciple would turn around and look back upon their path and discover that there was only one set of footprints. Why? Because Jesus doesn't leave footprints, since He only *seemed* to have a physical body. One can easily see why the Docetics believed as they did. They were dualists, influenced by the Greek concept of spirit and matter. If they affirmed that Jesus was truly *good*, they could not believe He was truly *human* with a physical body, since the body is evil. It is plain that there were Docetics around during the time of the apostles, for John left no uncertainty as to his view of their teaching:

> By this you know the Spirit of God: every spirit that confesses that Jesus Christ has come in the flesh is from God; and every spirit that does not confess Jesus is not from God; this is the spirit of the antichrist, of which you have heard that it is coming, and now it is already in the world. (1 John 4:2–3)[5]

With this background, we can now listen to Paul's words and test the various interpretations that are offered of his teachings in Colossians 1:15ff, as well as in Colossians 2:9.

IMAGE AND FIRSTBORN

Colossians 1:15–17 is so often cited by so *many* different groups, both orthodox and heretical, that we must be very careful to look as closely as possible at the text so as to be able to give a proper, God-honoring, consistent, and truthful answer to those who ask us concerning our belief in Christ as the eternally preexistent Creator of all things. A few points here might seem complex or obscure. However, keep in mind that the cultic groups that deny the deity of Christ *are often well prepared to utilize this passage to their benefit.* Knowing the passage well is your first line of defense in seeking to speak God's truth in love. Paul obviously felt it necessary to go into detail on this topic, so we should be prepared to work just as hard to understand his teaching.

> And He is the image of the invisible God, the firstborn of all creation. For by Him all things were created, both in the heavens and on earth, visible and invisible, whether thrones or dominions or rulers or authorities—all things have been created through Him and for Him. He is before all things, and in Him all things hold together. (Colossians 1:15–17)

At first glance, it seems obvious that we are describing the Creator in this passage. Yet many groups attempt to derail what seems like the obvious meaning of the passage by pointing out that verse 15 describes the Son as the "image of the invisible God" and as the "firstborn of all creation." Those who do not understand the doctrine of the Trinity will assert, "See, He's the *image* of the invisible God, not the invisible God himself," wrongly assuming that we believe the Father (the "invisible God") and the Son to be the same Person. In response, we point out that no *creature* can be the *image of the invisible God,* at least not in perfection. The Bible likewise describes Christ in similar language when it says that He is the "exact representation of His nature" (Hebrews 1:3). The Son can perfectly reflect the nature of God, and be the perfect *image* of the Father, because He, like the Father, is eternal and unlimited in His deity.

But what of the term "firstborn"? Many groups place heavy emphasis upon this term, though often for different reasons. Normally, the use of the term falls into two categories:

1. *Those who deny the deity of Christ will insist that the term indicates origination, creation—a beginning in time.* These groups will insist that the passage is teaching that the Son is the first thing created by God,

or the first element of the rest of creation. For most of these folks, "firstborn" is taken as completely synonymous with "first created."

2. *Those who believe this refers to some kind of relationship between the Father and the Son that indicates an inferiority on the Son's part.* Mormons, for example, take the term to refer to the idea that the Son was begotten by the Father in a premortal existence, making the Son a second God, separate from the Father.

The first major task in properly addressing this passage is dealing with the meaning of the Greek term *prototokos* (firstborn).[6] When Paul wrote this letter and used this term, what did he intend? How would his readers have understood him?

First, it is important to realize that this term already had a rich background in the Greek Old Testament, the Septuagint (LXX).[7] It appears there approximately 130 times, about half of those appearances coming from the genealogical lists of Genesis and Chronicles, where it bears the standard meaning of "firstborn." But it has a much more important usage in a number of other passages. The "firstborn" was entitled to a double portion of the inheritance or blessing (Deuteronomy 21:17; Genesis 27), and received special treatment (Genesis 43:33).

That *firstborn* came to be a title that referred to a position rather than a mere notion of being the first one born is seen in numerous passages in the Old Testament. For example, in Exodus 4:22 God says that Israel is "My son, My firstborn." Obviously Israel was not the first nation God "created," but is instead the nation He has chosen to have a special relationship with Him. The same thought comes out much later in Jeremiah 31:9, where God again uses this kind of terminology when He says, "For I am a father to Israel, and Ephraim is My firstborn." Such language speaks of Israel's *relationship* to God and Ephraim's *special status* in God's sight.

But certainly the most significant passage, and the one that is probably behind Paul's usage in Colossians, is Psalm 89:27: "I also shall make him My firstborn, the highest of the kings of the earth." This is a highly messianic Psalm (note verse 20 and the use of the term "anointed" of David), and in this context, David, as the prototype of the coming Messiah, is described as God's *prototokos*, the "firstborn." Again, the emphasis is plainly upon the relationship between God and David, not David's "creation." David had preeminence in God's plan and was given leadership and authority over God's people. In the same way, the coming Messiah would have preeminence, but in an even wider arena.

When we come to the New Testament,[8] we find that the emphasis is placed not on the idea of birth but instead upon the first part of the word—*protos*, the "first." The word stresses superiority and priority rather than origin or birth.[9] In Romans 8:29, the Lord Christ is described as "the firstborn among many brethren." These brethren are the glorified Christians. Here the Lord's superiority and sovereignty over "the brethren" is acknowledged, as well as His leadership in their salvation. In Hebrews 1:6 we read, "And when He again brings the firstborn into the world, He says, 'AND LET ALL THE ANGELS OF GOD WORSHIP HIM.'" Here the idea of preeminence is obvious, as all of God's angels are instructed to worship Him, a privilege rightly reserved only for God (Luke 4:8). The term "prototokos" is used here as a title, and no idea of birth or origin is seen.

In both Colossians 1:18 and Revelation 1:5, Christ Jesus is called the firstborn of the dead (or "from" the dead). These would refer especially to the leadership of Christ in bringing about the resurrection of the dead and inauguration of a new, eternal life.

And so we are now ready to tackle the question concerning Colossians 1:15 and "firstborn of all creation." In commenting on this passage, Kenneth Wuest said,

> The Greek word implied two things, priority to all creation and sovereignty over all creation. In the first meaning we see the absolute preexistence of the Logos. Since our Lord existed before all created things, He must be uncreated. Since He is uncreated, He is eternal. Since He is eternal, He is God. Since He is God, He cannot be one of the emanations from deity of which the Gnostic speaks. . . . In the second meaning we see that He is the natural ruler, the acknowledged head of God's household. . . . He is Lord of creation.[10]

It seems the eminent Greek scholar J. B. Lightfoot was behind at least the outline of Wuest's comments, as he provides much the same information in his commentary on the usage of *prototokos* in Colossians 1:15.[11] He sees a definite connection between Paul's use of "firstborn" here and its appearance in the Greek Septuagint at Psalm 89:27. He discusses both the aspects of priority to all creation as well as sovereignty over all creation. This understanding of the term is echoed by many other scholarly sources.[12]

So what can we conclude? Most importantly, we see that it is simply impossible to assume that the term "firstborn" means "first created." Even if one were to ignore all the background information above, the term would still not speak to *creation* but to *birth*, and such a term could easily refer to the Son's relationship with the Father, not to any idea of coming into existence as a creature. But when the Old Testament use of the term is examined, it primarily speaks to a position of power, primacy, and preeminence. So how does the concept of Christ's *preeminence* fit into Paul's teaching in this passage? Let's see.

ALL THINGS

Verse 16 of Colossians 1 begins, "For by Him . . ." This connects verses 16 and 17 to the thought of verse 15.[13] Why is Jesus called the "image of the invisible God, the firstborn of all creation"? Because, Paul says, all things came into being by Him. We are completely missing the point if, in fact, we think verse 15 is in any way *diminishing* the view of Christ being presented. Instead, Paul feels he must explain what he means by applying such exalted titles to Christ! "Image of the invisible God" is not a phrase to be used of a creature.[14] And when we read the phrase "firstborn of all creation," we should hear the emphasis upon *all creation*. When we say that someone is the champion in a certain sport "in all the universe," we are saying the person is the best there is, *period*. So when Paul says that Jesus Christ has preeminence over *all creation*, he is specifically denying that there is anything not under His sovereign power. He then explains how that can be by asserting that *all things* were created by, through, and for Christ.

It would be difficult to imagine how Paul could have been more thorough or more emphatic in what he says in this passage. He quite literally *exhausts the Greek language* to make His point. Take a moment to read again, slowly, in your own Bible, verses 16 and 17. Notice especially the prepositions Paul uses. *By* Him,[15] *through* Him,[16] *for* Him, *in* Him. He is *before* all things. Then notice that Paul isn't satisfied to simply say that "all things"[17] are created by Christ. He has to make sure we understand that he means *all* things. All things in heaven. All things in the earth (that's pretty much everything!). But he keeps going. All things visible. All things invisible. Now, *that* is everything! But he's not satisfied with just that. Things visible and invisible, whether they be thrones, dominions, rulers, or authorities. What's his point here? Even the heavenly realms and the spiritual authorities (concepts the Gnostics liked to talk about) exist simply because Jesus Christ made them! Everything, anywhere, at any time, looks to the Son of God as "Creator."

Not only did He make all things, but Paul says that all things were made for Him! Christians instinctively know that we exist for God's glory, God's pleasure, and God's purpose. Our hearts automatically agree with the sentiment, "You are the Potter, I am the clay." Yet here the Bible says that all things were made "for" Jesus, and that He is "before" all things! Can such language possibly be used of anyone but the eternal Creator himself? Can we make sense at all of using such terms of someone like Michael the Archangel[18] or any other created being? Of course not.

Finally, we are told that all of creation "holds together" or "consists" in Christ.[19] Echoing John's assertions about the Logos that we saw above, Paul places within the realm of Christ's power the very maintenance and continuation of the entirety of the universe! He makes everything "fit" and remain in its proper place. Is this not the function of God himself? It assuredly is.

SOME OBJECTIONS ANSWERED

Before we leave this passage, however, we need to listen to other objections that are raised. Indeed, this passage is translated in the *New World Translation*, published by the Watchtower Bible and Tract Society, in such a way as to attempt to hide the truths we have just seen. Rather than repeating the phrase "all things" over and over again, as Paul did, the Watchtower translation inserts another word, "other," into the phrase, making it read, "all [other] things."[20] The reason for the translation is transparent: since Watchtower theology insists Jesus is a creation, this passage *must* be rendered this way.

Apologists for the Watchtower Society have developed ingenious ways of defending the errors of the NWT. In this instance, two arguments are often put forward. The NWT tries to defend the insertion of the word "other" by referring the reader to passages where one could logically insert the word "other" to make sense of the passage.[21] However, there is no such need here, and the grammar of the passages cited is quite different than what we are considering in Colossians. The more complex argument goes like this: Jesus is the "firstborn *of* all creation." It is insisted that the Greek grammar indicates that this means Jesus is a *part* of the creation,[22] thus, one must translate "all things" as "all [other] things" to make sense of the passage.

Such an interpretation, however, is "excluded by the context,"[23] which makes a strong and undeniable distinction between the Son and "all things." Nowhere does Paul make the Son one of the "things."[24] The most telling objection, however, comes from the context that we established at the beginning of this chapter. Remember to read Paul in light of his intention to refute the early forms of Gnosticism that were coming into the Colossian church. The position taken by those who deny the deity of Christ *falls right into the trap of agreeing with the Gnostics against Paul!* In other words, if we interpret this passage as saying Jesus is a part of the creation, and not the Creator himself, we are left with a Jesus who looks very much like the Gnostic "aeon" that Paul is arguing *against!* The argument presented by deniers of the deity of Christ weakens Paul's entire argument against the Gnostics, leaving him arguing in circles! But when we allow the text to stand and speak for itself, Paul's point is devastatingly clear: the Gnostic cannot just stick Jesus into his "system" somewhere. Jesus can't be one of the "aeons" between the one true, good God and the evil demiurge who ends up creating the world. No, Paul makes it impossible for the

Gnostic to hold on to his false beliefs about the world *and* try to make room for an edited "Jesus" by firmly asserting that *everything that exists, including the physical universe,* came into existence through the creative activity of Jesus Christ. Keeping in mind the dualistic context of early Gnosticism helps us to see clearly the intention and purpose of Paul in this passage and, in so doing, helps us to avoid the misinterpretations rampant in non-Christian sects today. It might seem to some that such considerations are too "complex" or "obscure" to be important. Yet knowing these things, and being able to explain them to others, may well be used of the Lord to help deliver someone from deception and falsehood.

A SCENE IN HEAVEN

How fundamental is the eternality and creatorship of Jesus? Take a moment to consider this tremendous scene in heaven itself, recorded for us by the apostle John:

> Then I looked, and I heard the voice of many angels around the throne and the living creatures and the elders; and the number of them was myriads of myriads, and thousands of thousands, saying with a loud voice, "Worthy is the Lamb that was slain to receive power and riches and wisdom and might and honor and glory and blessing." And every created thing which is in heaven and on the earth and under the earth and on the sea, and all things in them, I heard saying, "To Him who sits on the throne, and to the Lamb, *be* blessing and honor and glory and dominion forever and ever." And the four living creatures kept saying, "Amen." And the elders fell down and worshiped. (Revelation 5:11–14)

Did you catch the key phrase? "And *every created thing*" joined in this song of praise directed to the One sitting on the throne *and to the Lamb. Every created thing.* If Jesus is a creation, a mere creature, then is He not likewise joining into this song of praise? Yet the song is directed to Him and to the Father. Obviously, those in heaven itself know that Jesus is not one of the created things. Creation knows its Master.

THROUGH WHOM HE MADE THE WORLD

The Father and the Son together are involved in the creation of all things. The last passage we will look at under this topic is found in the great first chapter of Hebrews, a chapter we will look at a number of times before we finish our study. Here the writer to the Hebrews makes reference to the roles of the Father and Son in creation:

> God, after He spoke long ago to the fathers in the prophets in many portions and in many ways, in these last days has spoken to us in His Son, whom He appointed heir of all things, through whom also He made the world. And He is the radiance of His glory and the exact representation of His nature, and upholds all things by the word of His power. When He had made purification of sins, He sat down at the right hand of the Majesty on high. (Hebrews 1:1–3)

God the Father has made the world *through* the Son. We have seen already the importance of recognizing the truth that creation is not *only* the work of the Father or *only* the work of the Son (or even of the Spirit). Instead, creation is the work of *Yahweh,* and the New Testament reveals to us with glorious clarity the differing roles the Father, Son, and Spirit play in that great exhibition of divine power. The Father decrees, the Son enacts, the Spirit conforms. Just as all three share the one divine name, so they also share the one divine description as "Creator," even while maintaining the distinction of roles that exists between them. Surely the believer marvels at the consistency, balance, and beauty of the Word's testimony to the relationship of the persons and their role in creation itself.

CHAPTER 8

Carmen Christi: The Hymn to Christ as God

The hymns sung by the church have always told of the faith that is hers. While few today dwell on what our hymns really *say,* the early church placed much more emphasis upon the *content* of her hymns. Fragments of the earliest "hymnal" are found in the text of the New Testament. We get a tantalizing glimpse at what the earliest Christians confessed in music. Probably the longest "song," and certainly the most important, is provided by the apostle Paul in his letter to the Philippians.

Philippians 2:5–11 has been identified as the *Carmen Christi,* the "Hymn to Christ as God." Some modern translations, such as the NIV, NRSV, TEV, and JB, set this passage apart in poetic form to indicate the fact that most scholars see in this passage something other than straight prose or teaching. Instead, what is found here may well be a section, maybe a verse or two, of an ancient Christian hymn.

If, in fact, Paul is referring believers to a commonly known song, we can imagine the effect his words had. In our day, it is common for a minister to incorporate a reference to a well-known and well-loved hymn so as to make a strong point. Many close a sermon on the grace of God, for example, by saying, "Amazing grace, how sweet the sound, that saved a wretch like me!" The minister doesn't need to tell us what hymn number he is referring to. He doesn't need to give us the name. Just a line or two is enough. "I once was blind, but now I see" is sufficient to bring to our minds the entire message contained in the song.

I believe that is exactly what Paul is doing in the second chapter of his letter to the Philippians. Verses 5 through 11 provide us with the "sermon illustration" Paul wishes to use. In these words he takes us to the highest points of scriptural revelation, speaking of great *eternal* truths. Yet he does so through the words of a familiar song.

A tremendous number of books and articles have been written concerning the meaning of Philippians 2:5–11. Yet many of them miss the most fundamental point of solid interpretation: context. Often the passage is separated from surrounding text and considered on its own. As we will see, the *context* of the passage will help us determine the *key* issue at stake here. And to that context we must first turn.

HUMILITY OF MIND

In this passage, Paul did not just break into a testimony to the greatness of Christ without a reason. He was trying to encourage the Philippians to live and act in a certain manner, and he gives as his example the Lord Jesus. To what kind of behavior was Paul exhorting his listeners? Let's read:

> Therefore if there is any encouragement in Christ, if there is any consolation of love, if there is any fellowship of the Spirit, if any affection and compassion, make my joy complete by being of the same mind, maintaining the same love, united in spirit, intent on one purpose. Do nothing from selfishness or empty conceit, but with humility of mind regard one another as more important than yourselves; do not *merely* look out for your own personal interests, but also for the interests of others. (Philippians 2:1–4)

How should Christians treat one another? This is what is being addressed in this passage. The apostle reminds his readers of the encouragement they have in Christ, the loving comfort they receive from Him, the fellowship of the Spirit they all enjoy. In light of these many benefits, Paul asks them to make his joy complete by living in a manner worthy of Christian people. They are to be of the same mind, not divided, going in different directions. They are to maintain godly love among themselves, being united in spirit, all moving toward the same goal. Now, how does one keep a diverse group of people together in this way? We all know that Christians sin against one another, and in so doing they disrupt the ideal of believing fellowship. So what is the key to contented and peaceful Christian community? Paul tells us.

"Do nothing from selfishness or empty conceit." The peace of the fellowship will exist only when believers do not act in a selfish or conceited manner. That is, when we look outside of ourselves and serve others, the unity of purpose and love and compassion will be served. But when we turn in upon ourselves and seek our own good before the good of others, things will fall apart. The key is found in the next phrase: "but with humility of mind regard one another as more important than yourselves." Here is the great secret of Christian fellowship: humble service toward others. Self-denial. Not "looking out for #1," but "making everyone else #1, and looking out for them!" The Christian church is to be filled with people who, while equal with one another ("There is neither Jew nor Greek, there is neither slave nor free man, there is neither male nor female, for you are all one in Christ Jesus," Galatians 3:28), are willing to put aside their own rights in service to others. The ministry of Jesus Christ is a panoramic picture of what selfless service to others is all about. And this humility of mind is what Paul preaches to his beloved Philippian congregation.

It is in the midst of this exhortation that we find the key verses, 2:5–11. Most often, these verses are examined as a single unit, distinct from the context around them. But it is quite clear that Paul is in no way "changing topics" between verses 4 and 5. In fact, a quick glance at verse 12 shows us that upon completing his comments about Christ, he moves right on with the practical exhortation to humility and obedience in the Philippian assembly. Why is this so important? Because it tells us Paul's *purpose* in setting forth this section of an ancient hymn. Paul is giving a "sermon illustration," a reminder that if we are to be like Christ, we must imitate His *humility* as well. All of the *Carmen Christi* is, in fact, a means of *illustrating* what it means to act in "humility of mind," to give one's life in the service of others. This is why verse 5 says, "Have this attitude in yourselves which was also in Christ Jesus."

The attitude of humility of mind that the Philippians are to have is best illustrated in Christ, so Paul directs them to have the same manner of thinking, the same outlook, as seen in Christ. This will become *determinative* when we look closely at the meaning of the passage itself.

THE FORM OF GOD

The first "verse" of this ancient hymn, if we divide things along lines of thought, would comprise verses 6 and 7:

> . . . who, although He existed in the form of God, did not regard equality with God a thing to be grasped, but emptied Himself, taking the form of a bond-servant, *and* being made in the likeness of men.

Here in a matter of just a few words, Paul provides us with some of the greatest insights into the nature of Christ *before* the Incarnation. Obviously, there are two ways to understand the passage, and one can find translations to fit either viewpoint. First, there are those who point to this passage as evidence that Christ is *not* truly God and was *not* divine prior to His coming to earth. Some of the translations that lean this direction include the *Today's English Version*, the *New English Bible*,[1] and, not surprisingly, the *New World Translation*. For example, the TEV says,

> He always had the very nature of God, but did not think that by force he should try to become equal with God.

This translation assumes that Christ *was not equal* with God, and that the attitude to be emulated is that shown by His not trying to become equal with God.

The second, and much larger, group of translations sees things quite differently. These translations make it clear that Christ was eternally *equal* with God. These include the *New International Version*, the *New Revised Standard Version*, the *Jerusalem Bible, Phillips Modern English*, and *The New Living Translation*. Note how, for example, the NIV renders the passage:

> Who, being in very nature God, did not consider equality with God something to be grasped, but made himself nothing, taking the very nature of a servant, being made in human likeness.

Likewise, the NRSV says,

> . . . who, though he was in the form of God, did not regard equality with God as something to be exploited, but emptied himself, taking the form of a slave, being born in human likeness.

And the *Phillips Modern English* expresses the meaning by saying,

> For he, who had always been God by nature, did not cling to his privileges as God's equal, but stripped himself of every advantage by consenting to be a slave by nature and being born a man.

We will be able to decide which translations have properly understood Paul's thrust shortly. First, a few specifics about the text itself.

Paul says that Jesus *existed* in the form of God. The Greek term used here,[2] just as in John 1:1, does not point to a time when Christ *entered into* this state. This is brought out by Phillips' translation, "who had *always* been God by nature." Certainly those who attempt to see in Christ a mere creature can find no solace in an assertion such as this.

What does it mean to exist *in the form of God*? The range of translations show us that the term can express a wide variety of things. The Greek term "form"[3] (*morphe*) means the "outward display of the inner reality or substance. Here it refers to the outward display of the divine substance, i.e., divinity of the preexistent Christ in the display of his glory as being in the image of the Father."[4] This is why a number of translations render the term "nature." "God's nature" would refer to the *state of being God*. This would not merely be referring to existence as a spirit, but to *divine existence*. It is hard to get away from the fact that Paul is plainly presenting the deity of the preexistent Christ. We shall see in a moment that, in fact, a later comment by the apostle leaves us with no doubt about this.

EQUALITY WITH GOD

Next Paul tells us that He who (eternally) existed in the form of God did not "regard equality with God a thing to be grasped" (NASB). What does this mean? The phrase "equality with God" is not difficult to understand. Paul is talking about full divinity, a status of equal power and glory with *God*. Obviously, if this status is something that Christ *had*, the discussion over the deity of Christ is pretty well over. But obviously, those who do not believe in the deity of Christ do not agree that the passage is saying this is something Christ ever really *possessed*. In fact, they strongly assert that the point of the passage is that Christ did not "grasp for" or attempt to obtain "by force" this very equality with God. And in all fairness, the Greek term translated "to grasp"[5] *can* be translated in this way. So can we know with certainty how Paul would have us to understand this term? When the early Christians sang this hymn, what did they mean? We will put all of this together shortly.

THE EMPTYING

Before we come to some final conclusions about which way we should understand this passage, we need a few more pieces of the puzzle. The hymn says that Christ did not "grasp" His equality with God but instead did something else. He "emptied Himself" is the literal translation. What does this mean?

Note first that *Jesus did this himself*. The passage does not say that Christ *was emptied*, as if some outside force or person acted upon Him.

This is voluntary. This is something Christ did himself. As we will see, this is vitally important.

Secondly, the term "emptied" is always used by Paul in a metaphorical sense. The term is used in such places as Romans 4:14, where Paul says, "For if those who are of the Law are heirs, faith is made void (literally, "emptied") and the promise is nullified." Paul is not talking about a literal "emptying" of faith, but a metaphorical "making empty," i.e., making void.[6] So it is here. The *King James Version* does an excellent job by rendering it "made himself of no reputation." Paul is not saying Jesus *ceased to be God,* or in any other way stopped being equal with the Father, but that He voluntarily laid aside the privileges that were His.[7] When the Lord walked this earth, men did not see Him as a glorious heavenly being, for His glory was hidden, veiled. With the single exception of the Mount of Transfiguration, where a chosen few saw Him in His true glory, the rest of mankind looked upon Him who, as Isaiah had said, "has no *stately* form or majesty that we should look upon Him, nor appearance that we should be attracted to Him" (Isaiah 53:2).

The act of *emptying* is followed by an act of *taking.* He "became flesh" (John 1:14) by *taking* the form of a bond-servant and being *made* in the likeness of men. It is no mere coincidence that Paul uses the *very same term* "form" here that he used in verse 6. Just as Jesus had the *form* of God in eternity past, so He took the *form* of a bond-servant in the Incarnation.[8] He who had eternally *been served* by cherubim and seraphim now takes on the form of a *slave* so as to serve others! And what service is He called to? "Being found in appearance as a man, He humbled Himself by becoming obedient to the point of death, even death on a cross." Here is ultimate obedience, ultimate service.

SO, ETERNALLY GOD OR NOT?

We have enough of the puzzle now to go back and ask the most basic question: is this passage identifying Jesus Christ as God or not? There are two basic understandings:

1. Many liberal theologians, as well as groups that deny the deity

of Christ, assert that here we have Paul saying that the Lord Jesus was *not* equal with the Father and did not give consideration to *becoming* equal with Him, but instead took on the form of a bond-servant to die upon the cross.

2. The majority of conservative scholars and historically orthodox groups believe that Paul is teaching the eternal deity of Christ. The Lord Jesus, though equal with the Father, lays aside His privileges so as to die upon the cross.

Can we determine which view is correct? I believe we can. Remember that I originally insisted that the *context* of the passage would be determinative to finding the real answer to this question. And it is just here that it unlocks for us the door to the understanding of this ancient hymn of the church.

TRUE HUMILITY

The apostle is presenting the grand act of humble service in the life of the Lord Jesus Christ as *the* example of what it means to walk in "humility of mind." Remember, we defined humility along the lines of having certain rights, *but giving up those rights in service to others.* Among Christians, this means that we are to look out for others rather than jealously guard our own rights and privileges. We are to *serve others*, even though we are all equals before the Lord.

In light of this, look again at Paul's example from the Lord Jesus. He tells us to "have this mind in you which was also in Christ Jesus." So here we have the ultimate example of humility. But which of the two understandings of the passage give us true humility? Let's look at each and find out.

The first viewpoint says that the Lord Jesus was not equal with the Father and did not attempt to become so. Yet, is this an example of humility? Do we regularly honor as "humble" those who hold an inferior position and do not seek to usurp the rights of someone in a superior position? Is it humble, for example, to be a newly hired employee who does not seek to immediately take over the position of the president of the company? Are you considered "humble" if you do not try to usurp your boss's authority? Do we look at the janitor at the

White House, for example, and say, "Oh my, what a humble man he is, for he did not today attempt to take over the president's job!" No, of course not. Such is not humility, it is simple common sense.

In the same way, *if* the Lord Jesus were merely a spirit being, a creature, how would it be "humble" of Him not to seek to become equal with God himself? Do we say someone is "humble" if they do not claim to be God? Certainly not. So if Jesus was an inferior creature, and He did not try to become equal with God, that would be no more humble than any other angelic creature abiding by their own station and not seeking to become something they were never intended to be in the first place.

On the other hand, what about the second understanding of the passage? Here we have the eternal Son of God, existing in the very form of God. He is equal with the Father, enjoying the privileges of deity itself. But He does not consider that position He has of equality something to be held on to at all costs. Instead, out of the great love He has for His people, He *voluntarily* lays aside those privileges and takes on the form of man. He becomes a servant in the fullest sense, for He lives His entire life in service to the very ones He has come to redeem. And in the ultimate act of service, He is obedient to the very point of death upon a cross.

Now, if humility consists of having privileges, and laying them aside in service to others, can we think of *any* example of humility more thrilling, more challenging, or more *clear* than this one? Certainly not! Therefore, we can reach only one conclusion: Paul is presenting this great early hymn as his highest example of humility of mind, and because of this, we *must* understand the passage to present Jesus as having eternally existed in the very form of God, having eternally possessed equality with the Father, and yet, out of His great love for us, He voluntarily laid aside those privileges so as to give His life as a "ransom for many." If context means anything at all, this is what the passage is teaching.

THE EXALTATION OF THE SON

But we are not left with only this assertion. Paul goes on to "seal the issue," so to speak. If the direct assertion of the eternal deity of

Christ wasn't enough, he goes on to use a passage from the Old Testament to demonstrate the deity of the Father and the Son:

> Therefore also God highly exalted Him, and bestowed on Him the name which is above every name, so that at the name of Jesus EVERY KNEE WILL BOW, of those who are in heaven and on earth and under the earth, and that every tongue will confess that Jesus Christ is Lord, to the glory of God the Father. (Philippians 2:9–11)

Some point to verse 9 and say, "See, God highly exalted Jesus, hence, Jesus can't possibly be God." Such a statement flows from a misunderstanding of the Trinity and the simple fact that *normally* Paul speaks of the Father simply as "God," and the Son simply as "Lord." Both are titles of deity, and since we are not in any way trying to confuse the Father and the Son, we can fully understand Paul's language. It is the Father who exalted the Son, just as it was the Son, not the Father, who took on human flesh. But notice carefully what Paul does with his words. He quotes from an Old Testament passage, Isaiah 45:23, which reads,

> "I have sworn by Myself, the word has gone forth from My mouth in righteousness and will not turn back, that to Me every knee will bow, every tongue will swear *allegiance*."

In context, this passage is specifically about *Yahweh*, the God of Israel (see Isaiah 45:21). Yet Paul quotes from this passage and says that it is to *Jesus* that every knee shall bow (when in Isaiah it is to Yahweh), to the glory of God the Father! How can Paul say this? Does he believe in more than one God? Certainly not! But he realizes that *both* the Father *and* the Son are worthy of the name Yahweh! To bow the knee to the Son, Jesus, is to bow to Yahweh. To do so is in no way to slight the Father, who, like the Son, shares the one divine name, Yahweh. The glorification of the Son results in the glorification of the Father as well. Perfect balance, perfect consistency with the entirety of divine revelation.

And so we understand Paul's exhortation to humility and take it to heart. As Christ laid aside His eternal privileges to serve His people, dying as the sacrifice for their sins, so we, too, are called to give ourselves in service to others. This is the primary meaning of the passage, but it comes to us only as we understand who Christ really *was* and *is*. The example only carries its weight when we realize that the Lord Jesus *eternally existed as the Father's equal* and laid aside His divine privileges out of love for us. A quasi divine Jesus, or a mighty creature, does not fit this passage but instead destroys the entire thrust. Rather, we rejoice in the truth that the Son, though eternally equal with the Father, made himself "nothing" so that we—those who name His name, love Him, and obey Him—might have eternal life.

CHAPTER 9

Jehovah of Hosts

When I share the truth about the Trinity and the deity of Christ
with Jehovah's Witnesses, I often begin with something like this:

> I believe in the Trinity because the Bible teaches the doctrine.
> No, the Bible doesn't use the specific word "Trinity" any more than
> it uses the specific word "theocratic" or "Bible." Instead, it teaches
> the doctrine by teaching the three pillars or foundations that make
> up the doctrine. The first such pillar is that there is only one true
> God, Yahweh, the Creator of all things. The second is that there
> are three divine persons, the Father, the Son, and the Spirit. The
> Father is not the Son, the Son is not the Spirit, and the Spirit is
> not the Father. Three persons who communicate with one another
> and love one another. Finally, the third pillar is the teaching that
> these three persons are completely equal in sharing in the divine
> Being. This would include the deity of Christ and the personality
> of the Holy Spirit. This is where we directly disagree. May I show

you from the Bible how it teaches these truths?

Jehovah's Witnesses believe the Trinity is nowhere to be found in Scripture, so they are quite confident that you will fail in attempting to support the Trinity from the Bible. So I press on:

> I assume you would agree with me that there is only one true God, Yahweh, or as you pronounce it, Jehovah. I believe the name "Jehovah" refers to the very divine Being, the eternal God who created every thing. We can agree, I assume, that the Father is identified as Jehovah.[1] But I believe that the Bible identifies Jesus as Yahweh, as well, and the Spirit is the Spirit of Yahweh. Each of these three *persons* share the one divine name, Yahweh or Jehovah. May I show you a few passages of Scripture that make this identification?

At this point I can go to a large number of passages where the New Testament writers think nothing of applying to the Lord Jesus passages from the Old Testament that were written in reference to Yahweh.[2] But I have found two particular passages to carry the most weight in communicating this truth to those who believe that Yahweh is God, believe the Bible is true, but reject the deity of Christ: Hebrews 1:10–12 in comparison with Psalm 102:25–27, and John 6:39–41 in comparison with Isaiah 6:1–10.

ETERNAL CREATOR

There can be no confusion about the intended meaning of the psalmist who penned these words in Psalm 102:25–27:

> Of old You founded the earth,
> And the heavens are the work of Your hands.
> Even they will perish, but You endure;
> And all of them will wear out like a garment;
> Like clothing You will change them and they will be changed.
> But You are the same, and Your years will not come to an end.

The first thing to establish in fairly and honestly dealing with the passage is what it meant in its original context. The entire psalm is written about Yahweh. Verse 1 indicates it is a prayer to the LORD. The use of the all-caps form LORD is the standard English means of indicating that the underlying Hebrew term is Yahweh, or Jehovah. Some Bibles, such as the Jerusalem Bible, or the *New World Translation* published by the Watchtower Society, use the term "Jehovah" or "Yahweh." Throughout Psalm 102 this term is found, indicating plainly that the psalm was originally written in praise of Yahweh. This is important, for it is the context of the words found in verses 25 through 27.

The psalmist speaks in these verses of the unchanging and eternal nature of Yahweh. He does so by contrasting the changing creation with the unchangeable Creator. One of the primary "evidences" God uses to demonstrate His unique nature and sole standing as the one true God is that He is the Creator.[3] This is the case here. Yahweh founded the earth (Psalm 24:1; 78:69; 89:11; Proverbs 3:19; Isaiah 48:13), and the heavens are described as a "work" of His hands (Psalm 19:1). On the most basic level, then, the universe itself is a dependent creation, while God is eternal and unchanging. They are temporal and will pass away, but God is eternal, and He will "endure." They are like an old garment that we throw away when it becomes old and useless. But He does not age. He does not change. His years have no number and will never come to an end. As Moses had said, "from everlasting to everlasting, You are God" (Psalm 90:2).

Why is it important to focus on what this passage means? Because it is speaking of characteristics that are *unique to the one true God*. This will become vitally important when we look at the means some use to avoid the weight of these passages as they are used in the New Testament.

The writer to the Hebrews shows no compunctions in taking this passage from the Psalter—a passage fit *only* for describing the eternal Creator himself—and applying it to Jesus Christ. Here is how he does it in Hebrews 1:8–12:

> But of the Son *He says*,
> "YOUR THRONE, O GOD, IS FOREVER AND EVER,

AND THE RIGHTEOUS SCEPTER IS THE SCEPTER OF HIS KINGDOM.
YOU HAVE LOVED RIGHTEOUSNESS AND HATED LAWLESSNESS;
THEREFORE GOD, YOUR GOD, HAS ANOINTED YOU
WITH THE OIL OF GLADNESS ABOVE YOUR COMPANIONS."
And,
"YOU, LORD,[4] IN THE BEGINNING LAID THE FOUNDATION OF THE
    EARTH,
AND THE HEAVENS ARE THE WORKS OF YOUR HANDS;
THEY WILL PERISH, BUT YOU REMAIN;
AND THEY ALL WILL BECOME OLD LIKE A GARMENT,
AND LIKE A MANTLE YOU WILL ROLL THEM UP;
LIKE A GARMENT THEY WILL ALSO BE CHANGED.
BUT YOU ARE THE SAME,
AND YOUR YEARS WILL NOT COME TO AN END."

An entire string of Old Testament passages are presented, each intended to demonstrate the superiority of Christ. Verse 8 begins by introducing the words of the Father regarding the Son. Verse 10 continues the same theme, again giving us the words of the Father relevant to the Son. It is vital to understand that verses 10 through 12 are, in fact, *addressed to the Son.* It is Jesus who is addressed as "LORD" in verse 10, and it is *His* activity in creation, and *His* unchanging nature, that is revealed in the rest of the passage. The significance of this is clear when one realizes that the writer to the Hebrews is directly applying the passage from Psalm 102:25–27[5] to the Son. The meaning of the original is beyond dispute. The fact that it is speaking of *unique characteristics of the true God* is likewise unarguable. Therefore, the fact that Hebrews applies such a passage to the Son tells us what the writer himself believed about the nature of Jesus Christ. *One simply could not meaningfully apply such a passage to a mere creature, no matter how highly exalted.*

What does it mean that the writer to the Hebrews could take a passage that *is only applicable to Yahweh* and apply it to the Son of God, Jesus Christ? It means that they saw no problem in making such an identification, because they believed that the Son was, indeed, the very incarnation of Yahweh.

The only way "around" this kind of direct identification of the Son as Yahweh is to point out that using an Old Testament passage of someone in the New Testament does not, of necessity, argue for identity of person. For example, in Hebrews 1:8, the writer applies a passage that was originally about one of Israel's kings (possibly Solomon) to the Lord Jesus. Does this mean that Jesus is Solomon? Aside from the impossibility of such an identification in the first place, such an argument misses a very important distinction. The connection between the Lord Jesus and Solomon has to do with a shared characteristic: kingship. But kingship is not a *unique* attribute of Solomon. There have been many kings. So while citing a passage about Solomon of Jesus doesn't make Jesus Solomon, citing a passage about a *unique characteristic* (creatorship, immutability, eternality) *of Yahweh* does make Jesus Yahweh, *for no one else shares that characteristic.* Being a king didn't make Solomon who he was, but being eternal and unchangeable *does* define who Yahweh is.

Allow me to illustrate. If I wanted to identify someone as Solomon by using a citation from the Old Testament, I would not do it by citing a passage that is merely about Solomon as a king, for that would not prove *identity* but rather *position.* There were other kings, like David, or Hezekiah. Simply identifying someone as a king wouldn't tell me *which* king I had in mind. If I instead applied a *unique* description of Solomon, *that* would convey identity. If I, for example, said that such and such a king had 700 wives and 300 concubines (1 Kings 11:3), who else could I be referring to but Solomon? That would distinguish which king I had in mind and would communicate *identity.* In the same way, if I were to merely call a person "loving," I would not, by so doing, be identifying that person as God, even though God is, indeed, loving. God is love, but there are others who express love and are loving. It is not unique to God to love. But if I were to say that someone is eternal, the Creator of all things, and unchanging, *that* would communicate identity, for there is only one who is eternal, unchanging, and the Creator of all things. And this is what the writer to the Hebrews does in 1:10–12. Hence the error of the attempt to avoid the force of the identification of Jesus as Yahweh here in Hebrews 1.[6]

WHO DID ISAIAH SEE?

Toward the end of Jesus' public ministry as recorded by John we find an incident where a group of Greeks seek out the Lord Jesus. The significance of the passage often goes right past us because we are looking more at the encounter than a little comment John tacks on to the end of his citation from Isaiah:

> But though He had performed so many signs before them, *yet* they were not believing in Him. *This was* to fulfill the word of Isaiah the prophet which he spoke: "LORD, WHO HAS BELIEVED OUR REPORT? AND TO WHOM HAS THE ARM OF THE LORD BEEN REVEALED?" For this reason they could not believe, for Isaiah said again, "HE HAS BLINDED THEIR EYES AND HE HARDENED THEIR HEART, SO THAT THEY WOULD NOT SEE WITH THEIR EYES AND PERCEIVE WITH THEIR HEART, AND BE CONVERTED AND I HEAL THEM." These things Isaiah said because he saw His glory, and he spoke of Him. (John 12:37–41)

The struggle with the meaning of the words from Isaiah often causes us to fly right past verse 41. Yet what does John mean when he says that Isaiah "said these things because he saw His glory and spoke of Him"? Who is the "Him" to whom Isaiah refers?

We have to go back a little to see that John cites two passages from the book of Isaiah. In verse 38 he quotes from Isaiah 53:1, the great "Suffering Servant" passage that so plainly describes the ministry of the Lord Jesus Christ. John says the unbelief of the Jews, despite their seeing signs, was a fulfillment of the word of Isaiah in Isaiah 53. He then goes beyond this to assert their *inability* to believe and quotes from Isaiah 6 and the "Temple Vision" Isaiah received when he was commissioned as a prophet:

> In the year of King Uzziah's death I saw the Lord sitting on a throne, lofty and exalted, with the train of His robe filling the temple. Seraphim stood above Him, each having six wings: with two he covered his face, and with two he covered his feet, and with two he flew. And one called out to another and said, "Holy, Holy, Holy, is the LORD of hosts, The whole earth is full of His glory." And the

foundations of the thresholds trembled at the voice of him who called out, while the temple was filling with smoke. (Isaiah 6:1–4)

In this awesome vision, Isaiah sees Yahweh (the LORD) sitting upon His throne, surrounded by angelic worshipers. The glory of Yahweh fills his sight. Isaiah recognizes his sin and is cleansed by the Lord, then commissioned to go and take a message to the people. But the message is not one of salvation, but of judgment.

> He said, "Go, and tell this people: 'Keep on listening, but do not perceive; keep on looking, but do not understand.' Render the hearts of this people insensitive, their ears dull, and their eyes dim, otherwise they might see with their eyes, hear with their ears, understand with their hearts, and return and be healed." Then I said, "Lord, how long?" And He answered, "Until cities are devastated *and* without inhabitant, houses are without people and the land is utterly desolate" (Isaiah 6:9–11).

John cites the heart of the message of judgment given to Isaiah and sees the hardheartedness of the Jews, who had seen the miracles of the Lord Jesus and heard His words of grace as the fulfillment of these words.

Then John says, "These things Isaiah said because he saw His glory, and he spoke of Him." John has quoted from two passages in Isaiah, Isaiah 53:1 and Isaiah 6:10. Yet the immediate context refers to the words from Isaiah 6, and there are other reasons why we should see the primary reference as the Isaiah 6 passage. John speaks of Isaiah "seeing" "glory." In Isaiah 6:1 the very same term is used of "seeing" the LORD, and the very term "glory" appears in verse 3.[7] Even if we connect both passages together, the fact remains that the only way to define what "glory" Isaiah saw was to refer to the glory of Isaiah 6:3.[8] And that glory was the glory of Yahweh. There is none other whose glory we can connect with Isaiah's words.[9]

Therefore, if we ask Isaiah, "Whose glory did you see in your vision of the temple?" he would reply, "Yahweh's." But if we ask the same question of John, "Whose glory did Isaiah see?" he would answer with the same answer—only in its fullness, "Jesus'." Who, then, was Jesus to John? None other than the eternal God in human flesh, Yahweh.

If the apostles themselves did not hesitate to apply to the Lord Jesus such unique and distinctive passages *that can only meaningfully be applied to deity*, to the Lord Jesus, how can we fail to give Him the same honor in recognizing Him for who He truly is?

Grieve Not the Holy Spirit

There is a reason why the Holy Spirit does not receive the same level and kind of attention that is focused upon the Father and the Son: it is not His purpose to attract that kind of attention to himself. Just as the Son voluntarily chose to take the role of Suffering Servant so as to redeem God's people, so, too, the Spirit has chosen to take the role as Sanctifier and Advocate of the people of God. But since it is the Spirit's role to direct the hearts of men to Christ, and to conform them to His image, He does not seek to push himself into the forefront and gain attention for himself.

One result of this voluntary role of the Spirit in the work of salvation[1] is that the evidences of His personality and deity are not as numerous or obvious as those for the Father or the Son. He is not "up front" and is not spoken of as often as the other persons. Some take this as evidence of inferiority, but as we have noted before, *difference in function does not indicate inferiority of nature.*

There are two issues to address when looking at the biblical witness to the Holy Spirit. Due to the fact that some deny His personality, we must establish the clear truth that the Holy Spirit is not merely a "force" or "power," but is, in fact, a person. Having established this, we must then demonstrate that He is an eternal person, Deity, along with the Father and the Son.

HE, NOT IT

One of the ways the *New World Translation* of Jehovah's Witnesses attempts to undermine the Trinity is by consistently rendering the phrase "Holy Spirit" as "holy spirit." When possible, they omit the article, resulting in strange renderings like "That one will baptize YOU people with holy spirit" (Matthew 3:11), "and he will be filled with holy spirit right from his mother's womb" (Luke 1:15), and "she was found to be pregnant by holy spirit before they were united" (Matthew 1:18). Their intention is clear: the Watchtower Society denies that the Holy Spirit is a person, hence, they desire their "translation" of the Bible to communicate the idea that the Holy Spirit is an "it," a force or power.

Of course, the argument that is often heard is that the phrase "Holy Spirit" in Greek is in the neuter gender, and it is.[2] But Greek genders do not necessarily indicate personality.[3] Inanimate things can have masculine and feminine genders, and personal things can have the neuter gender. We cannot automatically insert the pronoun "it" when referring to every neuter noun any more than we should always insert the pronoun "she" for "love," since love in Greek is feminine.[4] Instead, we determine whether the Holy Spirit is personal the same way we would demonstrate that the Father or the Son is a person. Does the Spirit exhibit personality by speaking, using personal pronouns, and doing other things that only persons can do? Does the Spirit have a will? Can we insult or resist the Holy Spirit?

One of the clearest indications of the personhood of the Spirit is His use of the personal pronoun in reference to himself. That is, I prove my own personhood by speaking of myself as "I" and "me." The Spirit likewise speaks of himself in this way. When the Spirit set aside

Barnabas and Saul, He did so personally:

> While they were ministering to the Lord and fasting, the Holy Spirit said, "Set apart for Me Barnabas and Saul for the work to which I have called them" (Acts 13:2).

The work of ministry is a work unto the Lord, but here the Spirit not only speaks of himself with the personal pronoun "Me," but we see that we are to view the calling to the service of God as a ministry unto the Holy Spirit himself. Earlier in Acts the Spirit had referred to himself in the same way:

> While Peter was reflecting on the vision, the Spirit said to him, "Behold, three men are looking for you. But get up, go downstairs and accompany them without misgivings, for I have sent them Myself" (Acts 10:19–20).

The Spirit speaks to Peter and again uses a personal pronoun, indicating His sovereign action in sending the men to Peter. Impersonal forces do not send men, speak, or use personal pronouns in reference to their actions.

Likewise, the Spirit is referred to by the Son as a person. When teaching the apostles about the future ministry of the Spirit among them, the Lord said,

> When the Helper comes, whom I will send to you from the Father, *that is* the Spirit of truth who proceeds from the Father, He will testify about Me. (John 15:26)

> But when He, the Spirit of truth, comes, He will guide you into all the truth; for He will not speak on His own initiative, but whatever He hears, He will speak; and He will disclose to you what is to come. He will glorify Me, for He will take of Mine and will disclose *it* to you. (John 16:13–14)

The Spirit here *testifies* about the Lord Jesus. The Spirit *guides* disciples, He *speaks,* and He *discloses* future events. He *glorifies* Christ as well. Each of these activities indicate personality.

The speaking of the Spirit is found throughout the text of the Bible. We have already seen some references in Acts. Two others should be noted:

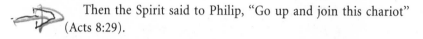

> Then the Spirit said to Philip, "Go up and join this chariot" (Acts 8:29).

> And coming to us, he took Paul's belt and bound his own feet and hands, and said, "This is what the Holy Spirit says: 'In this way the Jews at Jerusalem will bind the man who owns this belt and deliver him into the hands of the Gentiles'" (Acts 21:11).

But the Spirit speaks in another vital way as well:

> Because you are sons, God has sent forth the Spirit of His Son into our hearts, crying, "Abba! Father!" (Galatians 4:6).

This tremendously special manner of speaking is very much like what the Spirit does in His work of intercession for the elect as Paul discusses it in Romans 8:26–27:

> In the same way the Spirit also helps our weakness; for we do not know how to pray as we should, but the Spirit Himself intercedes for *us* with groanings too deep for words; and He who searches the hearts knows what the mind of the Spirit is, because He intercedes for the saints according to *the will of* God. (Romans 8:26–27)

Here the Spirit "helps," "intercedes with groanings," and "intercedes for the saints."[5] Impersonal forces do not help, groan, or intercede in this obviously intensely personal fashion. The very act of intercession demands personality. So, likewise, does the act of "searching" and "knowing the thoughts of God" predicated of the Spirit by Paul in his epistle to the Corinthians:

> For to us God revealed *them* through the Spirit; for the Spirit searches all things, even the depths of God. For who among men knows the *thoughts* of a man except the spirit of the man which is

in him? Even so the *thoughts* of God no one knows except the Spirit of God. (1 Corinthians 2:10–11)

Only persons "know" things. Electricity "knows" nothing, experiences nothing. Yet the Spirit knows the thoughts of God (the greatest task to which the creature man can be called). We dare not miss what else this means: The thoughts of God are infinite even as He is infinite. Therefore, the Spirit must likewise be omniscient, an attribute of deity itself.

The Spirit is likewise sovereign in His rule in the church. He sets apart elders and overseers in the congregation:

> Be on guard for yourselves and for all the flock, among which the Holy Spirit has made you overseers, to shepherd the church of God which He purchased with His own blood. (Acts 20:28)

An overseer (elder, bishop) is one who truly holds that office at the will of the Spirit, who guides and directs the church. Only a person can appoint elders with wisdom so as to meet the needs of the church.

The Spirit is also a *witness*:

> And we are witnesses of these things; and *so is* the Holy Spirit, whom God has given to those who obey Him" (Acts 5:32).

Another striking evidence of the personality of the Spirit is His role in bringing the very love of God for His people into their lives.

> . . . and hope does not disappoint, because the love of God has been poured out within our hearts through the Holy Spirit who was given to us. (Romans 5:5)

The love of God has been poured out in the hearts of the redeemed by the means of the Holy Spirit. How can such an assertion be understood apart from the personhood of the Spirit? Can love be poured into our hearts by electricity? Flowing water? Nameless, faceless cosmic forces? Love, by its very nature, requires that the one bearing it be personal. Otherwise, it becomes something far less than the true love of God. Paul takes up this theme elsewhere:

> Now I urge you, brethren, by our Lord Jesus Christ and by the love of the Spirit, to strive together with me in your prayers to God for me. (Romans 15:30)

The "love of the Spirit" was as common and understandable a reality to the Roman believers as was the person of the Lord Jesus Christ. There simply is no reason to believe that the Spirit was not viewed in as personal a category as the Lord himself. That is why Matthew would record these words of the Lord Jesus without ever thinking them strange:

> "Go therefore and make disciples of all the nations, baptizing them in the name of the Father and the Son and the Holy Spirit" (Matthew 28:19).

It is self-evident that the Father is a person; so also is the Son. How, then, could two persons share a single name with a nonperson, a mere force? The willingness of the Scripture writers to associate the Spirit in this way with both the Father and the Son is plain evidence of His personality.

Another of the many ways in which the personality of the Spirit is shown comes to us from Jesus' teaching on the "unpardonable sin." Both Matthew and Mark record the Lord's words:

> "Therefore I say to you, any sin and blasphemy shall be forgiven people, but blasphemy against the Spirit shall not be forgiven. Whoever speaks a word against the Son of Man, it shall be forgiven him; but whoever speaks against the Holy Spirit, it shall not be forgiven him, either in this age or in the *age* to come" (Matthew 12:31–32).

> "Truly I say to you, all sins shall be forgiven the sons of men, and whatever blasphemies they utter; but whoever blasphemes against the Holy Spirit never has forgiveness, but is guilty of an eternal sin" (Mark 3:28–29).

Everyone would recognize exactly what the Lord is speaking of when He refers to "speaking a word against the Son of Man." The Pharisees had been doing this all through His ministry. Their words of blasphemy had been directed at Him *personally*. In the same way, then, the words spoken "against the Holy Spirit" are placed in direct parallel with the words spoken against the Son of Man. We have no reason to believe that there would be any less personal element in their blasphemy when speaking of the Spirit than when speaking of the Son. They were attributing the work of Christ in doing good to evil sources. Jesus points out that in reality they are accusing the Holy Spirit of God of doing the very deeds of the devil. Such an action shows such spiritual blindness and perversity that the Lord warns that they are committing an "eternal sin" by blaspheming the Spirit of God.

Not only can someone blaspheme the Spirit, they can insult Him as well:

> How much severer punishment do you think he will deserve who has trampled under foot the Son of God, and has regarded as unclean the blood of the covenant by which he was sanctified, and has insulted the Spirit of grace? (Hebrews 10:29)

Likewise, the Spirit can be *grieved*:

> Do not grieve the Holy Spirit of God, by whom you were sealed for the day of redemption. (Ephesians 4:30)

An impersonal force cannot be grieved, pained, or injured, nor can a mere "force" or "power" seal believers for the day of redemption. And it was a serious accusation made by Stephen against the Jewish people when he accused them of resisting the Holy Spirit:

> "You men who are stiff-necked and uncircumcised in heart and ears are always resisting the Holy Spirit; you are doing just as your fathers did" (Acts 7:51).

But the single greatest indisputable testimony to the personality (and, in fact, the deity) of the Holy Spirit is found in His giving gifts to believers in the church. Paul explained to the Corinthians that there are different kinds of gifts given to members of the body of Christ, yet there is only one church, one body. One of the ways the unity of the church is seen is that there is only one source of these gifts: the Spirit of God. He emphasizes this truth in explaining the various manifestations of the gifts of the Spirit:

> . . . to another faith by the same Spirit, and to another gifts of healing by the one Spirit, and to another the effecting of miracles, and to another prophecy, and to another the distinguishing of spirits, to another *various* kinds of tongues, and to another the interpretation of tongues. But one and the same Spirit works all these things, distributing to each one individually just as He wills. (1 Corinthians 12:9–11)

There is only one Spirit bringing all the gifts to the redeemed. And He does this, not on the basis of how *we* think the gifts should be given, but instead He gives them "just as He wills." The word translated "wills" is the Greek term *boulomai*. It is used only of persons and refers to the volitional act of the will. For example, the Son *wills* to reveal the Father to His people:

> "All things have been handed over to Me by My Father; and no one knows the Son except the Father; nor does anyone know the Father except the Son, and anyone to whom the Son wills (*boulomai*) to reveal *Him*" (Matthew 11:27).

Likewise, the Father "wills" using the same term:

> In the same way God, desiring (*boulomai*) even more to show to the heirs of the promise the unchangeableness of His purpose, interposed with an oath. (Hebrews 6:17)

So if we can plainly see that the Son's *willing* is an act of a person, and the Father's *willing* is likewise the act of a person, how can we possibly avoid recognizing that the Spirit sovereignly and wisely gives His gifts to the church just as *He wills* to do so, and that this makes Him, inarguably, a person?

There is one concept used of the Spirit that is often thrown out as evidence against His personhood. We often hear, "The Spirit cannot be a person, because we are baptized in the Spirit, and hence, you can't be baptized in a person, but in a substance or a force." Yet, in reality, the Bible speaks of our being baptized into Christ Jesus in Romans 6:3 and Galatians 3:27, and neither passage is ever cited to make the point that *Jesus* is not a person. All through the New Testament we are said to be "in Christ" or "in Him," and this is never taken to mean that Jesus is not a person. Likewise, being baptized in the Holy Spirit does not deny He is a person—rather, it speaks to His omnipresence and spirituality.

THE SPIRIT AS GOD

It can be well argued that once the personality of the Spirit is established, the argument about His deity is over. The "Spirit of God" who is said to be omnipresent (Psalm 139:7), omniscient (1 Corinthians 2:10–11), and active in the very creation itself (Genesis 1:2; Psalm 104:30) hardly fits the description of some kind of lesser being. But the fact that this Spirit shares the one divine name with the Father and the Son (Matthew 28:19) makes His deity indisputable.

Yet there are a number of references to the deity of the Spirit that should be noted, especially since there are so many who denigrate the Spirit's glory and deny His rightful honor. The most often cited passage is found in the words of the apostle Peter:

> But Peter said, "Ananias, why has Satan filled your heart to lie to the Holy Spirit and to keep back *some* of the price of the land? While it remained *unsold*, did it not remain your own? And after it was sold, was it not under your control? Why is it that you have conceived this deed in your heart? You have not lied to men but to God." (Acts 5:3–4)

To whom did Ananias lie? To the Holy Spirit, or to God? Both, for to lie to the Spirit is to lie to God.

Another group of witnesses falls into the same pattern as those that testify to the fact that the Son is Yahweh. That is, we find the New

Testament writers applying passages to the Spirit that were originally written about Yahweh. Yahweh's words in the Old Testament become the Spirit's words in the New. For example, we again find the temple vision of Isaiah being used by the New Testament to reveal the richness of the nature and character of God. The very same passage from the commission of Isaiah is cited again, this time by Paul. In Isaiah Yahweh speaks and sends His prophet to the people with a message of doom (Isaiah 6:9). But note Paul's application:

> And when they did not agree with one another, they *began* leaving after Paul had spoken one *parting* word, "The Holy Spirit rightly spoke through Isaiah the prophet to your fathers, saying, 'GO TO THIS PEOPLE AND SAY, "YOU WILL KEEP ON HEARING, BUT WILL NOT UNDERSTAND; AND YOU WILL KEEP ON SEEING, BUT WILL NOT PERCEIVE" ' " (Acts 28:25–26).

It might immediately be objected that Paul is not intending to say that the Spirit literally spoke the words quoted, but instead caused them to be written in the Scriptures, that is, "inspired" them. And such would be a valid objection—but one that would only prove the point being made. It is quite true that the Spirit is often said to be the speaker of Scripture,[6] the One by whom the written Word was brought into being. As Peter put it,

> . . . for no prophecy was ever made by an act of human will, but men moved by the Holy Spirit spoke from God. (2 Peter 1:21)

Literally Peter speaks of the Holy Spirit "carrying along" the human writers of Scripture. This supernatural guidance results in it being quite proper to speak of the Spirit "speaking" in the Scriptures, so intimately is He a part of the very fabric of the Holy Writings. But it is just as true that the Scriptures are "God-breathed" and are the very speaking of Yahweh himself (2 Timothy 3:16). Since there is no way to separate out the Spirit from the Scriptures, and since they are literally the words of God, only one logical conclusion can be derived: the Spirit is fully divine. No mere force, no mere creature, could take the role in the giving of the Holy Scriptures that is taken by the Spirit of God.

The intimate relationship of the Spirit to the other divine persons is illustrated by the comparison of each of the Synoptic Gospels as they record the Lord Jesus' promise to be with His people when they face persecution for His name's sake:

> "When they arrest you and hand you over, do not worry beforehand about what you are to say, but say whatever is given you in that hour; for it is not you who speak, but *it is* the Holy Spirit" (Mark 13:11).

Here the Lord Jesus promises that the Holy Spirit will speak on behalf of His followers when they are brought before the authorities. But note Matthew's version of the same promise:

> "But when they hand you over, do not worry about how or what you are to say; for it will be given you in that hour what you are to say. For it is not you who speak, but *it is* the Spirit of your Father who speaks in you" (Matthew 10:19–20).

Here we see that it is the "Spirit of your Father" who speaks in believers at such times of danger and persecution. The Holy Spirit is the Spirit of the Father. But Luke's version adds another viewpoint:

> "So make up your minds not to prepare beforehand to defend yourselves; for I will give you utterance and wisdom which none of your opponents will be able to resist or refute" (Luke 21:14–15).

Here the Lord's promise is direct, that it is *He* who will give them utterance. This is not a denial of the Spirit's role, nor a contradiction of what is recorded in the other Gospels. Instead, the "interpenetration" of the divine persons is seen in this passage, just as it is seen in the promise of the Lord to be with His people:

> Jesus answered and said to him, "If anyone loves Me, he will keep My word; and My Father will love him, and We will come to him and make Our abode with him" (John 14:23).

Jesus promises that the Father and He will dwell with those who love

Him and keep His word (i.e., the true disciples). Yet how does the Lord do this? He does so by His Spirit, whom He sends in His place. This is the point of the entire passage in John 14 and 16: Jesus sends another Comforter to be with His people for all time. And that Comforter is the Spirit. But so intimate is the relationship, so perfect the union, that to be indwelt by the Spirit is to have the Father and the Son abiding with us. So close is the relationship of the persons that Paul could describe the Spirit as the Spirit of God and the Spirit of Christ within one short span:

> However, you are not in the flesh but in the Spirit, if indeed the Spirit of God dwells in you. But if anyone does not have the Spirit of Christ, he does not belong to Him. (Romans 8:9)

This powerful, life-giving person, the Spirit of God, is the one who brings spiritual life to God's people. He is the one who regenerates and causes us to be born again:

> "That which is born of the flesh is flesh, and that which is born of the Spirit is spirit" (John 3:6).

> He saved us, not on the basis of deeds which we have done in righteousness, but according to His mercy, by the washing of regeneration and renewing by the Holy Spirit. (Titus 3:5).

That is why the early Christians could place the Spirit with the Father and the Son in their worship and their praise, and could pronounce as a doxology the following words:

> The grace of the Lord Jesus Christ, and the love of God, and the fellowship of the Holy Spirit, be with you all. (2 Corinthians 13:14)

Grace is a divine gift and comes from a divine person, Jesus Christ. The love of God is divine and full and comes from the Father. And fellowship, likewise, is a rich term, full of meaning. We have been called into the "fellowship of His Son, Jesus Christ our Lord" (1 Corinthians 1:9). Paul spoke of "fellowship with His sufferings" (Philippians 3:10).

Believers have fellowship with the Father and the Son (1 John 1:3). The fact that the Spirit indwells all believers, and provides the ground of our supernatural unity, results in true Christian fellowship—a sharing that knows no bounds. It is a divine fellowship, brought about by a divine person, the Holy Spirit of God, the eternal third person of the blessed Trinity.

CHAPTER 11

Three Persons

As stated earlier, many Christians, without knowing it, hold a false view of the Trinity simply due to their inability to articulate the difference between believing in one *Being* of God and three *persons* sharing that one Being. As a result, even orthodox Christian believers slip into an ancient heresy known by many names: modalism, Sabellianism, Patripassionism. Today this same error is called Oneness or the "Jesus Only" position. Whatever its name might be, it is a denial of the Trinity based upon a denial of the distinction between the Father, Son, and Holy Spirit. It accepts the truth that there is only one true God, and that the Father, Son, and Spirit are fully God, but it denies that the Bible differentiates between the persons. Instead, advocates of this position either believe that the Father is the Son, and the Son is the Spirit, and the Spirit is the Father (the old actor on the stage example, wearing different masks to "play" different parts, but always being the same person), or they make the Son merely the "human nature" of Christ (hence denying His eternal nature). Jesus then becomes two "persons," the Father and the Son, the Father being the deity, the Son the human nature.

Most other groups who deny the Trinity do so thinking that orthodox Christian believers actually embrace some form of modalism. That is, many times Mormons or Jehovah's Witnesses will attack the Trinity on grounds that are really only relevant to the Oneness or modalistic position. They will point to the baptism of Jesus and say, "Well, was Jesus a ventriloquist or something?" The Oneness position is, in fact, liable to all sorts of refutation on the basis of Scripture, so it is easy to see why many who wish to deny the Trinity *prefer* to attack this perversion of it rather than the real thing. Christians who love the Trinity must be very quick to correct those who think that orthodox believers embrace a form of modalism—one *what*, three *whos*. That is the issue.

Scripture leaves no room for confusing the Father, Son, and Spirit. A brief survey of some of the more blatant ways in which this is confirmed will suffice for our purposes here. But do not think the brevity of the review indicates the issue is unimportant. As John taught,

> Whoever denies the Son does not have the Father; the one who confesses the Son has the Father also. (1 John 2:23)

Such a passage not only clearly differentiates between the Father and the Son, but it warns us how important God considers the truth about His nature.

FATHER, SON, AND SPIRIT

The scriptural truth that the Father is not the Son, nor the Son the Spirit, is rather easily demonstrated. We begin with the fact that the Father loves the Son and the Son loves the Father—actions incomprehensible outside of recognizing that the Father is a separate divine person from the Son:

> "The Father loves the Son and has given all things into His hand" (John 3:35).

"For the Father loves the Son, and shows Him all things that He Himself is doing; and greater works than these will He show Him, so that you will marvel" (John 5:20).

Just as the Father loves the Son, so the Son loves His disciples. The disciples are separate persons from the Son; hence, the Father is a separate person from the Son as well:

"Just as the Father has loved Me, I have also loved you; abide in My love" (John 15:9).

"I in them and You in Me, that they may be perfected in unity, so that the world may know that You sent Me, and loved them, even as You have loved Me. Father, I desire that they also, whom You have given Me, be with Me where I am, so that they may see My glory which You have given Me, for You loved Me before the foundation of the world" (John 17:23–24).

Certainly the best known example of the existence of three persons is the baptism of Jesus recorded in Matthew 3:16–17:

After being baptized, Jesus came up immediately from the water; and behold, the heavens were opened, and he saw the Spirit of God descending as a dove *and* lighting on Him, and behold, a voice out of the heavens said, "This is My beloved Son, in whom I am well-pleased."

Here the Father speaks from heaven, the Son is being baptized (and is again described as being the object of the Father's love, paralleling the passages just cited from John), and the Spirit is descending as a dove. Jesus is not speaking to himself but is spoken to by the Father. There is no confusing of the persons at the baptism of the Lord Jesus.

The transfiguration of Jesus in Matthew 17:1–9 again demonstrates the separate personhood of the Father and the Son:

While he was still speaking, a bright cloud overshadowed them, and behold, a voice out of the cloud said, "This is My beloved Son, with whom I am well-pleased; listen to Him!" (Matthew 17:5).

The Son's true preexistent glory is unveiled for an instant in the presence of the Father in the cloud. Communication again takes place, marked with the familiar love of the Father for the Son. Both the deity and the separate personhood of the Son are clearly presented in this passage. The Father spoke to the Son at another time, recorded in John 12:28:

> "Father, glorify Your name." There came then a voice out of heaven: "I have both glorified it, and will glorify it again" (John 12:28).

Again, the distinction of the person of the Father and of the Son is clearly maintained. This is a conversation, not a monologue.

Some of the most obvious passages relevant to the Father and the Son are found in the prayers of Jesus Christ. These are not mock prayers—Jesus is not speaking to himself (nor, as the Oneness writer would put it, is Jesus' humanity speaking to His deity)—He is clearly communicating with another person, that being the person of the Father. Transcendent heights are reached in the lengthiest prayer we have, that of John 17. No one can miss the fact of the communication of one person (the Son) with another (the Father) presented in this prayer. Note just a few examples of how the Son refers to the Father as a separate person:

> Jesus spoke these things; and lifting up His eyes to heaven, He said, "Father, the hour has come; glorify Your Son, that the Son may glorify You, even as You gave Him authority over all flesh, that to all whom You have given Him, He may give eternal life. This is eternal life, that they may know You, the only true God, and Jesus Christ whom You have sent" (John 17:1–3).

The usage of personal pronouns and direct address puts the very language squarely on the side of maintaining the separate personhood of Father and Son. This is not to say that their unity is something that is a mere unity of purpose; indeed, given the background of the Old Testament, the very statements of the Son regarding His relationship with the Father are among the strongest assertions of His deity in the Bible.

Striking is the example of Matthew 27:46, where Jesus, quoting from Psalm 22:1, cries out, "My God, my God, why have you abandoned me?" That the Father is the immediate person addressed is clear from Luke's account, where the next statement from Jesus in his narrative is "Father, into your hands I commit My spirit" (Luke 23:46).[1] That this is the Son addressing the Father is crystal clear, and the ensuing personhood of both is inarguable.

Jesus' words in Matthew 11:27 almost seem to be more at home in the gospel of John than in Matthew:

> "All things have been handed over to Me by My Father; and no one knows the Son except the Father; nor does anyone know the Father except the Son, and anyone to whom the Son wills to reveal *Him*" (Matthew 11:27).

Here the reciprocal relationship between the Father and Son is put forth with exactness, while at the same time dictating the absolute deity of both. Only God has the authority to "hand over all things," and no mere creature could ever be the recipient of the control of "all things" either. Jesus "reveals" the Father to those He wills to do so. Obviously, two divine persons are in view here.

It is just as clear that the Lord Jesus Christ is never identified as the Father by the apostle Paul but is shown to be another person besides the Father. A large class of examples of this would be the greetings in the epistles of Paul. In Romans 1:7 we read, "Grace to you and peace from God our Father and the Lord Jesus Christ." The same greeting is found in 1 Corinthians 1:3; 2 Corinthians 1:2; Galatians 1:3; Ephesians 1:2; and Philippians 1:2.

A COUPLE OF MISUSED PASSAGES

There are only a few passages that can be appealed to in the attempt to confuse the persons of the Father and the Son. Most are found in the gospel of John where the full deity of Christ is so strongly emphasized. Yet that Gospel is tremendously clear in its witness to the existence of three persons, the Father, the Son, and the Spirit. One of the most often cited passages is from Jesus' words in John 14:

> Jesus said to him, "Have I been so long with you, and *yet* you have not come to know Me, Philip? He who has seen Me has seen the Father; how *can* you say, 'Show us the Father'? Do you not believe that I am in the Father, and the Father is in Me? The words that I say to you I do not speak on My own initiative, but the Father abiding in Me does His works" (John 14:9–10).

Some insist that when Jesus says, "He who has seen Me has seen the Father," this is the same as saying, "I am the Father." But this ignores the very words that follow, where the Lord distinguishes himself from the Father by saying the Father abides in Him and does His (the Father's) works through Him. The truth that Jesus teaches here, however, does support the full deity of Christ, for no mere creature could ever say, "He who has seen Me has seen the Father." Jesus' words here do not make Him the Father, but they do tell us that the unity that exists between Father and Son is far more than a mere unity of purpose or intention. The Son reveals the Father, or to use the words of John himself, "He has explained[2] Him" (John 1:18).

The single most popular passage cited in defense of modalism, however, is one that is often cited in defense of the deity of Christ:

> "I and the Father are one" (John 10:30).

In this context, the assertion would be that the Father and the Son are one person. Yet this is not what the passage says at all. In fact, the simple citation of the passage, without due regard to its context and meaning, neither proves the modalistic viewpoint *nor* the deity of Christ! Its witness to the truth about Christ comes from the context, which is most often ignored.

Literally, the passage reads, "I and the Father, *we* are one." The verb translated "are" is *plural* in the Greek. Jesus is not saying, "I am the Father." The distinction between the Son and the Father remains even in the verb He uses. And in context, He is making specific reference to the oneness He shares with the Father in the redemption of His sheep:

> "And I give eternal life to them, and they will never perish; and no one will snatch them out of My hand. My Father, who has given *them* to Me, is greater than all; and no one is able to snatch *them* out of the Father's hand" (John 10:28–29).

This is the context of Jesus' statement, "I and the Father are one." They are one in giving eternal life, they are one in protecting the sheep, they are one in the covenant of redemption. All this must be said simply to be honest with the passage. And once we see what Jesus is speaking about, we can understand how this passage does, in fact, teach the deity of Christ, for no creature could claim this kind of oneness in redemption with the Father. Eternal life is divine life, and Jesus gives it to His own. God's people are in the Son's hand and are likewise in the Father's hand (cf. Colossians 3:3), and hence are safe and secure in their almighty grip. The Father has given a people to the Son and will not suffer any of them to be lost (cf. John 6:37–39). Here is the oneness that exists between the Father and the Son—a oneness in redemption. Yet since redemption is a divine act, here we have the testimony to the deity of Christ, for no apostle, no prophet, can be said to be "one" with the Father in saving believers in the way announced here. No mere creature can have this kind of perfect unity of purpose and action. No, Jesus Christ must be perfect deity to be able to say of himself in reference to redemption, "I and the Father are one."

JESUS CHRIST: ONE PERSON WITH TWO NATURES

If Jesus Christ is truly God and truly man, we are tempted to begin asking all sorts of questions concerning just how the "God-man" could exist. Thankfully, the Scriptures safeguard this unique and special act of the Incarnation and do not bow to our inordinate desire to know things God has not chosen to reveal. Instead, we are only given certain guidelines, certain truths that help us to avoid wandering off into error. We can say that the early church was correct in coming to the conclusion (at the Council of Chalcedon in A.D. 451) that Jesus Christ is one person with two natures, divine and human. He is not two persons, nor are His natures somehow mixed together so that He is not *truly* divine or *truly* man. He is both, concurrently, because He has both natures.

As we noted above, the prayers of Christ are very important in recognizing the separate person of the Son from the Father. Jesus was not "talking to himself" in His prayers, but was talking to the Father. In the same way, the Scriptures do give us at least some indication of the unipersonality of the Son while at the same time revealing to us His two natures. I briefly note one passage that is often referred to at this point, from Paul's first letter to the Corinthians:

> . . . *the wisdom* which none of the rulers of this age has understood; for if they had understood it they would not have crucified the Lord of glory. (1 Corinthians 2:8)

This passage represents a group of Scriptures that instructs us to view Jesus as one person with two natures. How so? Because of the phrase "crucified the Lord of glory." Obviously the "Lord of glory" has reference to the divine nature of Christ, yet Jesus was crucified as a man. Crucifixion is only meaningful with reference to his human nature (you cannot crucify the divine nature). When Paul speaks of the crucifixion of the Lord of glory, he is speaking of Christ as one person with two natures. The one action of crucifixion is predicated of one *person* though that *person* had two natures, divine and human.

Just as it is with the Trinity, so it is with the one act of revelation, wherein the Trinity is the most clearly revealed, the Incarnation of Christ: both present to us *unique* truths about God that defy our creaturely categorization. Just as we cannot present any one analogy that "grasps" the Trinity (due to the absolutely unique way in which God exists), so, too, the Incarnation defies our attempts to wrap our limited minds around all it means. God only became incarnate once in the Son; therefore, there is nothing else in the created order to which we can compare either the Incarnation or the resultant God-Man, Jesus

Christ. Instead of fretting over questions the Triune God has not chosen to answer in His revelation in Scripture, we should stand amazed at the *motivation* that brought the eternal Son into human flesh: His tremendous love for us!

CHAPTER 12

A Closer Look

The biblical verdict is clear: the three foundational truths we presented at the beginning of this work are definitely the teachings of Scripture. We can now see how richly this truth is found in the very fabric of Scripture itself. Take a moment to slowly read through the following passages, and in light of what has come before, consider what they communicate:

> . . . constantly bearing in mind your work of faith and labor of love and steadfastness of hope in our Lord Jesus Christ in the presence of our God and Father, knowing, brethren beloved by God, *His* choice of you; for our gospel did not come to you in word only, but also in power and in the Holy Spirit and with full conviction; just as you know what kind of men we proved to be among you for your sake. (1 Thessalonians 1:3–5)

> But we should always give thanks to God for you, brethren

beloved by the Lord, because God has chosen you from the beginning for salvation through sanctification by the Spirit and faith in the truth. (2 Thessalonians 2:13)

For I determined to know nothing among you except Jesus Christ, and Him crucified. I was with you in weakness and in fear and in much trembling, and my message and my preaching were not in persuasive words of wisdom, but in demonstration of the Spirit and of power, so that your faith would not rest on the wisdom of men, but on the power of God. (1 Corinthians 2:2–5)

Such were some of you; but you were washed, but you were sanctified, but you were justified in the name of the Lord Jesus Christ and in the Spirit of our God. (1 Corinthians 6:11)

Now there are varieties of gifts, but the same Spirit. And there are varieties of ministries, and the same Lord. There are varieties of effects, but the same God who works all things in all *persons.* (1 Corinthians 12:4–6)

Now He who establishes us with you in Christ and anointed us is God, who also sealed us and gave *us* the Spirit in our hearts as a pledge. (2 Corinthians 1:21–22)

The grace of the Lord Jesus Christ, and the love of God, and the fellowship of the Holy Spirit, be with you all. (2 Corinthians 13:14)

For the kingdom of God is not eating and drinking, but righteousness and peace and joy in the Holy Spirit. For he who in this *way* serves Christ is acceptable to God and approved by men. (Romans 14:17–18)

. . . to be a minister of Christ Jesus to the Gentiles, ministering as a priest the gospel of God, so that *my* offering of the Gentiles may become acceptable, sanctified by the Holy Spirit. (Romans 15:16)

. . . which has come to you, just as in all the world also it is constantly bearing fruit and increasing, even as *it has been doing* in you also since the day you heard *of it* and understood the grace of God in truth; just as you learned *it* from Epaphras, our beloved fellow bond-servant, who is a faithful servant of Christ on our behalf, and he also informed us of your love in the Spirit. (Colossians 1:6–8)

For through Him we both have our access in one Spirit to the Father. (Ephesians 2:18)

... that He would grant you, according to the riches of His glory, to be strengthened with power through His Spirit in the inner man, so that Christ may dwell in your hearts through faith. (Ephesians 3:16–17)

There is one body and one Spirit, just as also you were called in one hope of your calling; one Lord, one faith, one baptism, one God and Father of all who is over all and through all and in all. (Ephesians 4:4–6)

Do you see how the faith of the New Testament is an implicitly *Trinitarian* faith? None of these passages say, "Now, the doctrine of the Trinity is this ..." Nor do they need to. When you write to a friend, you don't start every letter by introducing yourself and going back over every shared experience you've had. No, there is an entire body of shared experiences and beliefs that form the background of such a letter to a close friend. In the same way, the early believers spoke easily of Father, Son, and Spirit without giving the slightest indication that they found anything strange in joining these divine persons in the one work of salvation and in the edification of the church. It was simply natural for them to speak in this way. That is why B. B. Warfield wrote, "The whole book is Trinitarian to the core; all its teaching is built on the assumption of the Trinity; and its allusions to the Trinity are frequent, cursory, easy and confident."[1]

THE REVELATION OF THE TRINITY

Warfield, one of my favorite theologians, had an insight into this subject that few have ever shared. In his article on the Trinity, he discusses how the Trinity has been revealed to us. Some of his insights simply cannot be phrased any better, so I draw heavily from him in attempting to communicate a very important element of how we are to understand the Trinity.

When we ask, "How was the Trinity revealed to us?" many answers are given. Some would assert that it is revealed in the Old Testament in the scattered allusions to the deity of Christ or the use of the plural pronoun "us" with reference to God (Genesis 1:26). But Warfield was right in noting,

> The Old Testament may be likened to a chamber richly furnished but dimly lighted; the introduction of light brings into it nothing which was not in it before; but it brings out into clearer view much of what is in it but was only dimly or even not at all perceived before. The mystery of the Trinity is not revealed in the Old Testament; but the mystery of the Trinity underlies the Old Testament revelation, and here and there almost comes into view. Thus the Old Testament revelation of God is not corrected by the fuller revelation which follows it, but only perfected, extended and enlarged.[2]

So when was it revealed? Many insist it developed over time "in the consciousness of the church," so that the Trinity does not become "doctrine" until well into the church age. But this is to confuse men's *knowledge* and *understanding* of God's revelation with the revelation itself. The Trinity as a doctrinal truth has *always* been true. But when did it become *knowable* to men? What "revealed" it to the human race?

The answer to that question is simply the Incarnation and the coming of the Holy Spirit. That is, the Trinity is revealed by the Son coming in the flesh and the Spirit descending upon the church. Therefore, the Trinity is revealed not in the Old Testament, or even in the New Testament, but rather *in between* the testaments, in the ministry of Christ and the founding of the church. These events are recorded for us in the New Testament, but they took place before a word of the New Testament was written. Warfield again puts it well:

> We cannot speak of the doctrine of the Trinity, therefore, if we

study exactness of speech, as revealed in the New Testament, any more than we can speak of it as revealed in the Old Testament. The Old Testament was written before its revelation; the New Testament after it. The revelation itself was made not in word but in deed. It was made in the incarnation of God the Son, and the outpouring of God the Holy Spirit. The relation of the two Testaments to this revelation is in the one case that of preparation for it, and in the other that of product of it. The revelation itself is embodied just in Christ and the Holy Spirit. This is as much to say that the revelation of the Trinity was incidental to, and the inevitable effect of, the accomplishment of redemption. It was in the coming of the Son of God in the likeness of sinful flesh to offer Himself a sacrifice for sin; and in the coming of the Holy Spirit to convict the world of sin, of righteousness and of judgment, that the Trinity of Persons in the Unity of the Godhead was once for all revealed to men.[3]

To grasp this reality is truly exciting! The Trinity is a doctrine not revealed merely in words but instead in the very action of the Triune God in redemption itself! We know who God *is* by what He has *done* in bringing us to himself! The Father, loving His people and sending the Son. The Son, loving us and giving himself in our place. The Spirit, entering into our lives and conforming us to the image of Christ. Here is the revelation of the Trinity, in the work of Christ and the Spirit.

This explains why we don't find a single passage that lays out, in a creedal format, the doctrine of the Trinity. Warfield continues:

> We may understand also, however, from the same central fact, why it is that the doctrine of the Trinity lies in the New Testament rather in the form of allusions than in express teaching, why it is rather everywhere presupposed, coming only here and there into incidental expression, than formally inculcated. It is because the revelation, having been made in the actual occurrences of redemption, was already the common property of all Christian hearts.[4]

The disciples were, indeed, "experiential Trinitarians." They had walked with the Son, heard the Father speak from glory, and were now indwelt by the Holy Spirit. Those early believers, hearing the testimony of the first followers of Christ, could not help but speak of the Father, the Son, and the Spirit. So it follows that

> Precisely what the New Testament is, is the documentation of the religion of the incarnate Son and of the outpoured Spirit, that is to say, of the religion of the Trinity, and what we mean by the doctrine of the Trinity is nothing but the formulation in exact language of the conception of God presupposed in the religion of the incarnate Son and outpoured Spirit.[5]

THAT CLOSER LOOK

The following section is meant to provide a base from which those who wish to "dig deeper" can begin. It is only meant as a starter. A number of works exist that can help the believer dig deeper into the many questions that have been asked, and answered, on the doctrine of the Trinity.[6]

Over the years, Christian theologians have struggled with these issues and, as a result, have produced expanded, more specific definitions of the Trinity that help us to more clearly understand how the truths presented in Scripture relate to one another.[7] It should be remembered that no matter how technical we become in our definition, we are still giving the same definition we gave in the first chapter: "Within the one Being that is God, there exist eternally three coequal and coeternal persons, namely, the Father, the Son, and the Holy Spirit." We expand upon the definition for the sake of clarity (believe it or not!), and we become more technical so as to exclude certain errors that have been promoted down through the history of the church. I will use the definition provided by Dr. Louis Berkhof in his *Systematic Theology*:

1. There is in the divine Being but one indivisible essence *(ousia, essentia)*.
2. In this one divine Being there are three persons or individual subsistences, Father, Son and Holy Spirit.

3. The whole undivided essence of God belongs equally to each of the three persons.
4. The subsistence and operation of the three persons in the divine Being is marked by a certain definite order.
5. There are certain personal attributes by which the three persons are distinguished.
6. The church confesses the Trinity to be a mystery beyond the comprehension of man.[8]

The "simpler" definition is really merely a "boiled down" version of what we have here. This longer rendition will help us to understand why we use the specific terms we do in defining the Trinity.

1. *There is in the divine Being but one indivisible essence (ousia, essentia).* This is Foundation One: monotheism. Yet, as we can see, it goes beyond the mere statement that there is only one true God numerically speaking. It makes a further statement: the divine Being is "indivisible." That is, you can't chop God up into parts. He is "simple," in the sense that He is not made up of different "parts." God's being is either entire, whole, or it is not God's being at all.

We struggle to express ourselves clearly here, for how does one describe the "being" of God? Terms have been used down through the centuries, such as *essence,* or in Greek, *ousia,* or in Latin, *essentia.* It's the "stuff of God." I like to say it is that "which makes God, God." Because He is unique, His being is unique as well. Whatever the "being" of God is, creatures don't have the same thing. Our biggest problem is that we think very physically. We want to think of being as something you can put under a microscope or weigh on a scale. But it isn't, especially since we know that "God is spirit."[9] He can say through Jeremiah, " 'Can a man hide himself in hiding places so I do not see him?' declares the LORD. 'Do I not fill the heavens and the earth?' declares the LORD."[10] And Solomon reminds us of this truth when he says of God, "Behold, heaven and the highest heaven cannot contain You; how much less this house which I have built."[11] God's being is not limited by time and space but is eternal and without bounds, omnipresent.

2. *In this one divine Being there are three persons or individual sub-*

sistences, Father, Son, and Holy Spirit. This is Foundation Two. Yet we note the fact that another term is offered to help define the word "person," that being "subsistences." Why suggest this term? Because we are wont to read into the term "person" all sorts of physical limitations that should not be thought of at all when speaking of the Trinity. Many people, when they hear of "three persons," visualize three men standing side by side. Yet this is not at all what we are talking about when we speak of "person." But then again, doesn't "subsistence" mean anything to most of us? What we are talking about are *personal distinctions* in the divine Being. We are talking about the "I, You, He" found in such passages as Matthew 3, where the Father speaks from heaven, the Son is being baptized, and the Spirit descends as a dove. While trying to avoid the idea of separate *individuals,* we are speaking of the *personal self-distinctions* God has revealed to exist within the one, indivisible divine essence.[12] Theologians speak of each of these subsistences as being marked by particular "incommunicable attributes." What we mean is that you can tell the Father from the Son, and the Son from the Spirit, by how they are related to each other, and by what actions they take in working out creation, salvation, etc.[13] We will talk more about this below. For now we emphasize the fact that the Father, Son, and Spirit are distinguished from one another, and yet these distinctions do not lead to a division in the one *Being* that is God. This leads us to the next point:

3. *The whole undivided essence of God belongs equally to each of the three persons.* This is Foundation Three. The statement asserts that the Father is in full possession of the entirety of the divine essence; the Son is in full possession of the entirety of the divine essence; and the Spirit is in full possession of the entirety of the divine essence. There are not three different *essences,* nor is the one essence divided equally into thirds. Each divine person is in full possession of the entirety of the divine nature. But the statement also goes beyond this to assert Foundation One again, for it reemphasizes the unity of the divine nature with its insistence that it is "undivided."

Right here we stumble, for in our experience *being* can only be shared fully by one *person.* Let's think about this. What is the difference between "being" and "person"? Everything that exists has being. A rock has the being of a rock,[14] a tree the being of a tree, a dog the being of a dog, and man is a human being. That which exists has being, but not everything that has being is personal. A rock is not personal. You can insult a rock all day long, and it won't really mind, since it is not personal. Same with a tree. My dog couldn't care less what I say to her, too—she's only concerned about *how* I say it, the tone of my voice. I might say, in a limited sense, that she has a "personality," but I don't mean that in the technical or specific sense I am using when discussing the Trinity. A dog is not a person in that sense, for my dog does not view herself as one dog over against all other dogs, nor does she understand the idea of "dog kind," nor does she work for the betterment of "dog kind."

Biblically speaking, there are three kinds of *beings* who are personal: God, men, and angels. I have being: I exist. Yet I am personal. My being is limited and finite. It is limited to one place geographically speaking, and one time temporally speaking. Despite all the Star Trek scenarios to the contrary, I am limited to one place at one time. Such is the essence of being a creature. My *being* is shared by only one *person:* me. My *being,* since it is limited, cannot be distributed among two, three, or any more *persons.* One being, one person: that's what it is to be a human.

What we are saying about God is that His being is not limited and finite like a creature's. His *Being* is infinite and unlimited, and hence *can,* in a way completely beyond our comprehension, be shared *fully* by three *persons,* the Father, Son, and Holy Spirit. The divine Being is one; the divine *persons* are three. While the Father is not the Son, nor is the Son the Spirit, each is fully and completely *God* by full and complete participation in the divine Being. Unless we recognize the difference between the terms *being* and *person,* we will never have an accurate or workable understanding of the Trinity.[15]

It is the full and equal participation in the divine Being that is most often denied by heretical and unorthodox religious groups. The truth of this claim is found in the scriptural witness to the deity of Christ and of the Holy Spirit.

4. *The subsistence and operation of the three persons in the divine Being is marked by a certain definite order.* To get a firm grasp on this concept, we need to define two terms that are often used in this discussion. The first is *ontological. Ontology* is the study of being. When we speak of the "ontological Trinity," we speak of the Trinity *as it exists in and of itself.* In contrast with this is the term *economical.* In this case, when we speak of the *economical Trinity,* we speak of the *operations and workings* of the Trinity, what the three persons *do* in creation and salvation. Obviously, the Father, Son, and Spirit have taken different roles in creation and in redemption. Hence, we find different relationships between them in the *economical* Trinity as we see them working out redemption and bringing about salvation. We must be *very* careful to distinguish between relationships *as we observe them outwardly* and the eternal relationship that exists between the persons *inside* the triune nature of God, that is, the *ontological* Trinity.

The "order" that is observed biblically is the Father first, the Son second, and the Spirit third. But immediately our time-bound minds hit a pothole and often jump the track. When we think of someone being "first" and someone else being "second," especially in relationships, we immediately begin to import time elements. "If the Father is *first,* then He must be *before* the Son." We need to dismiss this concept *immediately.* When we speak of the "order" of the Persons, we are not talking about an order *of being.* It is not an order *in time.* It does not refer to dignity or participation in the divine Being. The first is not "bigger" than the second or the third. The order is one of relationship. Stick with me here, for we are discussing aspects of God's nature that are very difficult and challenging. But the reward for the labor invested is well worth it.

When we speak of the relationship shared by the Father, Son, and Spirit, we use the terms *begotten* and *procession.* Again I sound the warning, "Define these terms within the context in which they are being used." That is, don't think of "begotten" in human terms, but divine; don't think of "procession" in a finite, creaturely sense, but in an eternal, unlimited, timeless sense. We must do so, for we are talking about the infinite, timeless being of God.

We use the term *begotten* of the relationship of Father and Son. The Son is *eternally* begotten by the Father. The Father is begotten by no one. Automatically we place this relationship within time and think of the Father *originating* the Son at a point in time. Most definitely not. The term as we use it here speaks of an eternal, *timeless*[16] relationship. It had no beginning, it will have no ending. It has always been. C. S. Lewis[17] likened it to a book that is lying on top of another. We say the top book owes its position to the bottom one. It wouldn't be where it is without the one on the bottom. Now, if you can, imagine this relationship as *always having been.* There never was a time when the top book was not where it was, never a time when the bottom book was alone. This is what we mean when we speak of the Father *begetting* the Son. The *relationship* of the first person of the Trinity to the second person is that of *begetting.*

The relationship of the Holy Spirit to the Father and the Son[18] is described by the term *procession.* He is said to "proceed" from the Father and the Son on the basis of such passages as John 15:26 and John 16:7.

5. *There are certain personal attributes by which the three persons are distinguished.* This refers back to the preceding point. Looking internally at the Trinity, these actions are called the *opera ad intra* and would be "generation" for the Father, "filiation" for the Son, and "procession" for the Holy Spirit. Because of the *relationship* the persons bear to one another, we cannot confuse them. Only the Father generates; only the Son bears the relation of Son to the Father (filiation); and only the Spirit proceeds from the Father and the Son.

6. *The church confesses the Trinity to be a mystery beyond the comprehension of man.* This is *not* a statement that the doctrine is inherently contradictory or irrational. It is *not* an excuse to ignore biblical passages or believe things not taught in Scripture. It *is* an admission that Deuteronomy 29:29 is true: there are certain secret things that belong only to the Lord. He has not chosen to reveal everything there is to know. Indeed, when it comes to the eternal relationship between Father, Son, and Spirit, could we even begin to grasp the eternal, perfect, infinite union that is theirs, even if we tried? Are not our finite

minds far too limited for such a task? The statement that the Trinity is a mystery beyond the comprehension of man does not differ from stating that how God exists eternally, outside the realm of time, is likewise a mystery beyond the comprehension of man. It is a statement about *our limitedness* over against the greatness of God's being, nothing more.

THE GREAT TRINITARIAN PASSAGE

We close our examination of the wonderful truth of God's triune nature with the single passage of the Bible that comes the closest to providing a "creedal" statement:

> And Jesus came up and spoke to them, saying, "All authority has been given to Me in heaven and on earth. Go therefore and make disciples of all the nations, baptizing them in the name of the Father and the Son and the Holy Spirit, teaching them to observe all that I commanded you; and lo, I am with you always, even to the end of the age" (Matthew 28:18–20).

The Lord is about to ascend into heaven. His words are measured and solemn. His disciples are listening very closely. He gives the entire church her charter, commanding believers of all ages to make disciples. Who is a disciple? One who has been baptized and taught. Baptized in whose name? There is only one name mentioned (the word "name" is singular here): that of the Father and the Son and the Holy Spirit. B. B. Warfield again touches the very heart of the truth by saying of this monumental passage,

> He could not have been understood otherwise than as substituting for the Name of Jehovah this other Name "of the Father, and of the Son, and of the Holy Ghost"; and this could not possibly have meant to His disciples anything else than that Jehovah was now to be known to them by the new Name, of the Father, and the Son, and the Holy Ghost. The only alternative would have been that, for the community which He was founding, Jesus was supplanting Jehovah by a new God; and this alternative is no less than

monstrous . . . We are not witnessing here the birth of the doctrine of the Trinity; that is presupposed. What we are witnessing is the authoritative announcement of the Trinity as the God of Christianity by its Founder, in one of the most solemn of His recorded declarations. Israel had worshipped the one and only true God under the Name of Jehovah; Christians are to worship the same one and only and true God under the Name of "the Father, and the Son, and the Holy Ghost." This is the distinguishing characteristic of Christians; and that is as much as to say that the doctrine of the Trinity is, according to our Lord's own apprehension of it, the distinctive mark of the religion which He founded.[19]

We see, then, why baptism in the name of the Father, Son, and Spirit is so important: because this is baptism in the name of our God, the triune God we worship and serve and adore, the triune God who has saved us. The Father—source of all, eternally gracious. The Son—Redeemer who left the glory of heaven to save His sheep. Spirit—indwelling Comforter who makes the truths of the Christian faith alive in our hearts. What other name would we wish to bear than the triune name of Father, Son, and Spirit? As the hymn writer so eloquently put it:

> *Holy, Holy, Holy! Lord God Almighty!*
> *All thy works shall praise thy Name*
> *In earth and sky and sea;*
> *Holy, Holy, Holy! Merciful and Mighty!*
> *God in three Persons, blessed Trinity!*

CHAPTER 13

From the Mists of Time: The Trinity and Church History

History is a wonderful guide but a lousy taskmaster. As long as we use history as a light to illumine but not an authority to obey we can profit greatly from its study. In the same way, history can shed much light on the doctrine of the Trinity, but only insofar as it shows us how the people of God have struggled to safeguard and defend the truth of God revealed to them in Christ.

There are many volumes written about the history of the doctrine of the Trinity, the deity of Christ, and the person of the Holy Spirit.[1] We will not even try to summarize the huge mountain of material that exists on the subject. Instead, let's answer one simple question: can we trace a belief in the fundamental doctrines we have examined in the Scriptures through the earliest writers of the Christian faith? That is, did they believe in only one true God? Did they believe in the deity of Christ? Did they differentiate between the Father, Son, and Spirit?

It would be nice if we could find a second-century "theology book" from the early church, a series of creedal statements, or some document or artifact that would give us a clear, exhaustive view of the beliefs of the early Christians in the decades immediately after the ministry of the apostles. But it is highly doubtful that we will ever find such a treasure. The reason is very simple: when you are running for your life, in-depth theological reflection, study, and writing is not a high priority. Until the beginning of the fourth century, the church experienced intense persecution. Sometimes it was localized, sometimes it spanned the Roman empire. There were a couple of periods when the church enjoyed a decade or two of peace. But on the flip side, there were other periods in which they experienced a decade or two of horrific persecution resulting in great bloodshed.

Even when the church had peace her attention was not focused upon the finer points of theology. While we can find a deep witness to a belief in one God and in the deity of Christ, from the beginning, the specific relationship of the Father, Son, and Spirit was not the first priority for those writers who put quill and ink to paper. A more basic defense of the validity of the Christian faith consumed those who wrote for "outsiders." As far as what was most important *within* the church, the issue of what to do about those who apostatized during periods of persecution but then desired admission back into the church was far more on the mind of people than anything else.

The end of persecution brought an almost immediate refocusing of the church's attention upon the issues of the Trinity and the deity of Christ. Indeed, the first major council of the church, called by Emperor Constantine in Nicaea in A.D. 325, addressed the issue of the nature of Christ a scant dozen years after the persecutions ended. The next centuries were spent working through the fine details of these concepts.

CLEMENT OF ROME

One of the earliest Christian writings outside of the New Testament is a lengthy letter written from the church at Rome to the church at Corinth regarding a rebellion that had taken place within the assembly at Corinth. Some unruly people had risen up and rebelled against the elders of the church, removing them from their positions of leadership. The church at Rome wrote to the church at Corinth, remonstrating with them as equals regarding this action. There is no specific name attached to the letter. Tradition eventually credited it to Clement, bishop of Rome. However, at the time, there was no one bishop in either Rome or Corinth. Instead, the biblical pattern of a plurality of elders prevailed. Clement may have been one of those elders, or even a scribe for the group.

Clement is soaked in Scripture. That there is only one true God, and that the Father, Son, and Spirit are separate persons, are clearly truths fundamental to Clement's beliefs. God has all power and is the Creator of all things:

> For by His infinitely great power He established the heavens, and by His incomprehensible understanding He set them in order. (33)[2]

There is only one true God:

> Surely he knew; but so that there might be no rebellion in Israel he did this so that the name of the true and only God might be glorified; to whom be glory for ever and ever. (43)

Clement clearly differentiates between the Father and the Son:

> Therefore, all these were glorified and magnified, not because of themselves, or through their own works, or for the righteous deeds they performed, but by His will. And we also, being called by His will in Christ Jesus, are not justified by means of ourselves, nor by our own wisdom or understanding or godliness or works which we have done in holiness of heart; but by that faith through which the Almighty God has justified all *those believing* from the beginning. To whom be glory for ever and ever, amen. (32)

> By love all the elect of God have been perfected; without love nothing is well-pleasing to God. In love has the Sovereign taken us to Himself. On account of the love He had for us, Jesus Christ

our Lord gave His blood for us by the will of God—and His flesh for our flesh, and His soul for our souls. (49)

This blessedness comes upon those who have been chosen by God through Jesus Christ our Lord; to whom be glory for ever and ever. Amen. (50)

But most significant for our study is the appearance of the very same kind of Trinitarian passages in Clement that we have found in the New Testament. Two such passages stand out:

For Christ is of those who are humble-minded, and not of those who exalt themselves over His flock. Our Lord Jesus Christ, the Scepter of the majesty of God, did not come in the pomp of pride or arrogance (though He could have!), but in a humble state, just as the Holy Spirit had spoken concerning Him. (16)

Even more specific is this passage, rich with theological meaning and content:

For as God lives, and the Lord Jesus Christ lives, and the Holy Spirit, who are the faith and hope of the chosen ones—the one who in humility of mind, with extended gentleness, without regret has done the ordinances and commandments given by God, this one will be enrolled and given a name among the number of the saved through Jesus Christ, through whom is the glory unto Him for ever and ever, amen. (58)

Just as in the New Testament, the intimate cooperation of the Father, Son, and Spirit (here using the common Trinitarian names used by Paul, God, Lord, and Spirit) in the work of salvation is prevalent in Clement's thinking. He describes the three persons as the "faith and hope of the chosen ones," a phrase that would make no sense outside of a belief in the full deity of all three. It would be blasphemous to speak of God, Michael, and some other lesser creature as the faith and hope of the elect.

IGNATIUS

The first major Christian writer to produce multiple letters of theological interest is Ignatius, bishop of Antioch (d. 107). While on his way to his martyrdom in Rome, Ignatius wrote a series of letters to various churches. While it was not his intention to produce a systematic theology by so doing, he did give us some very clear statements regarding important doctrinal beliefs of the early church. Most important for our purposes is his crystalline testimony to the deity of Christ. While some have attempted to hide his words,[3] they speak with great clarity and force. He speaks easily of Christ as God, borrowing from the apostle John (1:1; 20:28). Tradition says Ignatius knew John, which might explain the similarity of language. Yet there is no hint of polytheism (a belief in more than one God), and the Father is clearly distinguished from the Son and the Spirit. Notice how Ignatius begins his letter to the Ephesians:

> Ignatius, who is also called Theophorus, to her who has been blessed in greatness through the fulness of God the Father, ordained before time to be always resulting in permanent glory, unchangeably united and chosen in true passion, by the will of the Father and *of Jesus Christ, our God*, to the church which is in Ephesus of Asia, worthy of felicitation: abundant greetings in Jesus Christ and in blameless joy. (Ephesians 1)[4]

Ignatius speaks of such items as the conception of Christ and His deity as "givens," not explaining these beliefs, but instead viewing them as the New Testament writers did: as common convictions of those to whom he was writing. In this citation from his epistle to the Ephesians, Ignatius not only directly calls Jesus Christ "our God,"[5] but note the conjunction of the three persons:

> My spirit is but an offscouring of the cross, which is a scandal to the unbelieving, but to us it is salvation and life eternal. Where is the wise man? Where is the disputer? Where is the boasting of those who are called understanding? *For our God, Jesus the Christ*, was conceived by Mary according to a dispensation of *God*, from

the seed of David, yes, but of the *Holy Spirit* as well. (Ephesians 18)

Lest someone think that for Ignatius "our God" is something less than "God" himself, note these words concerning the Incarnation:

> . . . the ancient kingdom was utterly destroyed when *God appeared in the likeness of man* unto newness of everlasting life. (Ephesians 19)

Ignatius shows a true Trinitarian understanding of the nature of God when he can speak of the Father, the Son, and then of Jesus Christ as God. There is no confusion of the persons, just a clear recognition and repeated assertion of the deity of Christ:

> Ignatius, who is also called Theophorus, to her that has found mercy in the majesty of the Most High Father and of Jesus Christ His only Son; to the church that is beloved and enlightened through the will of Him who willed all things that exist, by faith and love toward *Jesus Christ our God*; even to her that has the presidency in the country of the region of the Romans. (Romans 1)

That the term "God" is not *merely* a synonym for the Father for Ignatius is seen in this passage:

> *For our God Jesus Christ*, being in the Father, is more plainly seen. The work is not of persuasiveness, but Christianity is a thing of might, whenever it is hated by the world. (Romans 3)

Ignatius can call Jesus God, and then the Son of God, in the same context without any difficulty:

> I glorify *Jesus Christ the God* who gave to you such wisdom, for I know that you are fully established in immovable faith, just as if you have been nailed to the cross of the Lord Jesus Christ, both in flesh and in spirit, firmly established in love in the blood of Christ, completely persuaded with reference to our Lord that He is truly of the race of David according to the flesh, but the Son of God

according to God's will and power, truly born from a virgin, having been baptized by John in order to by Him fulfill all righteousness. (Smyrneans 1)

The *depth* of Ignatius' doctrine of Christ demonstrates that such high views did not develop over time but are very primitive. That is not to say that others did not have less developed views, but that high views of Christ in regard to His deity, His natures, etc., can be found as early in the record as any other belief. Note what he wrote to Polycarp:

Await the One who is above every season, the Eternal, the In-visible, the One who for our sake became visible, the Untouched, the Impassible, who for our sake suffered, who endured in every way for our sake. (Polycarp 3)

Here Ignatius describes the Son as eternal, invisible, impalpable, and impassible. One is reminded of Paul's words to Timothy (1:17):

Now to the King eternal, immortal, invisible, the only God, be honor and glory forever and ever. Amen.

Surely Ignatius had no problem in describing the Son in this way. And the height of his Christology can be seen in this incredible de-scription of Jesus Christ:

There is one physician, of flesh and of spirit, generate and in-generate, God in man, true life in death, both from Mary and from God, first passible and then impassible, Jesus Christ our Lord. (Ephesians 7)

One could well say that even fifth-century Trinitarian thought does not represent any substantial advancement beyond the concepts ex-pressed here. Incarnation, the two natures of Christ—all clearly a part of the theology of the bishop from Antioch, the "birthplace" of Chris-tianity.

It is not overly surprising, then, to find Trinitarian passages, pre-senting all three persons associated together in the work of salvation, in Ignatius as well. One example will suffice:

> ... you being stones of a temple, prepared before as a building of *God the Father*, being raised up to the heights through the mechanism of *Jesus Christ,* which is the cross, and using as a rope the *Holy Spirit*... (Ephesians 9)

There is certainly nothing in Ignatius that can offer much solace to those who wish to deny the deity of Christ or present some aberrant view of the doctrine of God. And the fundamental elements of the Trinity—the three pillars of monotheism, the existence of three persons, and the deity of Christ and the Spirit—can easily be traced through his writings, providing a vitally important link between the New Testament writings and the first post-apostolic writings of the church.

MELITO OF SARDIS

Melito, bishop of Sardis, died around the year A.D. 180. Until recently, few students of church history paid much attention to him. One of the reasons might be that he ended up on the "wrong side" of the ancient debate over how to determine the date of Easter. Only recently a sermon on the Passover was found, penned by Melito. It provides us with a tremendous insight into the theology of the late second century. I reproduce here just one section, which requires no commentary, only a hearty "Amen!":

> And so he was lifted up upon a tree and an inscription was attached indicating who was being killed. Who was it? It is a grievous thing to tell, but a most fearful thing to refrain from telling. But listen, as you tremble before him on whose account the earth trembled!
>
> He who hung the earth in place is hanged.
> He who fixed the heavens in place is fixed in place.
> He who made all things fast is made fast on a tree.
> The Sovereign is insulted.
> God is murdered.

The King of Israel is destroyed by an Israelite hand.

This is the One who made the heavens and the earth,
    and formed mankind in the beginning,
The One proclaimed by the Law and the Prophets,
The One enfleshed in a virgin,
The One hanged on a tree,
The One buried in the earth,
The One raised from the dead
    and who went up into the heights of heaven,
The One sitting at the right hand of the Father,
The One having all authority to judge and save,
Through Whom the Father made the things which exist from
    the beginning of time.
This One is "the Alpha and the Omega,"
This One is "the beginning and the end"
. . . the beginning indescribable and the end
    incomprehensible.
This One is the Christ.
This One is the King.
This One is Jesus.
This One is the Leader.
This One is the Lord.
This One is the One who rose from the dead.
This One is the One sitting on the right hand of the Father.
He bears the Father and is borne by the Father.
"To him be the glory and the power forever. Amen."

The deity of Christ, His two natures, His virgin birth, His being
the Creator, His distinction from the Father—all part and parcel of the
preaching of the bishop of Sardis near the end of the second century.

THE COUNCIL OF NICAEA

It is repeated by believer and even nonbeliever alike around the
world. The Nicene Creed stands either for truth or for error for many
millions of people. Here is what it says:[6]

We believe in one God, the Father, the Almighty, the maker of all things visible and invisible.

And we believe in one Lord, Jesus Christ, the Son of God, begotten from the Father, the unique Son, that is, from the substance of the Father, God from God, Light from Light, true God from true God, begotten[7] not made, of one substance[8] with the Father, by Whom all things were made, whether things in heaven and things in earth, Who for us men and for our salvation came down and became incarnate, becoming man, suffered and rose again the third day, ascended into the heavens, and will come again to judge the living and the dead.

And we believe in the Holy Spirit.

But for those who say "There was a time when He was not,"[9] and "Before He was begotten He was not," and "He was made of things that were not,"[10] or who assert that He is of a different substance or essence [from the Father], or that He is created or subject to change or alterable—the Catholic Church anathematizes them.

These words were the result of the greatest church council ever convened—not in size, but in importance. Beginning on June 19, 325, around 300 bishops, almost all from the Eastern portion of the Roman empire, met and considered the issue of the deity of Christ. Many bore the scars of years of persecution that had only recently ended (A.D. 313). They had been willing to lay down their lives for the gospel of Christ, and now they were called upon to deal with a division in the church brought on by the teachings of a man named Arius.

A presbyter in a suburb of Alexandria, Egypt, Arius is said by historians to have been a good communicator—a slick speaker who could convince by his speech and personality. About seven years prior to Nicaea, Arius began to publicly disagree with his bishop, Alexander, because Alexander was teaching that the Son of God had eternally existed. Instead, Arius insisted, "There was a time when the Son was not." Christ, to Arius, was a highly exalted, yet created, being. Alexander attempted to deal with the issue locally, and Arius was condemned by a local synod in 321. But he simply moved elsewhere and continued to teach and preach.

Arianism, as it came to be known, disturbed the newly found

peace of the Christian church. Rather than persecution from outside, now strife from within occupied the energies of believers. The Roman Emperor Constantine learned of the battle. Seeking a unified empire, and fearing the results a split of the Christian church could bring, Constantine moved to encourage reconciliation and resolution. Failing this, he called a council[11] to meet at Nicaea in the summer of 325.

WHO BELIEVED WHAT

Hindsight is always 20/20, as they say, and it allows us to conveniently divide up the participants in the council in a way that might well make it look a little more simple than it was. Basically, there were three groups: the "different substance" party (Arius and his followers), the "same substance" party (Alexander, Hosius), and the "similar substance" party (Eusebius). The debate centered around whether Jesus is of the *same* substance as the Father (fully divine), a *different* substance (a created being, a creature), or a *similar substance*. The last option might sound like those holding to it were trying to introduce a second God, but that would be a misunderstanding. Instead, the "of a similar substance" group should be seen as a subset of the "same substance" group. The reason they hesitated to speak of Christ being "of the same substance as the Father" was that they feared this could be understood to teach an even older heresy that they detested as much as Arianism: modalism, the idea that Jesus is the Father. That is, modalists said the Father, Son, and Spirit were just three *modes of being*, and they denied that there were three coequal and coeternal *persons*. Many in the East had fought long and hard against modalism, so they were hesitant to affirm anything in the council that could be used by the very people they had been struggling against for generations. It took time to convince the "similar substance" group that their position could not be used to expose the errors of Arius and his followers, and that they were not, by accepting the statement that the Son is of the same substance as the Father, endorsing or supporting modalism.

Group/Leader(s)	Viewpoint
Arian/Arius	of a different substance— *heteroousios*
Orthodox/Alexander, Hosius, Athanasius	of the same substance— *homoousios*
Eusebian/Eusebius of Caesarea	of a similar substance— *homoiousios*

THE TERM "HOMOOUSION"

The key phrase that came out of the Council of Nicaea describes the relationship of the Son to the Father: "of one substance (*homoousion*) with the Father." This was the phrase that the Arians could not abide. By means of this assertion, the Council excluded them from the very fellowship of the church itself. The fact that it was precise in its meaning, specific and unambiguous, made it especially useful in clearly differentiating between the orthodox party and the Arians. The term had been used in other contexts before,[12] but this was the first time it was used to specifically assert the full, complete deity of Jesus Christ.

Many wonder about how appropriate it is to use a term that is not found in the Bible in the way the Council of Nicaea used it. Of course, the anti-Arian bishops would like to have used simple biblical terminology, but the duplicity of the Arians would not allow for such a conclusion to the matter. By redefining terms outside of their biblical context, the Arians were able to agree to pretty much any formulation placed on terms like "Son of God" or "Creator" or "God" or "Lord." But directly asserting that the Son and the Father share the same divine *being* forced the Arian's hand: they could not find a way of agreeing with such a statement. Surely the Bible taught the underlying truth— so the Council was maintaining the *essence* of biblical truth by using a more specific term. The other option involved the slavish use of biblical terminology *at the cost of the essence of biblical truth*. What good is it, though, to maintain the *language* of Scripture at the cost of the *meaning* of Scripture?[13] So concluded the Nicene Fathers, and hence they used the term *homoousion*. They did not feel they were going beyond Scripture's teaching to do so. Years later, Athanasius defended their actions in speaking against the Arians:

> Vainly they run about alleging that they have demanded councils for the sake of the faith. For indeed divine Scripture is sufficient above all things; but if a Council is needed concerning this, there are the acts of the Fathers. For the bishops who were at Nicaea did not neglect this issue, but also wrote so clearly, that the ones who legitimately consider their record are forced by them to remember the religion of Christ proclaimed in the divine Scriptures.[14]

IT DIDN'T END THERE

While some might believe that the pronouncement of a Council would simply end the matter for all concerned, such would be a gross oversimplification. The Nicene definition had to fight for its life not on the basis that it was an "infallible church council" and therefore had some special authority in and of itself, but on the only meaningful and solid foundation: its faithfulness to the Scriptures.

That's not to say that the opponents of the deity of Christ fought on the same grounds. In fact, the "Arian Resurgency" that took place in the decades after Nicaea was due mainly to political factors and the maneuvering of particular leaders who were opposed to the Nicene definition. Arian bishops courted the favor first of Constantine, and upon his death, his son Constantius. During the reign of Constantius numerous councils met, producing Arian and semi-Arian creeds. Great champions of the Nicene faith were forced from their positions. Athanasius was forced to flee his church in Athanasius five different times. During the middle of the fourth century things were so bad that, looking only on outward things, it appeared that Nicaea had been defeated. Later Jerome would say of that time period, "The whole world groaned and was astonished to find itself Arian."[15]

But political power cannot overthrow scriptural truth. Once the Arians consolidated their power, they turned upon each other. Their arguments were no more convincing then than they are today, and the simple believer, reading his or her Bible, could not help but see the truth of the full deity of Jesus Christ. The tide was turned, not by political power, but by the irresistible force of truth, and by the end of the century, Arianism was banished, at least from the mainstream of the church. It continues to exist today, in various forms, using the same arguments that were used many centuries ago.

Do Christians today believe in the Trinity and the deity of Christ just because the Council of Nicaea said so? Some might. I do not. I believe in the Trinity and the deity of Christ because it is the teaching of the Scriptures, as we have seen throughout this work. I accept the use of the term *homoousion* because it accurately reflects the teaching that there is one God, and that both the Father and the Son are described as being fully God, fully deity. Nicaea's authority, then, if we wish to use that term, is derived from its faithfulness to the scriptural testimony. It has validity today because what was true about Christ in A.D. 325 is true today, too. He is the same yesterday, today, and forever (Hebrews 13:8).

THE ATHANASIAN CREED

The so-called "Athanasian Creed" was not, historically, the work of Athanasius himself. But since it bore such a resemblance to his teaching, his name was attached to it. It is an expansion of the Nicene Creed penned probably in the fifth century or so. A careful reading of the text is most useful in recognizing the elements of the doctrine that must be kept in balance with one another.

We worship one God in Trinity, and Trinity in Unity, neither confounding the Persons nor dividing the Substance. For there is one Person of the Father, another of the Son, and another of the Holy Spirit. But the Godhead of the Father, of the Son, and of the Holy Spirit, is all one: the Glory equal, the Majesty coeternal. Such as the Father is, such is the Son, and such is the Holy Spirit. The Father uncreated, the Son uncreated, the Holy Spirit uncreated. The Father infinite, the Son infinite, and the Holy Spirit infinite. The Father eternal, the Son eternal, the Holy Spirit eternal. And yet they are not three eternals, but one eternal. As also there are not three uncreated, nor three infinites, but one uncreated, and one infinite. So likewise the Father is Almighty, the Son Almighty, and the Holy Spirit Almighty. And yet they are not three Almighties, but one Almighty. So the Father is God, the Son is God, and the Holy Spirit is God. And yet there are not three Gods, but one God. So likewise the Father is Lord, the Son Lord, the Holy Spirit Lord. And yet not three Lords, but one Lord. For as we are compelled by Christian truth to acknowledge every Person by himself to be God and Lord, so are we forbidden by the Catholic religion to say "There are three Gods, or three Lords." The Father is made of none, neither created, nor begotten. The Son is of the Father alone, not made, nor created, but begotten. The Holy Spirit is of the Father and of the Son, neither made, nor created, nor begotten, but proceeding. So there is one Father, not three Fathers; one Son, not three Sons; one Holy Spirit, not three Holy Spirits. And in this Trinity none is before, or after, another. None is greater, or less, than another. But the whole three Persons are coeternal, and coequal. So that in all things, as was said before, the Unity in Trinity, and the Trinity in Unity, is to be worshipped. Here therefore that will be saved must thus think of the Trinity.

CHAPTER 14

Does It Really Matter? Christian Devotion and the Trinity

The windshield wipers beat a regular rhythm as we drove along the Long Island Expressway. My friends Chris and Mike were driving me out to a motel way out in Patchogue, Long Island, where I would be speaking for the next few days. I had been on Long Island for almost a week, and I had another week left to go. Every little while I said the same thing. "You know, I really miss my wife." They would smile and nod. And a little while later, "Have I mentioned how much I really miss my wife?" They understood. All during my time away I was pulling out my wallet and showing off pictures of my wife to anyone who showed the slightest interest. I wanted everyone to know about my wife, how pretty she is, and how proud I am of her.

Everyone can understand my feelings. We have all had relationships where we so loved someone that we wanted everyone to know. And we wanted to tell others about that person, their accomplishments, their skills—all those things that make us proud of that person.

That's why I've written this book. I love telling folks about my God. I tell everyone who will listen the truth about Him. And the truth about God is that He is triune. He exists as Father, Son, and Holy Spirit.

I would not be happy if someone came along while I was showing off the pictures of my wife and said, "Oh, that's not your wife." Nor would I like it if someone said, "Oh, that's not your *only* wife!"

In the same way, I am tremendously bothered when someone comes along and says, "Jesus is not God." Or "There are other gods out there, too, you know." You see, such statements are untrue, and they dishonor the God who made me—and them. We are all naturally jealous that the *truth* about those we love be known. We are hurt when they are lied about, or misrepresented, or mistreated.

The same has to be true of our feelings about God. We *should,* if we truly love Him and His truth, be impacted by the denial of the truths He has revealed about himself. Impacted? How about upset? Even righteously angered? If we feel that way about loved ones who are our fellow creatures, how much more pure, holy, and intense should be our zealousness in defending the truth about the God we profess to worship and adore?

THE TRINITY AND WORSHIP

Does it matter? Jesus said that the Father is seeking worshipers who will worship in spirit *and in truth.* God is not honored by the worship of false gods. And we are hardly benefited by worshiping something or someone that does not exist.

True Christian worship is founded upon Christian truth. We have to have knowledge of our God to worship Him correctly. If we have defective knowledge, or worse, if we have *wrong* information and have been deceived, our worship is either lessened (due to simple ignorance), or it is completely invalid, as the worship of idols and false gods. That is not to say that we have to have perfect knowledge to worship God—none of us do. But our desire must be to grow in the grace *and knowledge* of God, and we must always remember that Jesus taught that eternal life was the possession of those who *know* the one true God. Knowledge does not save (that is the error of Gnosticism); but true worship does not exist without knowledge.

Almost every single imbalance in worship is due to a corresponding imbalance in our view of God. Some people become so enamored with the Spirit, for example, and their experience of Him that the Father and the Son are lost in the haze of emotions. Others are so focused upon the Father that they lose sight of the love of the Son and the joy and empowerment of the Spirit. One thing the doctrine of the Trinity does is always call us back to the balanced center point. We are never allowed to elevate one person to the expense of the others, since the fullness of deity dwells in each one completely.

Christian worship will be vital, consistent, and powerful when the proper attitude toward the triune God is maintained. When that truth is lost, Christian worship ends.

THE TRINITY AND THE GOSPEL

The Gospel is the means by which the Father, in eternal love and mercy, saves men through the redeeming work of the Son, Jesus Christ, and draws them to himself by the power and regenerating work of the Spirit. The Gospel, as it is proclaimed in Scripture, is Trinitarian. Remove the Father and you have no Gospel. Remove the Son, and the Gospel ceases to exist. Remove the Spirit, and the Gospel has no existence. There is no separating the work of the triune God in salvation from the truth of the Trinity itself.

Look at the "gospel" message of every single group that denies the doctrine of the Trinity. You will find error and perversion in every group. Why? Because the true Gospel must be based upon the work of the one true and triune God. Without that basis, the Gospel cannot stand. Look at Mormonism, which denies the pillar of monotheism: the Gospel becomes the means to becoming a god. Look at the Witnesses: the Gospel is a mere appendage, a message of how we can live forever in a paradise earth. Such is what happens when the Redeemer becomes Michael the Archangel, and the Spirit becomes an impersonal active force. And in the Oneness groups the Gospel becomes legalism, replete with "necessary" things one must "experience" to be *truly* saved.

Just as the Trinity requires us to be balanced and thorough in our reliance upon the Scriptures, so the Gospel demands the same care. The two go hand in hand, and it seems that those who lack clarity on the one inevitably end up in error on the other.

THE TRINITY AND YOU

So does it really matter? Only you can answer that question for yourself. If you are a believer, it matters greatly. You know the longing in your heart to honor and glorify God, and you know instinctively that God is not honored by falsehood. You long for His Word so that you can grow in His grace and truth. And you want everyone else to know the truth about your God who has redeemed you.

I love the Trinity. I honor the Father, the Son, and the Spirit. I have been baptized in that one divine Name, and I gladly call myself a servant of the triune God. Do you love the Trinity? I hope and pray that our journey through the Scriptures has solidified your faith in this divine truth and given you great boldness and courage to share that faith with others. But most of all, I hope and pray it has helped you to fulfill the greatest commandment of all: to love the Lord your God with all your heart, soul, mind, and strength. Truly I hope that you can join with me in singing,

> Praise God from Whom all blessings flow!
> Praise Him all creatures here below!
> Praise Him above ye heavenly host!
> Praise Father, Son, and Holy Ghost!
> Amen!

Notes

CHAPTER ONE

1. The great minister of Northampton (1703–1758), considered one of the greatest theologians America has ever produced.
2. Ian Murray, *Jonathan Edwards: A New Biography* (Edinburgh: The Banner of Truth Trust, 1987), 99–100.
3. William G. T. Shedd, "Introductory Essay" in Philip Schaff, ed., *The Nicene and Post-Nicene Fathers*, Series I (Grand Rapids: Eerdmans, 1956), 10–11.
4. Romans 8:7–8; 5:10.
5. John 3:3–6.
6. 2 Corinthians 5:1.

CHAPTER TWO

1. The great bishop of Alexandria, Athanasius (early to mid-fourth century) defended the deity of Christ against the Arian movement.

CHAPTER THREE

1. Throughout this work the *New American Standard Bible* is cited (1995 edition). The *NASB* follows the standard English custom of rendering the divine name of God in the Old Testament as LORD, using small capitals. This is meant to indicate to the English reader that the Hebrew term is יְהוָה, YHWH, or Yahweh (oftentimes badly mispronounced as Jehovah).
2. See the discussion in chapter 6 on the significance of this passage to the deity of Christ.
3. Jeremiah 10:11 is the only verse in Jeremiah's prophecy that is written in Aramaic

rather than Hebrew. As a result, many feel it is a gloss or interpolation. However, a much more logical reason exists. Charles Feinberg notes, "It should, however, be remembered that Aramaic was the lingua franca of the day; so the pagan idolators would be able to read the judgment of God on their idolatry." And in a textual note, he also says,

> No one has ever explained why an interpolator would introduce it here. It was a proverbial saying; so it was given in the language of the people (so Streane). The best explanation appears to be that it is in Aramaic so that the exiles could use these very words as a reply to solicitations by the Chaldeans to join in their idol worship.

Charles L. Feinberg, "Jeremiah" in *The Expositor's Bible Commentary*, 6:449–450.

4. The *KJV* translation, "God is a spirit," misses the point of the anarthrous use of "spirit" here. "God is spirit"=πνεῦμα ὁ θεός, where the position of the predicative nominative tells us something *about* God, that is, it is descriptive.

5. Hebrew: וּמֵעוֹלָם עַד־עוֹלָם, *me olam ad olam*. There is no stronger way to express ongoing, limitless existence than this. The psalmist is contrasting the created nature of the world with the uncreated and hence *eternal* nature of the Creator, Yahweh.

CHAPTER FOUR

1. The *imperfect* tense of the verb εἰμί (*eimi*) refers to continuous action in the past. One might compare it to saying, "I was eating," in contrast to "I ate" or "I had eaten." Specifically, and most importantly in this context, the verb does not point to a specific point of origin or beginning in the past.

2. ἐγένετο is in the aorist tense. The main emphasis of an aorist verb is *undefined aspect*, normally resulting in *punctiliar action* in the past. Such a verb points to a particular point of origin when used in the context of creation.

3. Some have argued against this use of ἦν by noting that the same verb is used of Mary's presence at the wedding in Cana of Galilee in John 2:1, "and the mother of Jesus was (*en*) there." Obviously John is not saying that Mary had *eternally* been in Cana. Such an argument, however, assumes that *every* use of ἦν indicates eternal existence in the past, and such is not the case. In John 2:1, a specific limitation is provided in the context (that speaks of "on the third day") and, of course, eternity itself is not even in view in the passage, unlike the prologue where that is, in fact, the specific "time" frame provided by the author himself.

4. To quote J. H. Bernard, the use of ἦν in John 1:1 "is expressive in each case of continuous timeless existence." *A Critical and Exegetical Commentary on the Gospel According to St. John*, International Critical Commentary (Edinburgh: T. & T. Clark, 1928), 1:2. Greg Stafford in *Jehovah's Witnesses Defended* (Huntington Beach, Calif.: Elihu Books, 1998), 168, attempts to avoid the weight of the distinction found in John's words:

> The contrast between ἦν in verses 1 and 2 . . . and ἐγένετο (*egeneto*, "came to be," in reference to the "things" created in this part of the "beginning") is simply a contrast between that which was existing (the Word) during the time period to which John refers, and that which came into existence, namely, the

physical universe. It is not necessarily a contrast between an *eternal* being and created things.

Stafford posits a complex concept of "the beginning," attempting to limit the Word's preexistence to a particular *part* of the "beginning." The inevitable result, however, is to say that the Word was *not* ἦν the "beginning" absolutely considered, but was only relatively preexistent to a relative beginning, which is just the opposite of what John is communicating. Stafford assumes, and imports into his exegesis, the "creation of the Logos" as an immutable fact, despite John's testimony against such an idea.

5. B. B. Warfield in *The Person and Work of Christ*, (Philadelphia: The Presbyterian and Reformed Publishing Company, 1950), 53, commented:

> "And the Word was with God." The language is pregnant. It is not merely coexistence with God that is asserted, as of two beings standing side by side, united in local relation, or even in a common conception. What is suggested is an active relation of intercourse. The distinct personality of the Word is therefore not obscurely intimated. From all eternity the Word has been with God as a fellow: He who in the very beginning already "was," "was" also in communion with God. Though He was thus in some sense a second along with God, He was nevertheless not a separate being from God: "And the Word was"—still the eternal "was"—"God." In some sense distinguishable from God, He was in an equally true sense identical with God. There is but one eternal God; this eternal God, the Word is; in whatever sense we may distinguish Him from the God whom He is "with," He is yet not another than this God, but Himself is this God. The predicate "God" occupies the position of emphasis in this great declaration, and is so placed in the sentence as to be thrown up in sharp contrast with the phrase "with God," as if to prevent inadequate inferences as to the nature of the Word being drawn even momentarily from that phrase. John would have us realize that what the Word was in eternity was not merely God's coeternal fellow, but the eternal God's self.

6. θεόν is the accusative singular form of θεός. Often people are confused by the fact that Greek nouns change form, depending upon their grammatical usage in a sentence. Greek is an inflected language, and its nouns are *declined,* meaning they take a different form when they are subject, object, indirect object, plural, etc. These changes in forms do not impact the actual meaning of the noun itself, only how it is being used in a particular sentence.

7. That is, believing in one God. Monotheism is the belief in one true God.

8. Daniel Wallace, *Greek Grammar Beyond the Basics: An Exegetical Syntax of the New Testament* (Grand Rapids: Zondervan, 1996), 207.

9. Ibid., 208.

10. Specifically, for the grammatically inclined, a preverbal, anarthrous predicate nominative, for θεὸς does not have the article, and appears before the verb, ἦν.

11. The great American Greek scholar A.T. Robertson in his work *Word Pictures in the New Testament* (Grand Rapids: Baker Book House, 1932), vol. 5, 4–5, commented:

> And the Word was God (*kai theos en ho logos*). By exact and careful language John denied Sabellianism by not saying *ho theos en ho logos*. That would mean

that all of God was expressed in *ho logos* and the terms would be interchangeable, each having the article. The subject is made plain by the article (*ho logos*) and the predicate without it (*theos*) just as in John 4:24 *pneuma ho theos* can only mean "God is spirit," not "spirit is God." So in 1 John 4:16 *ho theos agape estin* can only mean "God is love," not "love is God" as a so-called Christian scientist would confusedly say. For the article with the predicate see Robertson, Grammar, pp. 767f. So in John 1:14 *ho Logos sarx egeneto,* "the Word became flesh," not "the flesh became Word." Luther argues that here John disposes of Arianism also because the Logos was eternally God, fellowship of the Father and Son, what Origen called the Eternal Generation of the Son (each necessary to the other). Thus in the Trinity we see personal fellowship on an equality.

See also H. E. Dana, Julius Mantey, *A Manual Grammar of the Greek New Testament* (New York: The MacMillan Company, 1950), 148–149.

12. M. R. Vincent, *Word Studies in the New Testament* (Wilmington, Del.: Associated Publishers and Authors, n.d.), 1:384.

13. F. F. Bruce, *The Gospel of John* (Grand Rapids: Eerdmans, 1983), 31. Note also the words of the *Expositor's Greek New Testament*:

> The Word is distinguishable from God and yet θεὸς ἦν ὁ λόγος, the Word was God, of Divine nature; not "a God," which to a Jewish ear would have been abominable; nor yet identical with all that can be called God, for then the article would have been inserted. . . .

W. Robertson Nicoll, ed., *The Expositor's Greek Testament* (Grand Rapids: Eerdmans, 1983), 1:684.

14. The reader is directed to the presentation of Daniel Wallace, *Greek Grammar Beyond the Basics,* 256–270, and Murray Harris, *Jesus as God* (Grand Rapids: Baker Book House, 1992), 57–70, for excellent summaries of the scholarly material.

15. Some might include under this category the idea of "a godlike one." However, if John had wished to do this, he could have used the adjectival θειος in that case.

16. For those who are more refined in their presentation of this argument, and who wish to see only *pre-verbal* anarthrous predicates translated consistently in an indefinite form (a god): the context likewise militates against such a translation, for such an idea would be utterly foreign to John. Those who push this argument need to remember that the *meaning of the word being translated* must figure into the argument as well. What is more, the literature of those who attempt to defend the translation "a god" often confuses, and blends together, the case for a *qualitative* rendering ("the Word was as to His nature God") and also for an *indefinite* rendering. It should be noted that all arguments for a *qualitative* rendering are, in fact, arguments *against* the rendering "a god," which no more speaks to the *qualities* than does the bare rendering "God."

17. F. F. Bruce, *The Books and the Parchments* (Old Tappan, New Jersey: Fleming H. Revell Company, 1963), 60–61.

18. F. F. Bruce, *The Gospel of John,* 31.

19. Kenneth Wuest, *The New Testament: An Expanded Translation* (Grand Rapids: Eerdmans, 1956).

20. Daniel Wallace, *Greek Grammar Beyond the Basics,* 269.

21. It should be noted that when I use the term "divine," I am in no way indicating an *inferior* status. That is, "divine" should be taken as a synonym for "deity."

22. We do not enter here into the issue of how to punctuate this particular passage. Some texts (including the UBS 4th edition Greek New Testament) put a full break after "nothing was made." This results in the assertion that "what was made in Him was life." There is not much of a meaningful difference between the two renderings, but I prefer the phrasing used in most translations.

23. From the Greek term δοκεῖν meaning "to seem." They taught that Jesus only *seemed* to have a physical body.

24. I have addressed this passage in my book *The King James Only Controversy* (Minneapolis: Bethany House Publishers, 1995), 198–200, 258–260.

25. Harris, *Jesus as God*, 88–92, provides a full discussion.

26. The Greek term John uses to describe this revelation of the Father by the Son is simply beautiful: ἐξηγήσατο, a verb that means to "lead out, explain, make known, reveal." It is closely related to the noun from which we get our word *exegete*, to make known or reveal the meaning of a passage of Scripture. Jesus "exegetes" the Father, making Him known, explaining Him to His people, and He does so with such perfection that Jesus can say, "He who has seen Me has seen the Father" (John 14:9). Jan G. van der Watt noted in the *Westminster Theological Journal*, 57:2 (Fall 1995),

> The use of λόγος (v. 1 [John 1:1]) as well as ἐξηγήσατο (v. 18 [John 1:18]) emphasizes Jesus' position as Revealer. Theobald (*Im Anfang*, 31–32) has pointed out that both sections (vv. 1–2 [John 1] and 18 [John 1:18]) refer to Jesus as God, as the one with the Father or at his side, and as the Revealer (λόγος and ἐξηγήσατο).

27. Harris notes,

> It was not simply the only Son (ὁ μονογενὴς υἱός) who knew and revealed the Father. It was an only Son (μονογενής) who himself possessed deity (θεός) and therefore both knew the Father and was qualified to make him known (Harris, *Jesus as God*, 82).

Extended note on the meaning of μονογενής:

Traditional translations often have a great impact upon theology. This is certainly the case in regard to μονογενής. So imbedded in our thought is the phrase "only-begotten" as the translation of this word that it is difficult to discuss the term in its original context so as to arrive at the meaning it carried for those who used it, especially when we ask what it meant to the apostle John.

In English, "only-begotten" emphasizes the final element of the translation, the concept of begettal and generation. But the English meaning must, in all cases, be consonant with the Greek original, and we must take any emphasis from the *Greek*, not from the English.

The key element to remember in deriving the meaning of μονογενής is this: it is a compound term, combining μόνος, meaning "only," with a second term.

Often it is assumed that the second term is γεννᾶσθαι/γεννάω, "to give birth, to beget." But note that this family of terms has two nu's, "νν," rather than the single ν found in μονογενής. This indicates that the second term is not γεννᾶσθαι but γίγνεσθαι/γίνομαι, and the noun form, γένος. G. L. Prestige discusses the differences that arise from these two derivations in *God in Patristic Thought* (London: SPCK, 1952), 37–51, 135–141, 151–156.

γένος means "kind or type," and γίνομαι is a verb of being. Hence the translations "one of a kind," "one and only," "of sole descent." Some scholars see the -γενής element as having a minor impact upon the meaning of the term, and hence see μονογενής as a strengthened form of μόνος, thereby translating it "alone," "unique," "incomparable." An example of this usage from the LXX is found in Psalm 25:16, "Turn to me and be gracious to me, For I am lonely (μονογενής) and afflicted" (NASB).

There are numerous scholarly sources that substantiate the proper meaning of μονογενής. The lexicon of Johannes Louw and Eugene Nida, *Greek-English Lexicon of the New Testament Based On Semantic Domains* (New York: United Bible Societies, 1988), 591, says:

> μονογενής, -ές: pertaining to what is unique in the sense of being the only one of the same kind or class—"unique, only." τὸν υἱὸν τὸν μονογενῆ ἔδωκεν "he gave his only Son" Jn 3.16; τὸν υἱὸν αὐτοῦ τὸν μονογενῆ ἀπέσταλκεν ὁ θεὸς "God sent his only Son" 1 Jn 4.9; τὸν μονογενῆ προσέφερεν, ὁ τὰς ἐπαγγελίας ἀναδεξάμενος, "he who had received the promises presented his only son" or ". . . was read to offer his only son" He 11.17. Abraham, of course, did have another son, Ishamael, and later sons by Keturah, but Isaac was a unique son in that he was a son born as the result of certain promises made by God. Accordingly, he could be called a monogenes son, since he was the only one of his kind.

Newman and Nida, in *A Translator's Handbook on the Gospel of John* (New York: United Bible Societies, 1980, 24) notes:

> *Only Son* is the rendering of all modern translations. There is no doubt regarding the meaning of the Greek word used here (*monogenes*); it means "only" and not "only begotten." The meaning "only begotten," which appears in the Vulgate, has influenced KJV and many other early translations.

The major work of James Hope Moulton and George Milligan, *The Vocabulary of the Greek Testament* (Grand Rapids: Eerdman's, 1930, 416–417), likewise gives this indication:

> μονογενής is literally "one of a kind," "only," "unique" (*unicus*), not "only-begotten," which would be μονογέννητος (*unigenitus*), and is common in the LXX in this sense. . . . The emphasis is on the thought that, as the "only" Son of God, He has no equal and is able fully to reveal the Father.

This is cited with approval by Tenney, *The Expositor's Bible Commentary* (Grand Rapids: Zondervan, 1981, 33) with the additional comment, "God's personal revelation of himself in Christ has no parallel elsewhere, nor has it ever been repeated." George Beasley-Murray, likewise, said in the *Word Biblical Commentary on John* (Waco: Word Books, 1987, p. 14),

> μονογενής, lit., "the only one of its kind," unique in its γένος, in the LXX frequently translates יָחִיד (*yahid*) . . .

Likewise we read in Leon Morris's work, *The New International Commentary on the New Testament* (Grand Rapids: Eerdmans, 1971, 105),

> We should not read too much into "only begotten." To English ears this sounds like a metaphysical relationship, but the Greek term means no more than "only," "unique." [The footnote at this point reads as follows: It should not be overlooked that μονογενής is derived from γίνομαι not γεννάω . . . Etymologically it is not connected with begetting.]

So wide is the witness to this meaning that the standard lexical source, that of *A Greek-English Lexicon of the New Testament and Other Early Christian Literature* edited by Bauer, Arndt, Gingrich and Danker, 2nd ed. (Chicago: University of Chicago Press, 1979), includes in its definition of the term:

> μονογενής, -ές, only . . . of children: Isaac, Abraham's only son . . . Of an only son . . . —Also "unique" (in kind), of something that is the only example of its category . . .—In Johannine lit., μ is used only of Jesus. The mngs. *only, unique*, may be quite adequate for all its occurrences here (so M-M, RSV, et al.; DMoody JBL 72, '53, 213–19; FCGrant, ATR 36, '54, 284–87).

Finally, Murray Harris, in *Jesus as God*, 87, said,

> This leads us to conclude that μονογενής denotes "the only member of a kin or kind." Applied to Jesus as the Son of God, it will mean that he is without spiritual siblings and without equals. He is "sole-born" and "peer-less." No one else can lay claim to the title Son of God in the sense in which it applies to Christ.

CHAPTER FIVE

1. Nature, then, and function are two different things. Human beings share the same type of nature, but we have many different functions. This is the difference between making an *ontological* statement about what something or someone *is* and making an *economical* statement about what something or someone *does*.

2. Such a phrase is, I realize, a misnomer. Eternity is timeless existence, hence, to speak of eternity past is only to speak of the timeless existence of God that, from our perspective in time, "preceded" us.

3. I note in passing that some Christian theologians have identified Michael as the preincarnate Son. However, they are not in the same class as the Witnesses, for they likewise confirm the deity of Christ. Hence, for those Christians who identify Jesus as Michael, they are, in effect, saying that Michael is a *theophany*, an appearance of God in some physical form, while the Witnesses are instead denying the deity of Christ and making Him a mere creature.

4. Some have gone to great lengths in the vain attempt to get around this plain truth. Some have said that here Thomas is directing his words not to Jesus but to God, in a sudden outburst of praise. Yet, the text clearly shows that these words were

spoken to Jesus, not to anyone else. See the discussion in Murray Harris, *Jesus as God* (Grand Rapids: Baker Book House, 1992), 105–129.

5. Attempts by Stafford in *Jehovah's Witnesses Defended* (Huntington Beach, Calif.: Elihu Books, 1998), 202–206 (Stafford mainly follows David D. Schuman's unpublished work, *Did the Apostle Thomas Call Jesus "God" at John 20:28?*), to obscure such a plain passage are circular at best. Stafford and others point to the fact that Thomas uses the nominative forms κύριός and θεός rather than the vocative forms (the vocative case being the case of direct address). However, as A. T. Robertson pointed out, this is hardly relevant. In his *A Grammar of the Greek New Testament in the Light of Historical Research* (Nashville: Broadman Press, 1934), 465–466, Robertson points out uses of the nominative in the place of the vocative (such as Revelation 4:11, Αξιος εἶ, ὁ κύριος καὶ ὁ θεὸς ἡμῶν, "Worthy are You, O Lord our God—", where both "Lord" and "God" are identical in form to John 20:28, and yet no one would argue that God himself is not being directly addressed), and says of our passage:

> In Jo. 20:28 Thomas addresses Jesus as ὁ κύριός μου καὶ ὁ θεός μου, the vocative like those above. Yet, strange to say, Winer calls this exclamation rather than address, apparently to avoid the conclusion that Thomas was satisfied as to the deity of Jesus by his appearance to him after the resurrection. Dr. E. A. Abbott follows suit also in an extended argument to show that κύριε ὁ θεός is the LXX way of addressing God, not ὁ κύριός καὶ ὁ θεός. But after he had written he appends a note to p. 95 to the effect that "this is not quite satisfactory." For xiii. 13, φωνεῖτέ με ὁ διδάσκαλος καὶ ὁ κύριος, and Rev. 4:11—ought to have been mentioned above." This is a manly retraction, and he adds: "John may have used it here exceptionally." Leave out "exceptionally" and the conclusion is just.

Therefore, we have examples of the use of the nominative used for the vocative in John (John 13:13 and Revelation 4:11). Therefore, there can only be one reason why the plain, obvious meaning of this passage is denied, and that reason comes out plainly in Stafford's comments. While admitting that Jesus can be called "Lord and God," he limits this to a mere representative position, focuses not upon the passage but upon John 20:17 (see comments in text), and concludes, "What is certain about John 20:28 is that Thomas' words are in no way an affirmation of anything agreeable to Trinitarianism, for Thomas had no concept of a consubstantial Trinity." This merely begs the question while ignoring the impact of the words of Thomas.

6. Another element of the argument is that if Jesus says the Father is the "God" of the disciples, then He himself could not likewise be their God, as Thomas would confess. Yet, this again *assumes* what it is meant to prove: unitarianism, the idea that *both* the Father and the Son could not, simultaneously, be "God" to the disciples.

7. Stafford, 205.

8. For discussions of this passage and the various translational issues involved, see C. E. B. Cranfield, *A Critical and Exegetical Commentary on the Epistle to the Romans* in *The International Critical Commentary* (Edinburgh: T&T Clark, 1979), II:464–

470; Henry Alford, *The New Testament for English Readers* (Grand Rapids: Baker Book House, 1983), II:920–921; Douglas Moo, *The Epistle to the Romans* in *The New International Commentary on the New Testament* (Grand Rapids: Eerdmans, 1996), 565–568.

9. Specifically, there is no reason to include ὁ ὢν in the final phrase if there is no direct connection to what has gone before.

10. Paul has spoken of the fleshly nature of the Messiah, and now speaks of the Messiah's spiritual nature as God. Breaking up the sentence leaves Paul speaking only of the Messiah "according to the flesh."

11. Romans 1:25; 11:36; 2 Corinthians 11:31; Galatians 1:5; 2 Timothy 4:18.

12. There is one possible exception at Psalm 67:19, though the text seems questionable at that point.

13. B. M. Metzger, "The Punctuation of Rom. 9:5" in *Christ and Spirit in the New Testament: In Honour of Charles Francis Digby Moule*, ed. B. Lindars and S. Smalley (Cambridge: Cambridge University, 1973), 107.

14. Metzger mentions Irenaeus, Tertullian, Hippolytus, Cyprian, Athanasius, Epiphanius, Basil, Gregory of Nyssa, John Chrysostom, Theodoret, Augustine, Jerome, and Cyril of Alexandria, among others, as reading the passage in support of the deity of Christ.

15. Specifically, in verses 2–3, 6–8, and 10–12.

16. Harris's treatment is quite adequate, *Jesus as God*, 205–227.

17. See chapter 7 on the meaning of this term.

18. Some, including Jehovah's Witnesses, attempt to downplay the use of the verb "worship" here, insisting that it doesn't *always* mean "worship" in the full sense. While that is quite true, it is also true that the context will determine the meaning of the word, and if there is any place where true and religious worship is in sight, it is here in the very heavenly realms itself. No mere "relative worship" or "obeisance" will meet the meaning of this term.

19. Indicating, of course, that the Son is not an angel.

20. A "marriage-ode" or an "epithalamium."

21. Harris, *Jesus as God*, 227.

22. Another way the context dictates the understanding of this passage is seen in the parallel between the vocative (i.e., direct address) use of "Lord" in verse 10 and that of "God" in verse 8. Both passages are spoken *to* the Son, and in verse 10 the speaker uses the vocative. Hence, the parallel would indicate that the vocative is being used in verse 8 as well.

23. As found in the LXX translation of the Psalm.

24. Granville Sharp (1735–1813) was an English abolitionist with a keen interest in theological subjects. His strong belief in the deity of Christ led him to study various grammatical forms in the New Testament relevant to the topic. For the most in-depth treatment of the subject, see Daniel Wallace, "The Article With Multiple Substantives Connected by Καί in the New Testament: Semantics and Significance" (Ph.D. dissertation, Dallas Theological Seminary, 1995). For those not inclined toward the reading of dissertations, Dr. Wallace's tremendous Greek gram-

mar, *Greek Grammar Beyond the Basics: An Exegetical Syntax of the New Testament* (Grand Rapids: Zondervan, 1996), 270–290, provides a most useful summary.

25. Granville Sharp's rule, according to Granville Sharp, is:

> When the copulative καί connects two nouns of the same case [viz. nouns (either substantive or adjective, or participles) of personal description, respecting office, dignity, affinity, or connexion, and attributes, properties, or qualities, good or ill, if the article ὁ, or any of its cases, precedes the first of the said nouns or participles, and is not repeated before the second noun or participle, the latter always relates to the same person that is expressed or described by the first noun or participle: i.e., it denotes a further description of the first named person.

Granville Sharp, *Remarks on the Uses of the Definitive Article in the Greek Text of the New Testament: Containing Many New Proofs of the Divinity of Christ, From Passages Which Are Wrongly Translated in the Common English Version* (Philadelphia: B. B. Hopkins and Co., 1807), 3.

26. Wallace comments in his *Greek Grammar* (p. 276) on Titus 2:13:

> It has frequently been alleged that θεός is a proper name and, hence, that Sharp's rule cannot apply to constructions in which it is employed. We have already argued that θεός is not a proper name in Greek. We simply wish to point out here that in the TSKS construction θεός is used over a dozen times in the NT (e.g., Luke 20:37; John 20:27; Rom 15:6; 2 Cor 1:3; Gal 1:4; Jas 1:27) and always (if we exclude the christologically significant texts) in reference to one person. This phenomenon is not true of any other proper name in said construction (every instance involving true proper names always points to two individuals). Since that argument carries no weight, there is no good reason to reject Titus 2:13 as an explicit affirmation of the deity of Christ.

27. Five, if you include 2 Peter 3:2, which differs in some respects from the other examples.

28. Wallace, *Greek Grammar*, 277.

29. There is the possibility that the Greek text used by the KJV translators added a word at 2 Peter 1:1, resulting in their less-than-clear translation, but no such reason exists at Titus 2:13.

30. Robertson, *The Minister and His Greek New Testament* (Grand Rapids: Baker Book House, 1977), 66. Further scholarly corroboration of this interpretation of these passages can be found in A. T. Robertson's *Word Pictures in the Greek New Testament* (Grand Rapids: Baker Book House, 1932), vol. 6, 147–148; in Nicoll's *Expositor's Greek Testament* (Grand Rapids: Eerdmans, 1983), vol. 5, 123; and in B. B. Warfield, *Biblical and Theological Studies* (Philadelphia: Presbyterian and Reformed, 1968) 68–71. Grundmann, in Kittel's *Theological Dictionary of the New Testament* (Grand Rapids: Eerdmans, 1968), vol. 4, 540, says, "Hence we have to take Jesus Christ as the *megas theos*. This is demanded by the position of the article, by the term *epiphaneia* . . . , and by the stereotyped nature of the expression. . . . Hence the best rendering is: 'We wait for the blessed hope and manifestation of the glory of our great God and Saviour Jesus Christ.' "

31. This passage is at times misused in the attempt to make Jesus the Father. See the discussion of this error in chapter 11. Suffice it to say that the phrase "Eternal

Father" cannot be read in New Testament terms, as the revelation of Father, Son, and Spirit had not yet been made. What is more, the Hebrew phrase so translated, אֲבִיעַד avi-ad, can be rendered "Father (or Creator) of eternity" as well. I believe this refers to Christ's role as Creator. Paul said that all things were not only made *through* Him but also *for* Him, so the description would be quite appropriate.

32. F. Delitzsch, *Isaiah* in *Commentary on the Old Testament in Ten Volumes* (Grand Rapids: Eerdmans, 1983), 252–253.

33. For a summary, see Harris, *Jesus as God*, 131–141.

34. For a discussion of textual variations and the process used to determine the original text of the New Testament, see James White, *The King James Only Controversy* (Minneapolis, Minn.: Bethany House Publishers, 1995), or J. Harold Greenlee, *Scribes, Scrolls, and Scripture* (Grand Rapids: Eerdmans, 1985).

35. κυριου is read by P74 A C* D E Ψ and others. θεου is read by א B and others. The Majority text conflates the two earlier readings into κυριου και θεου. In the ancient script of the New Testament, the difference between the two words would be minor: **KY** vs. **ΘY**. Most scholars feel that the phrase "His own blood" would have caused a scribe to alter "God" to "Lord" rather than the other way around.

36. Should someone object that Jesus is a highly exalted creature, not "merely" a creature, we respond by pointing out that no matter how highly exalted a creature might be, *it is still a creature, dependent and finite.* There is a vast, uncrossable chasm between the infinite and eternal and the finite and temporal.

37. Walter Bauer, *A Greek-English Lexicon of the New Testament and Other Early Christian Literature* 2nd ed., ed. Gingrich and Danker (Chicago: University of Chicago Press, 1979), 358.

38. Joseph Henry Thayer, *The New Thayer's Greek-English Lexicon of the New Testament* (Lafayette, Ind.: Book Publisher's Press, 1981), 288.

39. Hence the Jehovah's Witnesses' mistranslation of the passage in the *New World Translation* as "divine quality" completely misses the mark. Stafford, in *Jehovah's Witnesses Defended,* fails to deal with the meaning of the passage, but instead shifts the focus from Colossians 2:9 to Colossians 1:19, confusing the undefined "fullness" that dwells in the Son by the decree of the Father with the fullness *of deity* that is said to dwell in the Son in Colossians 2:9. It is again beyond defense to say that the fullness of "that which makes God God" dwells in Michael the Archangel, so it is understandable why this passage causes those who would defend Arianism much trouble. Likewise, Stafford then confuses the undefined "fullness" that dwells in believers (Colossians 2:10) with the fullness *of deity* found in verse 9. Obviously, however, Paul was not saying that the fullness of *deity* dwells in believers.

40. Richard Trench, *Synonyms in the New Testament* (Grand Rapids: Eerdmans, 1953), 7–8.

41. B. B. Warfield, "The Person of Christ" in *The Works of Benjamin B. Warfield*, (Grand Rapids: Baker Book House, 1981), II: 184.

42. Greek: ὁ πρῶτος καὶ ὁ ἔσχατος

43. Greek: ἡ ἀρχὴ καὶ τὸ τέλος. It is important to note that the term ἀρχή does not have to mean "first created thing," but can be a title of deity.

44. The Watchtower insists we must do this, but the reasons given are shallow at best. The only real reason they do so is theological: they refuse to accept the Word's testimony to the deity of Christ. It should be noted that men such as Stafford, in attempting to defend the Watchtower's position in denying that Jesus is the Alpha and Omega (the WT has flipped back and forth on this topic many times) are forced to do mental gymnastics to get around the clear teaching of Revelation on this subject, yet they will insist that "wisdom" in Proverbs 8 *must* be Jesus Christ. The basis of the connection between Christ and wisdom in Proverbs 8 rests upon a *fraction* of the biblical data that can be mustered for seeing Jesus as the Alpha and the Omega, the first and the last, the beginning and the end. The role played by an authoritarian group (in this case, the Watchtower Society) in the "exegesis" of those who deny the deity of Christ is clear. We are not here dealing with an exegesis of the text—the meaning of the text has already been determined by the ultimate authority of the religious group.

45. Stafford points to Isaiah 40:10, "Behold, the Lord GOD will come with might, with His arm ruling for Him. Behold, His reward is with Him and His recompense before Him." Yet the argument is not only circular, but actually proves the opposite of what the author intends. Isaiah 40 is often cited of the Lord Jesus, and the fact that it is the Lord who comes and His reward is with Him to render to every man (Revelation 22:12) only proves that Jesus is again being identified as Yahweh, just as He is in John 12 and Hebrews 1.

46. Specifically, the Jews use the phrase ἴσον, which is the masculine singular accusative form; Paul uses ἴσα, the neuter form. What is the difference? Lightfoot, in his commentary on Philippians (*St. Paul's Epistle to the Philippians* [Grand Rapids: Zondervan, 1978], 112), put it this way: "Between the two expressions . . . no other distinction can be drawn, except that the former refers to the *person*, the latter to the *attributes*." The biblical teaching is not that the Son is ἴσον the Father (leading to modalism) but He is ἴσα the Father (equal in attributes and deity, but a different divine Person).

47. Benjamin Breckenridge Warfield, *The Biblical Doctrine of the Trinity*. This article is found in three sources: *The International Standard Bible Encyclopedia*, 1939 edition, 3012–3022, in *Biblical and Theological Studies*, ed. Samuel G. Craig (Philadelphia: Presbyterian and Reformed, 1968), 22–59, and in *The Works of Benjamin B. Warfield*, II:133–172. References in this work are from the latter source, 158–159.

CHAPTER SIX

1. The specific phrase ego eimi occurs twenty-four times in the gospel of John. Thirteen of these times it is followed by a clear predicate (John 6:35; 6:41; 6:51; 8:12; 8:18; 10:7; 10:9; 10:11; 10:14; 11:25; 14:6; 15:1; 15:5). Some of these instances would be John 6:35, "I am the living bread" or John 10:11, "I am the good shepherd" (*ego eimi ho poimen ho kalos*). Three times the usage does not fall into a clear category—these would be 4:26, 6:20, and 9:9. In 4:26 Jesus says to the woman at the well, "I am, the one speaking to you" which is strangely reminiscent of the LXX

rendering of Isaiah 52:6. In 6:20 it seems to be a rather straightforward self-identification to the frightened disciples in the boat. And in 9:9 we find the man who had been healed of his blindness insisting that he was indeed the man of whom they spoke. This last instance is similar to the sayings as Jesus utters them, in that the phrase comes at the end of the clause and looks elsewhere for its predicate. Given the above, we are left with seven uses that have been described as "absolute." These would be John 8:24; 8:28; 8:58; 13:19; 18:5; 18:6; and 18:8. It is very significant that in each of these instances, the phrase comes at the end of the clause. We will note why it is important when we look at the usage of the phrase in the Septuagint.

2. A. T. Robertson, *A Grammar of the Greek New Testament in the Light of Historical Research* (Nashville: Broadman Press, 1934), 879–880, describes the "progressive present":

> This is a poor name in lieu of a better one for the present of past action still in progress. Usually an adverb of time (or adjunct) accompanies the verb.... Often it has to be translated into English by a sort of "progressive perfect" ('have been'), though, of course, that is the fault of English.... "The durative present in such cases gathers up past and present time into one phrase" (Moulton, Prol., 119).... It is a common idiom in the N.T.... In Jo. 8:58 εἰμί is really absolute.

3. *See* A. T. Robertson, *Word Pictures in the New Testament* (Grand Rapids: Baker Book House, 1932), 5:158–159.

4. Daniel Wallace in *Greek Grammar Beyond the Basics: An Exegetical Syntax of the New Testament* (Grand Rapids: Zondervan, 1996), 530–531, has commented on the translation of this passage:

> The text reads: πρὶν Ἀβραὰμ γενέσθαι ἐγὼ εἰμί ("before Abraham was, I am"). On this text, Dennis Light wrote an article in defense of the *New World Translation* in the *Bible Collector* (July–December, 1971). In his article he discusses ἐγὼ εἰμί, which the *New World Translation* renders, "I have been." Light defends this translation by saying, "The Greek verb *eimi*, literally present tense, must be viewed as a historical present, because of being preceded by the aorist infinitive clause referring to Abraham's past" (p. 8). This argument has several flaws in it: (1) The fact that the present tense follows an aorist *infinitive* has nothing to do with how it should be rendered. In fact, historical presents are usually wedged in between aorist (or imperfect) *indicatives*, not infinitives. (2) If this is a historical present, it is apparently the only historical present in the NT that uses the equative verb εἰμί. The burden of proof, therefore, lies with the one who sees εἰμί as *ever* being used as a historical present. (3) If this is a historical present, it is apparently the only historical present in the NT that is in other than the third person.
>
> The translators of the *New World Translation* understand the implications of ἐγὼ εἰμί here, for in the footnote to this text in the *NWT*, they reveal their motive for seeing this as a historical present: "It is not the same as ὁ ὤν (*ho ohn*, meaning 'The Being' or 'The I Am') at Exodus 3:14, *LXX*." In effect, this is a negative admission that if ἐγὼ εἰμί is *not* a historical present, then Jesus is here claiming to be the one who spoke to Moses at the burning bush, the I AM, the eternally existing One, Yahweh (cf. Exod 3:14 in the LXX, ἐγώ εἰμι ὁ ὤν).

5. See the preceding discussion of the prologue of John, chapter 4.

6. Irenaeus, *Against Heresies* in Philip Schaff, *The Nicene and Post-Nicene Fathers* (Grand Rapids: Eerdman's, 1983), 1:478.

7. Origen, *Against Celsus* in Alexander Roberts and James Donaldson, *The Ante-Nicene Fathers* (Grand Rapids: Eerdman's, 1981), 4:463.

8. *A Treatise of Novatian Concerning the Trinity* in Roberts and Donaldson, *The Ante-Nicene Fathers*, 5:624–625.

9. Chrysostom, *Homilies on St. John* in Schaff, *The Nicene and Post-Nicene Fathers*, 14:199.

10. Henry Alford, in his *New Testament for English Readers* (Grand Rapids: Wm. B. Eerdman's Publishing Company, 1983), 2:547, added,

> As Lucke remarks, all unbiassed (*sic*) explanation of these words must recognize in them a declaration of the essential pre-existence of Christ. All such interpretations as "before Abraham became Abraham" i.e., father of many nations (Socinus and others), and as 'I was predetermined, promised by God' (Grotius and the Socinian interpreters), are little better than dishonest quibbles. The distinction between was made (or was born) and am is important. The present, I am, expresses essential existence (see Col. 1:17) and was often used by our Lord to assert His divine Being. In this verse the Godhead of Christ is involved; and this the Jews clearly understood, by their conduct to Him.

11. Hebrew: אֲנִי־הוּא. This connection is either directly made or alluded to by Leon Morris, *The New International Commentary on the New Testament: The Gospel According to John* (Grand Rapids: Eerdman's, 1971), 447, 473; by Merrill C. Tenney, *The Expositor's Bible Commentary: John* (Grand Rapids: Zondervan, 1981), 99; and by F. F. Bruce, *The Gospel of John* (Grand Rapids: Eerdman's, 1983), 193, 288.

12. Morris, *The Gospel According to John*, 473.

13. In the LXX this is rendered thus: ἵνα γνῶτε καὶ πιστεύσητε καὶ συνῆτε ὅτι ἐγώ εἰμι (*hina gnote kai pisteusete kai sunete hoti ego eimi*).

14. In Greek the last phrase is ἵνα πιστεύσητε ὅταν γένηται ὅτι ἐγώ εἰμι (*hina pisteusete hotan genetai hoti ego eimi*).

15. M. James Penton, "The 'I Am' of John 8:58," in *The Christian Quest* (Winter): 1988, 64.

16. R. C. H. Lenski, *The Interpretation of John's Gospel* (Minneapolis: Augsburg Publishing House, 1943), 614–615.

17. Indeed, many of the denials of the rather clear usage of *ego eimi* in John 8:24; 8:58; 13:19; and 18:5–6 find their origin in preconceived theologies that are nearly unitarian, subordinationist, or so enamored with naturalistic rationalism as to be antisupernatural. A good example is given by C. K. Barrett: "It is not however correct to infer either for the present passage or for the others in which *ego eimi* occurs that John wishes to equate Jesus with the supreme God of the Old Testament. . . . Note that in v. 28 it is followed by 'I do nothing of myself, but as the Father taught me I speak these things . . . I always do the things that are pleasing to him', and in 13:19 by 'He who receives me receives him who sent me' (13:20). Jesus is the obedient servant of the Father, and for this reason perfectly reveals him. *ego eimi* does

not identify Jesus with God, but it does draw attention to him in the strongest possible terms." The assumption of the unipersonality of God as well as the ontological subordination of the Son that underlies Barrett's comments and clouds his normally clear exegesis is striking.

18. We will look more closely at the identification of Jesus as Yahweh in chapter 10.
19. *Tractate XLIII* in Schaff, *The Nicene and Post-Nicene Fathers*, series I, 7:244.
20. Leon Morris, *The Gospel According to John*, 473. A footnote on the same page reads:

> ἐγώ εἰμί in LXX renders the Hebrew אֲנִי־הוּא which is the way God speaks (cf. Deut. 32:39; Isa. 41:4; 43:10; 46:4, etc.). The Hebrew may carry a reference to the meaning of the divine name hwhy (cf. Exod. 3:14). We should almost certainly understand John's use of the term to reflect that in the LXX. It is the style of deity, and it points to the eternity of God according to the strictest understanding of the continuous nature of the present eimi. He continually IS. *Cf.* Abbott: "taken here, along with other declarations about what Jesus IS, it seems to call upon the Pharisees to believe that the Son of man is not only the Deliverer but also one with the Father in the unity of the Godhead" (2228).

21. B. B. Warfield, *The Person and Work of Christ* (Philadelphia: Presbyterian and Reformed, 1950), 60.
22. Ryle, *Expository Thoughts*, 573.
23. Martin Luther, "Sermons on the Gospel of John Chapters 6–8," in *Luther's Works*, Jerislav Pelikan, ed. (Saint Louis: Concordia Publishing House, 1959), 365.
24. A. T. Robertson, *Word Pictures in the Greek New Testament*, 5:158–159.
25. William Hendrickson, *New Testament Commentary: The Gospel of John* (Grand Rapids: Baker Book House, 1953), 67.
26. Greg Stafford, *Jehovah's Witnesses Defended* (Huntington Beach, Calif.: Elihu Books, 1998), 144, goes so far as to say that the falling back of the soldiers "need mean no more than that 'the men who came to make the arrest . . . were so overcome by His moral ascendancy that they recoiled in fear.'" Stafford goes on to speak of the soldiers being "taken aback by his fearless demeanor." Of course, men had been taken aback by the Lord's pure moral stature many times in His ministry—but had never fallen over as a result.

CHAPTER SEVEN

1. That the context of the passage is vital to its proper understanding seems a given; yet those who attempt to assert that the Son is a creature on the basis of Colossians 1:15 uniformly ignore the context of Paul's anti-gnostic polemic. For example, Greg Stafford in *Jehovah's Witnesses Defended* (Huntington Beach, Calif.: 1998), 91–101, completely ignores the issue of gnosticism and, in the process, ends up gutting Paul's apologetic, leaving it utterly irrelevant to the gnostic view.
2. Greek: γνῶσις. It should be noted that there is nothing "wrong" with knowledge. The NT uses the term in highly favorable ways. It is the misuse of knowledge, and the elevation of knowledge to a means of salvation, that is in error.
3. Greek: πλήρωμα. For discussions of Gnosticism, its development, and its relationship to Paul's epistle to the Colossians, see J. B. Lightfoot, *Saint Paul's Epistles to the Colossians and to Philemon* (Grand Rapids: Zondervan, 1978), 76–113, and

John Rutherfurd, "Gnosticism," in *The International Standard Bible Encyclopedia,* James Orr, ed. (Grand Rapids: Eerdmans, 1959), II:1240–1248.

4. Greek: δοκεῖν.

5. The *Textus Receptus* version of the Greek New Testament repeats the phrase "come in the flesh" in verse 3, and hence the KJV and NKJV, which are based upon the *TR*, likewise repeat the phrase. For a discussion of the passage, see my comments, *The King James Only Controversy* (Minneapolis: Bethany House, 1995), 184–185.

6. Greek: πρωτότοκος.

7. In the LXX the Greek term πρωτότοκος regularly translated the Hebrew term בכור. (*bekhor*). It is significant that *bekhor* is not related in its root meanings to either "first" or "to give birth." As Michaelis says concerning *prototokos* in the *Theological Dictionary of the New Testament* (Grand Rapids: Eerdmans, 1968), IV:873, ". . . it was quite possible that as an equivalent of בכור this might become increasingly remote and even detached altogether from the idea of birth or the whole question of origin." See also Tsevat, בכור, *Theological Dictionary of the Old Testament* (Grand Rapids: Eerdmans, 1968), II:123–127, and Oswalt, ובכר, *Theological Wordbook of the Old Testament* (Chicago: Moody Press, 1980), 108–110.

8. The term *prototokos* appears eight times in the New Testament: Luke 2:7; Romans 8:29; Colossians 1:15, 18; Hebrews 1:6; 11:28; 12:23; and Revelation 1:5.

9. "This expression . . . is also used in some instances where it is uncertain whether the force of the element —τοκος is still felt at all." Walter Bauer, *A Greek English Lexicon of the New Testament and Other Early Christian Literature,* 2nd ed. (Chicago: University of Chicago Press, 1979), 726.

10. Kenneth Wuest, "Ephesians and Colossians," *Wuest's Word Studies in the Greek New Testament* (Grand Rapids: Wm. B. Eerdmans Publishing Company, 1981), 183.

11. Lightfoot, *Saint Paul's Epistles to the Colossians and to Philemon,* 148.

12. Hence, *The Expositor's Greek Testament* says of the term *prototokos,* "in its primary sense expresses temporal priority, and then, on account of the privileges of the firstborn, it gains the further sense of dominion." W. Robertson Nicoll, ed., *The Expositor's Greek Testament* (Grand Rapids: Eerdmans, 1983), 502. Likewise, R. M. Clark says, "The original meaning of the word is giving birth for the first time. Later it came to mean the first-born or first in rank. This is the N. T. meaning. In the N. T. the "-tokos" element is clearly implied only in Luke 2:7, in other places it tends to recede into the background." R. M. Clark, "Words Relating to the Lord Jesus Christ," *Bible Translator,* 13 (April 1962) :84. The *Linguistic Key to the Greek New Testament* by Fritz Reinecker and Cleon Rogers distills down the scholastic information and says, "The word emphasizes the preexistence and uniqueness of Christ as well as His superiority over creation. The term does not indicate that Christ was a creation or a created being." Fritz Reinecker, Cleon Rogers, *Linguistic Key to the Greek New Testament* (Grand Rapids: Zondervan Publishing House, 1982), 567.

13. Stafford is in error (*Jehovah's Witnesses Defended,* p. 100) when he says, "The fact that he [Jesus] is excluded from 'all things' (*ta panta*) does not mean he is excluded from 'all creation' (*pases ktiseos*)." However, it is clear that the connection between

verse 15 and verses 16–17 is unmistakable, and it would again be a complete capitulation to Paul's opponents to make the distinction he makes between "all things" and "all creation." The exhaustive way in which Paul explains what "all things" includes shows that Stafford is forced into untenable eisegesis so as to safeguard Watchtower theology. "All creation" is exactly what Paul is describing in verses 16–17 as "all things." Admitting that the Son is excluded from "all things" makes the Son the Creator.

14. When man is said to be created *in* the "image of God," the Scriptures there speak of man's spiritual nature and ability to have fellowship with God. Being a creature in the image of God is not the same as being *"the* image of the invisible God." One speaks to our spiritual nature, the other to the exhaustive and perfect revelation of the Father made by the Son.

15. The phrase "For *by Him* were all things created" could be translated "in Him," as the Greek, ἐν αὐτῷ, is often translated this way in other contexts.

16. The Greek preposition "through" is διά. It is used in the exact same context in another passage that teaches the creatorship of Jesus Christ, Hebrews 1:2. More importantly, it is a term used of the Father's role in creation as well in Romans 11:36 and Hebrews 2:10. Those who deny the deity of Christ insist that Jesus is merely the *instrument* of creation, but not the Creator himself. Yet the fact that the inspired text can use the same prepositions of both the Father and the Son demonstrates that the use of διά does not make Jesus any less the Creator than the Father.

17. The Greek phrase used by Paul is τὰ πάντα. I believe it is significant that Paul does not use the more popular terms πᾶς (*pas*) or πᾶν (*pan*), both of which had meanings in Greek philosophy that allowed for the creation to be part of God or God a part of creation (as in *pan*theism). Instead, he uses a term that makes the creation a concrete, separate entity with *real* existence.

18. I refer again to the belief of Jehovah's Witnesses that Jesus Christ, prior to the Incarnation, was Michael the Archangel, a created being. Some Christian theologians have identified Christ with Michael, but in the process, have insisted that Christ is eternal and uncreated, meaning that His appearance as Michael would not imply creatureliness or limitedness. I do not accept such an identification in light of the discussion of Michael in Jude 9.

19. Greek: συνέστηκεν.

20. When the *NWT* first came out, the word "other" wasn't in brackets. However, such a hue and cry was raised, later editions included the brackets. However, the Society gladly drops the brackets when paraphrasing the passage (as in the 1991 publication, *The Greatest Man Who Ever Lived,* prologue, and the 1995 publication, *Knowledge That Leads to Everlasting Life,* 39).

21. The current editions of the *NWT* refer the reader to Luke 11:41–42, where the word "other" is inserted for clarity.

22. A construction known as a "partitive genitive." Stafford, 100, "Thus the genitive *pases ktiseos* is properly seen as partitive, including Christ in the collective group of created things, but dignified above it as 'firstborn.'"

23. Nicoll, *The Expositor's Greek Testament*, 503. Specifically, "Grammatically is it possible to make πάσης κτίσεως a partitive genitive? But this is excluded by the context, which sharply distinguishes between the Son and τὰ πάντα, and for this idea Paul would probably have used πρωτόκτιστος. The genitive is therefore commonly explained as a genitive of comparison." Likewise, A. T. Robertson, in his *Word Pictures in the Greek New Testament* (Grand Rapids: Baker Book House, 1932), IV:478:

> The use of this word does not show what Arius argued that Paul regarded Christ as a creature like "all creation (*pases ktiseos* . . .) It is rather the comparative (superlative) force of *protos* that is used . . . Paul is here refuting the Gnostics who pictured Christ as one of the aeons by placing Him before "all creation" (angels and men) . . . Paul takes both words to help express the deity of Jesus Christ in his relation to the Father as *eikon* (Image) and to the universe as *prototokos* (First-born).

24. Stafford attempts to get around this and, by so doing, defend the insertion of the term "other" in the text, by saying that while indeed Jesus is not part of "all things," He *is* part of "all creation." Hence, he insists that Jesus created "all things" but not "all creation," since He himself is a creation. Of course, the text does not make the differentiation that Stafford alleges between "all creation" and "all things." The two are synonymous.

CHAPTER EIGHT

1. We should note in fairness that the NEB provides a marginal translation, "yet he did not prize his equality with God." Such a translation would allow for the understanding that the preexistent Christ was, in fact, equal with the Father.
2. Greek: ὑπάρχων, a verb of being or existence, in the present active participial form.
3. Greek: μορφή.
4. Fritz Reinecker, *A Linguistic Key to the Greek New Testament*, ed. Cleon Rogers, Jr. (Grand Rapids: Zondervan, 1980), 550.
5. Greek: ἁρπαγμόν.
6. See also the examples in 1 Corinthians 1:7; 9:15; 2 Corinthians 9:3.
7. The NASB provides a marginal note, "laid aside His privileges."
8. Surely, then, if taking the *form of a bond-servant* in verse 7 means Jesus was truly human, truly a man, then having eternally existed in the *form of God* in verse 6 must, logically, mean that He had eternally been deity.

CHAPTER NINE

1. For Mormons who reject this identification (Mormonism identifying the Father as "Elohim" and the Son as "Jehovah"), see such passages as Isaiah 53:6 and Matthew 22:41–45, where the Father is identified as Yahweh. See also James White, *Letters to a Mormon Elder* (Minneapolis, Minn.: Bethany House Publishers, 1993), 67–75.
2. Here is a partial listing of other passages that can be developed along these lines:

> Matthew 1:21; Psalm 130:8; Isaiah 35:4 [God will save His people]

Matthew 3:12; Revelation 6:16; Psalm 2:12; Psalm 76:7 [Fear God]
Matthew 5:18; Mark 13:31 [God's Word is eternal; Jesus' Word is eternal]
Matthew 25:31–46; Psalm 50:6; 59:11; 96:13 [God is Judge, Jesus is Judge]
John 1:3; Isaiah 44:24 [Yahweh alone created all things]
John 1:7–9; Isaiah 60:9 [God is light]
John 7:37–38; Jeremiah 2:13 [Yahweh the fountain of living water]
John 10:11; Psalm 23:1; 100:3 [The Good Shepherd]
John 12:41; Isaiah 6:1 [The vision of Isaiah—Yahweh's glory]
John 14:6; Psalm 31:5 [God is truth]
John 14:14; 1 Corinthians 1:2 [Prayer to Jesus]
John 14:26; 16:27; Romans 8:9; 1 Peter 1:11; Nehemiah 9:20; 2 Samuel 23:
    2–3 [Spirit of YHWH/God/Christ]
John 17:5; Isaiah 48:11 [Will not give His glory to another]
Acts 1:8; Isaiah 43:10 [Witnesses of Whom?]
Acts 4:24; 2 Peter 2:1; Jude 4 [Who is our Master?]
Romans 10:13; Joel 2:32 [Call on the name of . . .]
Ephesians 4:8–9/Psalm 68:18 [God leads the captives . . .]
Philippians 2:10–11; Isaiah 45:23 [Every knee will bow . . .]
Colossians 1:16, Ephesians 5:25, 27; Romans 11:36 [All things are to God . . .]
Colossians 1:17; Acts 17:28 [We exist in God]
Colossians 2:3; 1 Timothy 1:17 [Only wise God . . . treasure of wisdom]
2 Timothy 1:12; Jeremiah 17:5 [Trust in Yahweh—believe in Jesus]
Hebrews 1:3; 1 Timothy 6:15 [Jesus' power—God is only sovereign]
Hebrews 1:10; Psalm 102:25 [Jesus is Yahweh]
Hebrews 13:8; Malachi 3:6 [God changes not]
James 2:1; Zechariah 2:5 [Lord of glory]
1 Peter 2:3; Psalm 34:8 [Taste that Yahweh is good]
1 Peter 3:15; Isaiah 8:13 [Sanctify Yahweh]
Revelation 1:5–6; Exodus 34:14 [Glorify Jesus]
Revelation 1:13–16; Ezekiel 43:2 [God's voice is the voice of Jesus]
Revelation 2:23; 1 Kings 8:39 [Jesus searches the hearts]
Revelation 3:7; Revelation 15:4 [God alone is holy]

3. See the discussion of this fact in chapter 3.
4. The *New World Translation* of Jehovah's Witnesses inserts the name "Jehovah" 237 times in the text of the New Testament. When the NT cites an OT passage that uses the name Yahweh, the NWT will use "Jehovah," replacing the Greek term "Lord" or "God" that appears in the text. At other times, the NWT will simply remove the term "Lord" and replace it with "Jehovah." The translation is inconsistent, however, in when it will insert the divine name. In a number of places, replacing "Lord" with "Jehovah" would teach the deity of Christ. For example, Paul says that no man can say "Jesus is Lord" except by the Holy Spirit (1 Corinthians 12:3). Even though some of the Hebrew documents the Watchtower Society cites in support of their insertion of Jehovah have "Jesus is Yahweh," the Society would not, of course, translate it that way. In the same way, if the NWT was consistent, they would have the word "Yahweh" here at Hebrews 1:10, replacing the word "Lord." But this would teach the deity of Christ, hence, the replacement is not made.

5. The wording is almost identical to that found in the Greek Septuagint translation of Psalm 102:25–27.

6. This argument is put forward by Greg Stafford in *Jehovah's Witnesses Defended* (Huntington Beach, Calif.: Elihu Books, 1998), 49–50. The circularity of Stafford's arguments is illustrated by the comments that precede this discussion. In trying to avoid the plain teaching of Hebrews 1:10–12 that Jesus is the Creator of all things, Stafford notes that God created all things through the Son (Hebrews 1:2), and writes, "Clearly, then, in context Hebrews 1:10–12 could not be teaching that Jesus is the Creator, for here, in the opening words to the Hebrews, it is clearly stated that *God* made all things "through" His Son" (p. 48). This is circular argumentation, for it assumes the conclusion Stafford wishes to reach. It assumes unitarianism. The fact that the Son is differentiated from the Father is admitted by all. But unless one assumes that the term "God" must always and only refer *solely* to the Father (unitarianism), the entire argument collapses. The Son is the one through whom the Father made all things (Hebrews 1:2) *and* He is Yahweh, the eternal Creator, for the Father, Son, and Spirit are all identified as Yahweh. There is no contradiction between allowing *both* truths to coexist. Only the authority of the Watchtower forces Stafford to downplay the plain meaning of the one passage to uphold his unitarian interpretation of the other.

7. The connection is actually closer than first glance might indicate, for the Greek Septuagint (the LXX) contains both the verb form John uses in verse 1, εἶδον, and departing from the Hebrew text, it contains at the end of the verse the reading τῆς δόξης αὐτοῦ meaning "the house was full of His glory." This is the same phraseology used in John 12:41, τὴν δόξαν αὐτοῦ, (the accusative for the genitive) meaning "he saw His glory." The use of the same phraseology makes the connection to the John 6 passage unbreakable.

8. Or, more likely, the term "glory" used in the LXX in verse 1.

9. Stafford insists that we look only at Isaiah 53 for the reference to John 12:41, but he does not deal with the verbal parallels to the Greek LXX. In fact, one will search in vain in Isaiah 53 for εἶδεν/εἶδον being used with "glory"; and one will not find the phrase τὴν δόξαν αὐτοῦ or anything similar to it. The term "glory" only appears once in Isaiah 53, and that in a completely separate context.

CHAPTER TEN

1. That is what theologians call the Eternal Covenant of Redemption, that agreement between the Father, Son, and Spirit, regarding the roles each person would take in bringing about the redemption of God's people.

2. The phrase appears in a number of forms, the simplest being πνεῦμα ἅγιον.

3. I note in passing as well the use of the masculine form of the demonstrative pronoun ἐκεῖνος of the Holy Spirit at John 16:13–14 as another reference to the personality of the Holy Spirit. While the normal pronouns used for the Spirit are neuter (matching the neuter gender of the word "Spirit"), ἐκεῖνος is masculine, translated "He."

4. Specifically, I refer to the term ἡ ἀγάπη.

5. For a discussion of the alternate understanding of this last phrase, see Douglas Moo, *The Epistle to the Romans* in *The New International Commentary on the New Testament* (Grand Rapids: Eerdmans, 1996), 526–527.
6. Another relevant example, also identifying the Spirit as Yahweh, is found at Hebrews 10:15–17, where Jeremiah 31:31–34 is cited as the words of the Spirit.

CHAPTER ELEVEN

1. The words of Jesus at Matthew 27:46 have come in for many kinds of interpretation. Unfortunately, many of the theories have compromised the Bible's teachings on the nature of the relationship between the Father and the Son. The Father was never separated from or abandoned the Son. This truth is clear from many sources. Jesus uses the second person when speaking to the Father—"why have *You* forsaken Me?" rather than "why did *He* forsake Me?" as if the Father is no longer present. Immediately on the heels of this statement Jesus speaks to the Father ("Father, into your hands . . ."), showing no sense of separation. Whatever else Jesus was saying, He was not saying that, at the very time of His ultimate obedience to the Father, the Father abandoned Him. Rather, it seems much more logical to see this as a quotation of Psalm 22 that is meant to call to mind all of that Psalm, which would include the victory of v. 19ff, as well as verse 24, which states, "For He has not despised nor abhorred the affliction of the afflicted; neither has He hidden His face from him; but when he cried to Him for help, He heard."
2. The Greek here is simply beautiful, as noted in chapter 4 on the prologue of John, footnote 25.

CHAPTER TWELVE

1. B. B. Warfield, "The Biblical Doctrine of the Trinity," *The Works of Benjamin B. Warfield*, (Grand Rapids: Baker Book House, 1981), II:143.
2. Ibid., 141–142.
3. Ibid., 144.
4. Ibid., 145.
5. Ibid., 146.
6. The systematic treatments by Grudem, Hodge, Berkhof, and others, cited in this chapter, would provide fertile soil for those who wish to enter into the philosophical considerations of the doctrine of the Trinity.
7. The issues of the use of nonbiblical terminology to communicate biblical truths is beyond the scope of our study. A brief word from Warfield (p. 133) will have to suffice:

> A doctrine so defined can be spoken of as a Biblical doctrine only on the principle that the sense of Scripture is Scripture. And the definition of a Biblical doctrine in such un-Biblical language can be justified only on the principle that it is better to preserve the truth of Scripture than the words of Scripture. The doctrine of the Trinity lies in Scripture in solution; when it is crystallized from its solvent it does not cease to be Scriptural, but only comes into clearer view. Or, to speak without figure, the doctrine of the Trinity is given to us in Scripture, not in formulated definition, but in fragmentary allusions; when we assembled

the *disjecta membra* into their organic unity, we are not passing from Scripture, but entering more thoroughly into the meaning of Scripture. We may state the doctrine in technical terms, supplied by philosophical reflection; but the doctrine stated is a genuinely Scriptural doctrine.

8. Louis Berkhof, *Systematic Theology* (Grand Rapids: Eerdmans, 1941), 87–89. One could just as well use the definition provided by Charles Hodge in his *Systematic Theology* (New York: Scribner's, 1872; reprint. Grand Rapids: Eerdmans, 1986), I:442ff., or any number of others.

9. John 4:24.

10. Jeremiah 23:24.

11. 2 Chronicles 6:18.

12. John Calvin put it well in the *Institutes of the Christian Religion, Book I, XIII, 6,* and we would do well to ponder his words (repeatedly, if necessary):

> By person, then, I mean a subsistence in the Divine essence, a subsistence which, while related to the other two, is distinguished from them by incommunicable properties. By subsistence we wish something else to be understood than essence. For if the Word were God simply and had not some property peculiar to himself, John could not have said correctly that he had always been with God. When he adds immediately after, that the Word was God, he calls us back to the one essence. But because he could not be with God without dwelling in the Father, hence arises that subsistence, which, though connected with the essence by an indissoluble tie, being incapable of separation, yet has a special mark by which it is distinguished from it. Now, I say that each of the three subsistences while related to the others is distinguished by its own properties.

13. That is, in the *opera ad intra* (internal operations) and *opera ad extra* (external operations).

14. Or, if one wishes to be very technical, the constituent parts of the rock, the various minerals, have the "being" of those minerals. A rock is normally a composite item, made up of different materials.

15. The Athanasian Creed put it well long ago: "We worship one God in Trinity, and Trinity in Unity; *neither confounding the Persons nor dividing the Substance.*"

16. It is important to note that when we speak of "eternal" in relationship to the nature of God, we are, in fact, talking about a timeless existence, a type of existence that knows no succession of moments. It is not merely a "very, very long time," but it is not *time* at all.

17. C. S. Lewis, *Mere Christianity* (New York: Macmillan Publishing Company, 1952), 149–151.

18. We do not here enter into the controversy between East and West concerning the procession of the Spirit from the Father only (as in Eastern theology) or from the Father and the Son (Western theology). See the discussion in Wayne Grudem, *Systematic Theology* (Grand Rapids: Zondervan, 1994), 246–247.

19. Warfield, 155.

CHAPTER THIRTEEN

1. *See* the listings of works in the "Notes on Books" on the relevant chapters in J. N. D. Kelly, *Early Christian Doctrines* (San Francisco: Harper and Row, 1978), 108, 137, 162, 251, 279, 309, 343.

2. All citations of the early church Fathers in this section are translated by the author from the texts as found in the *Thesaurus Linguae Graecae* D CD ROM (Los Altos, Calif.: Packard Humanities Institute, 1993), unless otherwise noted. Section numbers follow the standard numbering in most printed editions.

3. The most egregious example of attempting to hide the testimony of this early Father is found in the *Watchtower* magazine of February 1, 1992, 21. By ignoring all the genuine epistles of Ignatius, and quoting only from the spurious epistles written by later writers, the Watchtower managed to conclude that Ignatius did not believe in the deity of Christ. Even a brief examination of his actual writings proves otherwise.

4. All emphases added.

5. One might consider the common argument used by some that Jesus can be called a "god" in the sense of "an angel" or a "mighty being" in light of a phrase such as this. Would someone say "by the will of the Father and of Michael the Archangel"? Does that make any sense?

6. This translation is based upon the edition of the creed preserved by Eusebius in his *Epistola ad Caesarienses*, drawn from the TLG CD-ROM, which differs in only a few places from that given in G. L. Dossetti's edition, reproduced in J. N. D. Kelly, *Early Christian Creeds*, 3rd ed. (New York: Longman, 1972), 215–216.

7. The Greek term is γεννηθέντα, and it speaks of relationship as it is used here.

8. This is the key term, *homoousion*, ὁμοούσιον, or in Latin, *consubstantialem*.

9. The catch-phrase of the Arians, ἥν ποτε ὅτε οὐκ ἦν.

10. Or, "that he came into existence out of nothing," rendering the Greek phrase ἐξ οὐκ ὄντων ἐγένετο, from which the nickname "Exukontians" arose.

11. The council may have been the idea of others, most likely Hosius, bishop of Cordova, or Eusebius of Caesarea.

12. In fact, it had been condemned by Eastern writers and councils due to the possibility of its use by modalists, though that was a different context than its use at Nicaea. Also important is the assertion by some that the emperor was the source of the term. There is no reason to believe this. As Philip Schaff pointed out in his *History of the Christian Church* (Grand Rapids: Eerdmans, 1985), 3:628, "The word . . . was not an invention of the council of Nice, still less of Constantine, but had previously arisen in theological language, and occurs even in Origen and among the Gnostics . . ." The only reason put forward by some comes from the words of Eusebius, written to his home church, in which he writes of Constantine, "He encouraged the others to sign it and to agree with its teaching, only with the addition of the word 'consubstantial' (i.e., *homoousios*)." The term translated "encouraged" could be rendered as strongly as "commanded" or as mildly as "encourage" or "advise." It seems Eusebius is only referring to the fact that once the Council

reached a decision, Constantine put his support behind it—at least at that time. He would later change his views.

13. This issue is discussed more fully in chapter 12.

14. Athanasius, *De Synodis* 6.

15. Jerome, *Adversus Luciferianos* 19, *Nicene and Post Nicene Fathers*, 2nd series (Grand Rapids: Eerdmans, 1980), II:6:329.

Index

Adoration, God worthy of, 39
"Aeons," 108
Alford, Henry, 210
"All things were created," 113–116
"Alpha and Omega," 86–87
Alternate understanding providing for, 56
"Amazing Grace" (hymn), 120
Ananias, 147
Anarthrous *theos*, 56, 198–200
Angels, Christ worshipped by, 74–75
Ani hu, 99–100
Anti-intellectualism, 16
Apologetics, 31, 193–194
Aramaic language, 197–198
Archangel Michael. *See* Michael the Archangel
Arianism, 186–187, 189
Arian Resurgency, 189
Arius, 186–187
Armstrong, John, 33
Arrogance, 34
Article (of speech), 53–54
Athanasian Creed, 190–191
Athanasius, 33, 189, 197
Attitude toward God, proper, 21–22, 34–35
Augustine, 33, 101

Balanced knowledge
of the doctrine of the Trinity, 30
of God the Father, 15
Barnabas, 141
Beasley-Murray, George, 203
"Became flesh," 59–60
"Beginning," 49
Believers, individual
and the Trinity, 196

Berkhof, Louis, 168–169
Bible, monotheism in, 55–56
Blaspheming the Holy Spirit, 145
Boundaries set by God, 34–35
Bruce, F. F., 54, 56–57
"By Him all things were created," 113–116

Calvin, John, 33, 218
Carmen Christi. See "Hymn to Christ as God"
Christ. *See* Jesus Christ
Christian apologetics, 31, 193–194
Christian devotion and the Trinity, 193–196
Christian fellowship, 121–122, 150–151
Chrysostom, 97–98
Church
false teachers entering, 60, 106–107
persecution of, 178
"purchased with His own blood," 82–83
Church history and the Trinity, 159, 177–191
"Church of God," 82–83
Clement of Rome, 178–180
Comforter. *See* Holy Spirit
Confession of Thomas, 68–71
Conservative theologians, 126
Context, considering, 56–57
Council of Chalcedon, 159
Council of Nicaea, 178, 185–190
aftermath of, 189–190
who believed what, 187–188
Creator of all
Christ as, 105–117

eternal, 132–135
God as, 36, 43–45
Logos as, 58
Cults opposing deity of Christ, 110

Defining the Trinity, 23–31
essentially undefinable, 24–26
Definite interpretation of *theos*, 55–58
Deity of Jesus Christ, 65–93
cults opposing, 110
defending, 197
Delitzsch, F., 81–82
"Demiurge," 108–109
"Different substance" party, 187–188
Divine existence, 124
Docetism, 60, 109
Doctrine of the Trinity. *See* Trinity, doctrine of the
Dualism, 107

Economical Trinity, 172
Edwards, Jonathan, 197
example of, 19
on loving God, 18–20
Egeneto, 50–51, 59
Ego eimi. See "I am He"
Electricity, analogy to, 143
El gibbor. See "Mighty God"
"Emptied Himself," 124–125
metaphorical sense of, 125
Ephraim, 111
"Equal with God," 87–89, 124
"Eternal Covenant of Redemption," 66
Eternal Creator, 132–135
Eternal existence, 27–28
Eternal life, 83–84, 194
Eternal Word, 51, 57

Eternity
defined, 42
invading time, 59–61
Sovereign Lord of, 44
of the Word, 51
Eusebius, 219–220
Exaltation of the Son, 127–129
Expositor's Bible Commentary,
The, 198, 202
Expositor's Greek New Testament,
200

False gods, 35–38
trial of the, 36–38
False teachers entering the
church, 60
Father, God the. *See also* God
balanced knowledge of, 15
"Father is greater than I," 89–92
Feinberg, Charles, 198
Filiation, 173
"Firstborn of all creation," 110–
113
Flesh, 59–60, 109
"Form of God," 122–124
Foundations of the Trinity, 28–
30, 163, 169–171
"Fullness of Deity," 84–86
Function, difference in, 66–68,
70, 91, 139

Glory, seeing, 137
Gnosticism, 60, 106–109, 115–
116, 195
God
beyond realm of Time, 41–43
boundaries set by, 34–35
a brief introduction to, 33–45
Creator of all, 43–45, 58–59
as Eternity, 59–61
first and last, 37
form of, 123
greatness of, 20–22, 38–40
Holy Spirit as, 147–151
intuitive recognition of, 105
morning prayer to, 35–38
omnipresence of, 40
oneness of, 38–40
only Son of, 61–64
only true, 91
personality of, 55

proper attitude toward, 34–35
smarter than we, 20
as spirit, 40–41
unchanging nature of, 43
uniqueness of, 36–40, 133
unlike man, 41
worshiping as He is, 18, 20–21
worthy of worship and
adoration, 39
Godly attitude, 21–22
"God over all," 71–74
Gods
false, 35–36
"perishing," 40
Gospel, and the Trinity, 195–196
Grace, 150
Grammar, 53–54, 74
Grammar of the Greek New
Testament in the Light of
Historical Research, A, 203,
209
Granville Sharp's Rule, 77
Greatness of God, 20–22, 38–40
Greek-English Lexicon of the New
Testament and Other Early
Christian Literature, 203
Greek-English Lexicon of the New
Testament Based On
Semantic Domains, 202
Greek Grammar Beyond the
Basics: An Exegetical Syntax
of the New Testament, 209
Greek language, 48–58, 96–104,
114
Greek philosophy, 50
Grieve not the Holy Spirit, 139–
151

Harris, Murray, 75, 201, 203
Hebrew language, 98
Hebrew thought, 43–44
Hedonism, 107–108
Hendrickson, William, 102
History. *See* Church history
History of the Christian Church,
219
Holiness of God, The, 34
Holy Spirit. *See also* God
blaspheming, 145
as God, 40–41, 147–151

He, not It, 140–147
leading into deeper
knowledge, 17
not grieving, 139–151
Homoousion, 188–189
Humility, 121–122, 126–128
in "Hymn to Christ as God,"
120–122, 126–127
Hymns, 120, 175, 196
"Hymn to Christ as God"
(*Carmen Christi*), 119–129

"I am He," 95–104
Old Testament background of,
98–100
translating, 96–98, 198, 208
Idolatry, 36–38
Ignatius, Bishop of Antioch,
181–184
"Image of the invisible God,"
109–110
Incarnation, the, 160–161, 183
Indefinite interpretation of *theos,*
55–58
Inferiority of nature, 66–68, 70,
91, 111, 139
Inspiration, 47
Institutes of the Christian
Religion, 218
Interpretation
punctuation in, 72–73
of *theos,* 55–58
"In the beginning," 49
Intuitive recognition of God,
105
Irenaeus, 97
Isaiah, 80, 148
vision of, 136–138
Israel, 35–36, 111

Jehovah of Hosts, 131–138
eternal Creator, 132–135
Jehovah's Witnesses, 14, 68, 114–
115, 140, 154
witnessing to, 131–132
Jehovah's Witnesses Defended,
198–199, 204, 207, 211–
213, 216
Jeremiah, 39–41
Jesus as God, 203

Jesus Christ. *See also* God; Son of God
"Alpha and Omega," 86–87
a blessed hope in, 76
"by Him all things were created," 113–116
"Church of God," 82–83
as Creator of all, 105–117
deity of, 65–93
distinguishes himself from Father and the Spirit, 67, 88
"emptied Himself," 124–125
"equal with God," 87–89, 124
eternal Creator, 132–135
"Father is greater than I," 89–92
"firstborn of all creation," 110–113
in the "form of God," 122–124
"fullness of Deity," 84–86
God in human flesh, 65–93
"historical," 106
humility of, 121–122
"I am He," 95–104
"image of the invisible God," 109–110
"mighty God," 80–82
"my Lord and my God," 69
"no God but one," 92–93
not a creation, 116
"of one substance," 188–189
one with the Father, 158–159
"only begotten," 201–202
"our great God and Savior," 75–80
preexistence of, 96, 124, 156
revealing the Trinity, 14–15
"through whom He made the world," 117
transfiguration of, 155–156
"true God and eternal life," 83–84
two natures of, 159–161
worshiped by angels, 74–75
"Jesus Only" position, 153
John, 116
John, Gospel of, 95–104
misused passages from, 157–159

prologue to, 47–64
understanding message of, 100–104

Liberal theologians, 125–126
Lightfoot, J. B., 113
Logos. See "Word"
Lord Jesus. *See* Jesus Christ
Louw, Johannes, 202
Love, meaning of, 16
Loving God
Jonathan Edwards on, 18–20
Luther, Martin, 33, 102

MacArthur, John, 33
Melito of Sardis, 184–185
Messiah, 74, 80
Michael the Archangel, identity of, 68, 195, 203, 213
"Mighty God," 80–82
Milligan, George, 202
Modalism, 30, 153–154, 159, 187
Monogenes, 61–64
Monotheism, 27, 34, 52, 169, 199
in the Bible, 55–56
Mormonism, 14, 154, 195, 214
Morris, Leon, 101, 203, 211
Moses, 45
Moulton, James Hope, 202
"My Lord and my God," 69

Nature, inferiority of, 66–68, 70, 91, 139
New International Commentary on the New Testament, 203
New Testament for English Readers, 210
New World Translation (NWT), 114–115, 215
Nicene Creed, 185–186
Nicene Fathers. *See* Council of Nicaea; individual Church Fathers
Nida, Eugene, 202
"No God but one," 92–93
Novatian, 97

"Of one substance," 188–189
Omnipresence of God, 40, 147
Omniscience of God, 147
Oneness groups, 153–154, 195

Oneness of God, 38–40
"Only begotten of the Father," 60–61, 201–202
Ontological statements, 203
Ontological Trinity, 172
Opera ad intra, 173
Origen, 97
Orthodox theologians, 126
"Our great God and Savior," 75–80

Passion for truth, 17
Patripassionism, 153
Paul, 15, 73–77, 113–114, 120–128, 148, 157, 160
travels of, 82
Person and Work of Christ, The, 199
"Person," defining, 25–27, 88, 140, 153, 171
Personhood of Holy Spirit, 140–147
Peter, 141, 147–148
"Pleroma," 108
Polytheism, 30, 35–36
no defense for, 39
Prayer to God, 35–38
Predicate nominative constructions, 53–54
Preexistence of Jesus Christ, 96, 124, 156
Present tense, 97
Prestige, G. L., 202
Pride, 34
Progressive present tense, 97
Prophecy, 44
Pros, 52
Prototokos, 111–113, 212
Punctuation, 72–73
"Purchased with His own blood," 82–83
Puritans, the, 33

Qualitative interpretation of *theos*, 55–58
Questions, rhetorical, 38

Revelation, incomplete, 34
Rhetorical questions, 38
Robertson, A. T., 79–80, 97, 102, 199–200, 204, 209, 214

Ryle, J. C., 102

Sabbath, healing on, 87–89
Sabellianism, 153
Salvation, 104
    foundation of, 43
Samaria, 40
"Same substance" party, 187–
    188
Saul, 141
Schaff, Philip, 219
Sharp, Granville, 77–78, 205–206
Sharp's Rule, 77
Shema, 35
"Similar substance" party, 187–
    188
Slave, taking on form of, 125
Solomon, 135
Son of God
    distinguishes himself from
        Father and the Spirit, 67
    exaltation of, 127–129
    who is God, 61–64
Son of Man
    speaking against, 144–145
Sovereign Lord of eternity, 44
Spirit. See Holy Spirit
Spiritual experiences, 19
Spiritual riches, 15
Sproul, R. C., 33–34
Spurgeon, Charles Haddon, 33
Stafford, Greg, 198–199, 204,
    207–208, 211–214, 216
Subordinationism, 30
Systematic Theology, 168

Temple Vision. See Vision of
    Isaiah
Theology, 33–34, 125–126, 178
Theos, interpretations of, 55–58
Thomas, confession of, 68–71
Three foundations of the Trinity,
    28–30, 163
Three persons of the Trinity,
    153–161
    Father, Son, and Spirit, 154–
        157
    Jesus' two natures, 159–161

misused Bible passages, 157–
    159
"Through whom He made the
    world," 117
Time
    God beyond realm of, 41–43
    invaded by Eternity, 59–61
Timeless existence, 198–199
Translation, tenets of, 56
Translator's Handbook on the
    Gospel of John, A, 202
Trench, Richard, 85–86
Trinitarian Bible passage, 163–
    165
    greatest, 174–175
Trinity, definition of
    attacks against, 154
    basic, 26–28
    biblical, 28–29
    diagram, 30
    difficulties with, 24–26
    expanded, 168–174
    great Trinitarian Bible passage,
        174–175
    incorrect, 16, 23–24, 88, 153–
        154
Trinity, doctrine of the
    balanced knowledge of, 30,
        195
    blessing of, 14–15
    bringing deeper
        understanding of, 16–18
    and Christian devotion, 193–
        196
    and church history, 177–191
    closer look at, 163–175
    defending, 193–194
    functions within, 66–68
    and the Gospel, 195–196
    as greatest revelation of God,
        14–15
    and the individual believer,
        196
    loving, 13, 31, 196
    revelation of, 28–29, 165–168

three foundations of, 28–30,
    163, 169–171
three persons of, 66–67, 153–
    161
why forgotten, 13–22
and worship, 194–195
"True God and eternal life," 83–
    84
Two natures of Jesus Christ,
    159–161

Undefinables, defining, 24–26
Uniqueness
    of God, 25, 38–40, 133
    of the Trinity, 29
Unitarian view, 67

van der Watt, Jan G., 199
Vision of Isaiah, 136–138
Vocabulary of the Greek
    Testament, The, 202

Wallace, Daniel, 57, 209
Warfield, B. B., 33, 86, 93, 101,
    165–168, 174–175, 199
"Was," 50–51
"Was God," 52–55
Watchtower Society. See
    Jehovah's Witnesses
Winer, George, 79
"With God," 51–52
Woman at the well, 40
"Word," 49–51, 57–59. See also
    Eternal Word
Word Biblical Commentary on
    John, 203
Word Pictures in the New
    Testament, 199–200, 214
Worship
    God worthy of, 39
    and the Trinity, 194–195
Wuest, Kenneth, 57, 112–113
Wycliffe, John, 33

Yahweh, 35–38, 44, 67, 76–77,
    87, 100–101, 128, 147–148,
    197, 215
    confusion over, 132–135
    words of, 98
    work of, 117